OVERLANDING

The Ultimate Roadtrip

Tim English

Pen Press Publishers Ltd

ISBN 1-904754-40-6

First published in Great Britain in 2004
Pen Press Publishers Ltd
39-41, North Road
Islington
London N7 9DP

A full catalogue record of this book is available from
the British Library

Maps © Francesca Romanin

Cover design: Jacqueline Abromeit

You may find yourself … in another part of the world

You may find yourself … behind the wheel of a large automobile

You may ask yourself … how did I get here?

You may ask yourself … where does that highway go to?

And you may tell yourself – MY GOD! WHAT HAVE I DONE?

'Once in a lifetime'.
(David Byrne/Talking Heads, 1980)

ABOUT THE AUTHOR

 Tim English was raised in the quaint market town of Stamford. Spreading his wings wide, he then studied at Trent Poly, Nottingham. Overland driving is one of seventy-three career choices since that time. Now a special needs teacher in London, he spends much of his unfeasibly long holidays in Africa, where he has helped build and stock two libraries, and South America, where he is researching his next book: *Finding The Source of The Amazon.*

ACKNOWLEGEMENTS

I always assumed that writing was a lonesome affair. I always therefore assumed that acknowledgements were a slightly forced part of any book, like saying 'hello to everyone that knows me' when you eventually get through to Radio Two with a birthday request for your favourite Dire Straits track.

Manuscript finished, I can safely revise those assumptions. Writing 'Overlanding' has been collaborative, to say the least. Here follows a list of people - and I will now happily steal a well worn phrase from every other acknowledgement - 'without whom this book would never have been possible':

For services to struggling writers well beyond the call of friendship: Sara Whitaker and Sarah Seavers, who between them typed up the first manuscript; all 250,000, hand-scrawled, rambling and unintelligible words of it. Ta - I don't know how you did it.

For ploughing through the first draft, still 180,000 words long, and offering unprofessional but nonetheless invaluable advice on which chunks needed chucking: chief Kilifi editor - Kate Nokes (plus a still impressive half effort from James Nokes); chief Dar-Es-Salaam editor/mechanical advisor/overlanding technicality monitor - Adrian Mumby; Alun Davies, Sarah Forde; chief African facts advisor - Collins Owuor; Mark Archer, Jim Danbury, Aunt Mary; Al Ross-Bell and Ione Minett, Dave Ellis, Gabs Rowles, Jes Robinson, Heidi Tryland, and my brother, Mike English. Thanks a lot; all you lot.

For allowing themselves to be hounded into performing a similarly demanding and equally useful job on the second, 150,000-word draft: Mark Waddell, Graham Cooke, Stuart Bell, Tony Rogers, Marcus English, Polly Evans, Mike English (again!) and Adrian Mumby (likewise). Many pints still owed to all.

For a truly honest and genuinely professional edit of the 140,000 word version: Alex Games. For finally unlocking the door to getting it down to an acceptably-sized 120,000 words, your constructive criticism beginning with the words 'I don't actually like travel books, but ...': Buick McCann. Cheers, you both.

For slipping the monumental effort of a withering copy edit between consulting for the great and the greedy and creating future works of art: Cheryl Field (with occasional advice from Richard Field). You deserve more Bolly.

For directing her artistic grace at such a dull, technical project as drawing up maps: Francesca Romanin. You were severely underpaid, I know. (But as an artist, you better get used to it).

For providing, to a roving, restless brother-in-law, a seaview study in a Kenyan home of such warmth: Caz Lightowler. Thanks to you and Mike for eight months encouragement, food (actually - that one goes to Joseph), fitness and fun; go on Caz - you can read it now. And to their boys, Atti, Rex, Solo and George, and the whole Kilifi community (thanks, Kath Maitland, for your attempted contact); your company was my energy.

For coming in late with a few well chosen words: Phil Jackson and Dal Nagra.

For providing the well needed expertise to actually get this group effort 'on the road', everyone at Pen Press.

And finally, thanks to all the folks I met on the road, whose spirit of adventure, humour and joie-de-vivre provided me with such a wealth of material and characters to choose from. I hope I have captured at least some of the amazing highs and plunging lows of overland travel. It *was* fun - wasn't it?

Oh, and if you actually found this, bought it and read it - thanks to you too.

CONTENTS

TRANS-AFRICA

Saharan Journey
Senegal - Mali - Niger - Algeria - Morocco

Crossing The Congo
Uganda - Zaire (DRC)

Central to West
Central African Republic - Cameroon - Nigeria

North to West
England - Morocco - SADR - Mauritania - Mali

SOUTH AMERICAN CIRCLE

Andean Adventure Part One
Brazil - Paraguay - Argentina - Chile - Bolivia - Peru

Andean Adventure Part Two
Ecuador - Peru - Bolivia - Chile

Across The Amazon
Columbia - Venezuela - Brazil

TRANS-AFRICA

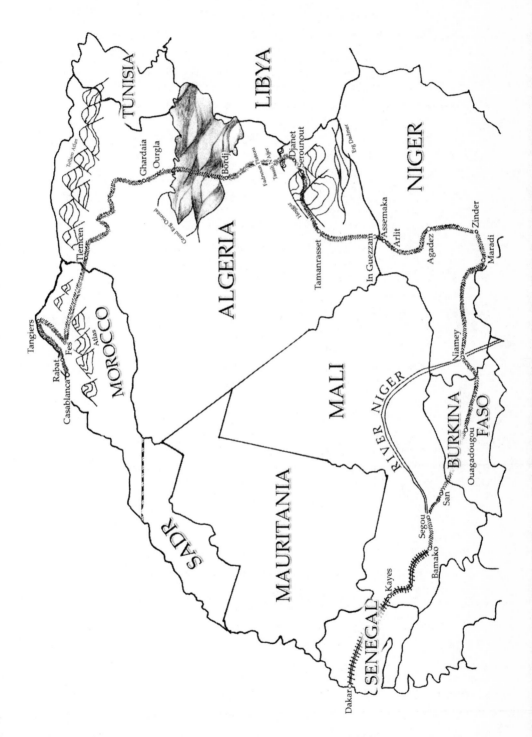

As we pulled into Niamey campsite, clouds of white smoke billowed from the truck's exhaust and leaking oil left a trail of blacks gobs in the dust.

"You need an engine doctor," the gateman offered helpfully.

"No kidding," Pete replied.

From our elevated position in the cab we could see everything the establishment had to offer us. An area the size of a dozen football pitches, the scorched sand was dotted with limp acacia trees casting patchy shade. Just by the gate a container-bar served locals and campers alike, and immediately behind the rudely converted metal box stood what looked like dreadful toilets. With the essentials – the market and Post Office – just around the corner, it looked as if it would make an adequate overlanding home.

As it turned out, it would have to.

I had dealt with my personal necessities twice already that day, but frequent gurgles from below indicated that I had contracted a debilitating dose of diarrhoea. As soon as we parked up I sprinted straight for the toilet block, where outside appearances hid a still more sordid scene inside. Evidently not cleaned since the day they were built, the long-drops were infested by flies and threw up a choking stench from their uncharted depths. It was a gruelling ten minutes.

As I strolled back to our camp I surveyed the scene, familiar now after a week on the road. The converted Bedford army truck had its canvas cover rolled up to reveal the two rows of seats in which the twenty group members spent endless hours facing one another. Next to the truck, the open trailer was being emptied of the last few backpacks by the two trailer-packers. The rest of the group, with their practised efficiency, had already erected the large blue cooktent and the smaller two-man tents they shared. Ten blue triangles, set out in a semicircle, neatly defined our boundary from absolutely no one. The drab capital of Niger was not a popular trans-Africa stopover; we were here strictly by necessity.

Having built a home for twenty in minutes, most of the group were already absorbed in their own pursuits. I grimaced in reply to enquiring looks from those marshalling their wash kit and nodded to others chatting on stools in front of their tents. I found the remainder playing cards in the cooktent, keeping out of the way of that day's cook team who were busying themselves preparing lunch. Pete, predictably, was under the truck, the oil-stained legs of his boiler suit protruding into the space where he had neatly laid out his tools.

The rest of Pete gradually appeared as he wriggled out on his elbows. In his left hand a used oil-filter dripped its contents down his wrist; in his right he held a makeshift plastic bucket full of more oil; between his teeth he gripped a spanner like a horse's bit. I relieved him of the spanner and asked him to repeat his latest wise words.

"I said – a bit more advice, Tim." He was looking up at me with the blank expression I'd become accustomed to. "When you're on your own, you haven't got time to be ill."

As Pete's trainee, I was at his beck and call. He didn't abuse his position, but was as hard on me as he was on himself. Nearly. Our company's drivers usually ran trans-Africa overland trips solo, tough going even when things were going well, but having a trainee on board only gave Pete even more to think about. I had joined him over halfway through his trip and was constantly amazed at his diligence in preparing me for the rigours ahead.

"I'll be right with you," I replied. "Anything we need under there?"

"A new engine would be good. But we can't have it all. The sleeves I ordered should be here tomorrow, so I'm just doing the usual maintenance for now."

"I'll get the grease gun then."

"You're learning." Pete allowed himself a flicker of a smile.

The spanner felt heavy in my hand and I found it a struggle to even make it through the morning. My stomach problem had escalated overnight, but I had refrained from mentioning it to Pete. At dawn we had taken the truck to 'the best workshop in Niamey', the description in our trip notes compiled by previous drivers. The shelterless compound looked like a car dump and had no concrete surface for us to work on, only sand, a nightmare as it stuck to everything. I was relieved to be given the job of taxiing to the airport in the afternoon to pick up our spares.

Arriving back at the workshop, I held up the bag of parts. The sight of them seemed to strike some deeply concealed vein of joy in Pete's worst-case scenario mindset. He grabbed the bag and ran around laughing, punching air with delight. The three resident mechanics, whom Pete generally tried to keep as far from the truck as possible, appeared from under a nearby bonnet to see what the commotion was about. Clocking Pete leaping about, they joined in with their own impromptu dancing and hollering. Feeling so feeble, I just watched – it was a joy to see how the local mechanics took on Pete's jubilation without having a clue what it was about.

"A bit of luck at last," Pete called out breathlessly. All four men were now arm-in-arm, hugging like winning footballers, the bag held aloft like a cup. "I ordered these weeks ago, the last lot got stuck in a strike at Paris airport."

The engine still in situ, Pete rigged up a jack against the tilted cab to push a sleeve into one of the four cylinders. With hindsight it was never going to make it; Pete screamed in real pain as the brittle metal shattered half way in. The mechanics, in the West African manner of trying to reconcile problems immediately, only managed to incense him further. With a chorus of "pas de probleme", they started picking up anything vaguely cylindrical to measure up against the holes in the engine block.

"Pas de probleme? Pas de sodding probleme?!" Pete shouted, hitting every inanimate object he could find with the jack handle that was still in his hand. I ushered the lads back to their work and waited for calm. I deeply wished I had something to offer, but I was no mechanic. Minutes of mobile rage ceased only when Pete had reached the roof of the truck. Taking stock of the situation from his perch, a deadpan voice finally expressed his conclusion: "Now we're really in the shit, Tim."

During our week on the road to Niamey from Bamako, I had noticed that Pete usually spent each evening alone in the cab. Head down over his paperwork, he left me to sit around the fire with the group. As the enthusiastic rookie, I was more than happy with this arrangement. I could chat the night away under the stars or revel in the silence of the wide-open spaces of the Sahel. He sometimes appeared for a few warm whisky night-caps with the stragglers, but generally I got the impression he was keen not to be with the group for any longer than was necessary. In fact, Pete had clearly had enough: of groups, of trucks – in short, of overlanding.

That evening, however, after Pete had delivered the news of further delay, I listened as he made himself available to a litany of barracking from the group. My illness having left me languid and liquid, I had retreated to my tent but could hear him replying quietly and factually as each person vented their complaints. In a bid to take on board more of his myriad expertise, I tried to concentrate. Eventually, however, my own grim situation took precedence in my mind, a shallow smile forming on my face as I mulled over a burgeoning thought: *how on earth did I get here?*

Little more than a month before, I had been living in my brother's flat in London, attempting entrepreneurialism. The purchase of an ancient Ford Transit had enabled me to start a one-man removals service, but with business as slow as the van I had spent my frequent downtime converting it into a camper. One evening, after another day of removing nothing except more money from the bank, I listened as my brother and his flatmate Paul swapped tales of junior doctoring. As they described a life of long hours, commitment and academic prowess, I pondered that it was a far cry from my own post-university achievements. When the conversation eventually came round to me, the imminent demise of my dream venture raised the same old question: what should I do? With my new search for enjoyable employ as tedious as any discussion about it, my brother soon left the table to begin his evening's studying.

Paul had a moment's more energy. On the way out to his own desk, he pulled a thick colour brochure from his briefcase and slung it at me. "Why don't you try working for that lot?" he called over his shoulder.

The cover featured a photograph of a large, orange truck. I had seen similar vehicles on UK motorways, always with a couple of dozen soldiers hanging out of the back flicking Vs. This one, however, was in the desert. And instead of military recruits, young travellers hung out of the open sides, sunglasses on, waving at the camera; all obviously having the time of their lives.

I read the brochure from cover to cover. Noting the route map of each trip the company offered, I saw red lines snaking across whole continents. Those lines quickly decided it: overland driving was the job for me. OK, there wasn't much cash in it, but no bills, rent or trying not to chip the family china – just the open road, twenty people to play with and the possibility of the odd surprise more exciting than the amazing size of Granny's aspidistra.

A week later I found myself in Northampton with ten other hopefuls. The interview had gone well – particularly as Tony, the workshop manager, liked the fact that I had converted my Transit myself.

"Besides," Tony had concluded, "we like to give potential a chance. The workshop does the rest. Trainees spend at least six months in there, and only one in twenty make it through. Start on Saturday."

My first encounter in the workshop was instructive, albeit humiliating. Under the tilted cab of a three-ton Bedford truck, Scott was bent over the oily block. He cast his eyes over me with utter disdain as he spat out his admonishment "It's an engine, you tosser…"

He paused.

A tall, brash, New Zealander, his look lingered on the two doughnuts of turnup at the bottom of my one-size-fits-all boilersuit. Obvious now, but every engine I'd seen until then had been kept under a bonnet, not under a driver's seat. I simply hadn't thought it through before taking a chance on striking up my first workshop friendship with a jaunty 'What's that under there, mate?'

"… what the hell d'you think it is?"

Staring back at Scott, and drinking in the biggest sneer a mean face could produce, it began to dawn on me that overland driving wasn't about leading singsongs around the campfire. It was a tough job, and I was in a very competitive environment. Putting vacuous questioning above intelligent reasoning wasn't going to get me out on the road.

I kept out of Scott's way and he disappeared before dawn the following Saturday, Friday being pay and 'discussion' day with Tony. There was nothing of the traditional leaving do after that discussion; you just melted away, one of the failures. Although a top mechanic, Scott had found it difficult living and working together for twenty-four hours a day, and had argued with several trainees. Above all else we had to prove to Tony that we could get on well in a group.

Another prerequisite for successful graduation to the wheel was mechanical skill. And I possessed none. Quickly realising the need to divert attention from my obvious deficiencies, I sought out alternative ways to gain credibility and show team-spirit.

Noting Tony's obsession with environmental issues, I put out recycling boxes for the huge number of beer cans that passed through the shared house. I used my meagre plumbing skills to mend the shower that leaked through its base, into a room shared by four trainees below. When it was my turn to cook for a houseful of hungry men, I quietly supplemented the tight food budget to produce steak and cartons of cheap wine. In the workshop, my technique was simpler still: I became the permanent assistant, learning quickly enough to repeat most of what I had just seen. In the store, a room full of the incredible variety of items necessary for each trip, from dried foods to spare parts, I put in place a proper stocktaking system gleaned from a previous job. And now it had no use, I let the workshop chickens roost in my van, collecting fresh eggs each evening and boiling them for lunch the following day.

To my surprise, it was neither a sacking nor my veneer of usefulness that got me out of the workshop in record time, but my degree. As the only one qualified in such a wishy-washy way, I had kept the fact very quiet. The other trainees were for the most part well-qualified tradespeople, highly trained ex-servicemen, motor mechanics or farmers. Of these real skills I was envious in the extreme, particularly as I could find no way of applying my shaky knowledge of business law or 'Maslow's Hierarchy of Needs' to the challenges I was encountering. But a year in France and half a degree in French meant I could speak French; indeed, under the 'Languages' section on my CV, French had 'fluent' next to it.

Waking with a start, I patted my hand around the corners of my tent in search of my torch. I shone it at my watch and realised I had dozed off. Darkness had descended over the campsite promptly at six but it was still only eight. It felt like midnight. Outside, the grumbling voices were still in full flow. My guts grumbled in reply. It wouldn't be long before I had to make another trip to the dreaded longdrop.

Pete was speaking again and I became conscious that some of the group had concocted the notion that it was a conspiracy; the truck was dead and the company was playing a waiting game to get as many people as possible to leave before paying off the staunch remainder. I heard at least half the group backing Pete as he calmly tried to counter the accusation.

I lay there, hollow with the consideration of how I might behave in his shoes, as the driver. I felt around in the darkness once more and found my bog-roll where I'd put it, under my pillow. Reassured, I listened as the two opposing sides of the group began to argue. With the quarrel escalating, I forced myself to think of something else. My mind ended up back in the workshop.

It was the Friday night of my fourth week in Northampton when I was called into the office 'for a chat'. Hawkins, the company owner, who had pretty much invented overlanding twenty-five years previously, was up from the London office and wanted to see me. I knew I'd been rumbled, but couldn't work out why Hawkins himself would be there to deliver the blow. Peering through the crack in the door, I could see him, hands behind his back, pacing the office and clearly talking to himself in his clipped military manner. *Go gracefully*, I told myself as I knocked. *You've had fun and learned a lot – you can try again.* Word had it that other overland companies sometimes employed our ex-trainees, so there was still a chance.

"Ah, English. Come in, come in. Smoke? No, not here, not quite right I suppose."

Hawkins sat down behind a desk. I sat opposite him, wondering if I should have saluted.

"Thing is, the Touareg. The nomads from Niger, Mali – you know. We got word today that they've hijacked one of our trucks. Of course, everyone's OK, don't worry about that."

The trainees had heard a rumour at tea break that bandits in the Sahara had hit Chris Keating and his group. We had no more details to go on, but had spent the rest of the day in various tough poses, depicting what we would have done in his situation. Hijacking stories and robberies were not unheard-of in overlanding lore, and each of us maintained a blasé attitude while, at least in my case, secretly praying that it would never actually happen.

Hawkins explained that Chris' truck had been stopped by tribesmen armed with machine-guns. Their Landcruisers had easily caught him up after appearing true ambush style from behind a rocky outcrop in the Sahara section of Niger. The Touareg had apparently been extremely courteous while they stripped the group of all their valuables. They gave them each back their passports, full waterbottles and a few dollars, escorted them to within sight of a small settlement and then drove off with the truck. Having organised the storeroom, I realised what a list of booty the truck would have contained, even before adding in the belongings of twenty touring Westerners.

"Noble thieves these Touareg," Hawkins continued, "but a bloody nuisance."

Wondering why he was telling me all this before, I still presumed, a quick goodbye, I elected to remain silent, forcing him to get quickly to the point.

"Your bag though, isn't it? French that is. Fluent I hear. Halfway decent reports from the workshop too. Heard all that this after' and drove straight up. Ops have got a job for you."

I could suddenly see a chink of light, a route out of my oily purgatory. Once out of the workshop, I felt I could keep my mechanical deficiencies under wraps and blag my way to solutions. I had plenty of skills. It was just that the workshop was a place I couldn't use them.

"Just a quick trip though. You'll be back here with the boys in no time."

Hawkins' smiled reassurance smashed my plans as if he was reading my mind. "I hear you need a few more months on the spanners."

Oh well, it'll be a start, I thought. I asked when I would go.

"Visas and jabs Monday morning. Tickets and briefing in the office. Then you're off."

I walked back into the workshop to help clear up before heading to the pub, and immediately experienced the averted eyes I'd seen after other Friday night 'discussions'. It appeared no one else had any doubt as to my fate either – they just couldn't work out why I was lingering in the shed. I chose to remain silent. I needed time to think what to say, and as the latest arrival it had to be handled delicately.

The trainees filled two tables, commandeering over half of the Three Queens' available space. Earlier I had cornered Jack, a quiet Scotsman I'd become good friends with, and explained the situation. He had suggested that I should say I had a return ticket for a week only and that no driving was involved. Essentially true, for all I knew, though I deeply hoped it wasn't the case.

"But I've been in that shed near seven bleedin' months!" Collier wheezed after downing his second pint. As the natural leader of our group, both through strength of personality and length of service – he had theoretically been next to fly out – his reaction mattered greatly to me.

"But well done, ya scrawny ponce. Slip a slim one up Hawkins' jacksy while you were in there, did ya? By the way – what's this, eh?" he said, holding up the glass for all to see.

"It's an empty beer glass…" the whole table chimed in unison "…what the hell d'you think it is!?"

That was it. I'd pulled it off. If the standing gag was out I was OK. Although it was always aimed at me, I still found it funny when any silence was broken with a "What's this?" While some item was held aloft a cry would go up, "It's a spatula,…" or a chicken, a bag of groceries, or the favourite, "an aluminium beer can recycling box … what the hell do you think it is?!"

Still clutching my bog-roll, I got up to do what I could put off no longer. Dizzy with the sudden movement, I opened the tent flap and looked out. The group had dispersed and Pete was sitting alone. Arms folded, he was staring into the fire.

"Can I help, Pete?" I asked weakly, gulping down air as a wave of nausea washed over me.

"No. You can keep out of this one. This isn't part of the training." Pete shook his head to break his stare and looked up at me. "Overlanding's not supposed to be like this. Truck problems? … yeah, plenty. Dodgy officials? … everywhere. Malaria. It's all par for the course. But this, Tim, this is a new one. Even on me."

"You're so together though."

"I might look it. Hey, maybe you can learn one thing from this after all. In this job, Tim, you have to be patient. That's leadership. Especially when the shit hits."

"Have they finished arguing now?"

"No. I've just called time out. It was getting a bit heated."

I looked at Pete's face. He looked as tired and drawn as when I had first seen him.

"Go on, mate." He waved me away. "You look like you need to empty out in a hurry. A three-way splash coming up, I reckon." I nodded gratefully and made to go. Then I noticed Pete's weak smile flicker across his face as a further thought struck him. "The worst thing is," he told the flames once more holding him in a trance, "I haven't even told them about the Touareg problem yet."

I weaved off towards the toilet block. Squatting over a hole I started to piss, then immediately threw up between my legs. The reek was reason enough, but it was the flies that had made chunder inevitable. As I opened the door squadrons of bee-sized black bugs had swirled around me in formation. Now presented with the opportunity of a fresh meal, they didn't even wait politely for delivery. In a cloud of frenzied buzzing at the operative end, they were pulling it out for me. I glanced around me. Surely this was the darkest hour of my life. Yet only two weeks previously, I thought I'd struck gold.

On the Monday, I'd arrived at the London office, 8am sharp, for my briefing. There, I found a dozen people already working. Most were ex-EM's – 'expedition members', as we were obliged to refer to them, avoiding at all costs the word 'passenger'. Hawkins was sharp on such detail. His personality laid thick seams through the company culture: "call them that and they'll expect a bus trip. We run *expeditions* do we not?"

The five office mainstays were Hawkins, the director; Amanda, who had the daunting task of dealing with accounts in dozens of currencies; Diane, whose marketing strategies brought in thousands of customers each year; and the Ops team, Dean & Graham, both ex-expedition leaders of long standing and vast experience. The groundfloor shopfront was decorated with beautiful photographs and enormous maps, while up the stairs the Accounts and Marketing teams buried themselves under mounds of paper. Operations nestled in the basement, to which I headed down.

Within arm's reach of the Hotline, a dramatic-looking red telephone occupying pole position in the centre of a desk, Dean and Graham were in deep discussion about what to do in Niger. Chris and the other hijack victims were currently making their way south on the back of an open transporter. Travelling in direct Sahara sunlight, they were dealing with a lack of food, water and equipment; Dean and Graham were fleshing out a plan for them to be met by another driver who had been waiting for deployment in Kano, Nigeria.

I stopped listening and looked around the room. Hawkins had slipped in and was sitting in a deep armchair with his eyes closed. I took in the cluttered but orderly scene around him; it had all the hallmarks of a Second World War command bunker.

On the wall were three large magnetic boards entitled Africa, South America and Asia. Details of each truck and leader were written below a dateline header that stretched out for six months. At the right of each line was the leader's photo. Looking at them, I could picture what each might be doing at that very instant; digging the truck out of mud; driving through the jungle, desert or mountains; arguing with border guards or eating with the group around a campfire. And there, along from the title 'Saharan Journey', was Chris. A cheeky smile beamed below curly, ginger hair. I realised he looked no more the part than I did, but was obviously coping admirably with his day's work, odd though it was.

I counted twenty-three trips travelling at that very moment across three continents. And that was just our company. I looked back at Graham and Dean in admiration. They had to be up to date with the progress of every one of them. They had to solve problems from thousands of miles away, but also had to be weeks ahead in preparing the ground: getting money to banks, spares delivered and all the people to the right place.

Tuning back in, I heard everyone laughing and saw Graham's hand outstretched towards me.

"Bonjour. My French speaker?"

"Hi. Tim. Yeah, I believe so," I replied, trying to catch Hawkins' recently opened eye for some confirmation of my role.

"Yes, yes, that's right," said Hawkins as he leapt to his feet and started to pace the cramped basement. "Graham, what do you think? I reckon Tim here should just get on with the job and leave Chris to it. The replacement truck's fully equipped, yes? We can send him dollars, and he can get anything he needs in Niamey."

Graham was renowned for his intelligence. Every sentence was carefully considered before he delivered it. "I want the group to feel everything possible has been done for them," he said levelly, "but this incident jeopardises our entire trans-Africa overlanding operation. I think it's more important for Tim here to collect the next Saharan Journey group in Dakar and lead them to Bamako to meet Pete. His expedition's the next to travel through Touareg territory and Tim can help Pete investigate the problem as they go north."

The Senegal-bound Air France plane flew over the Sahara. Studying it from aloft, I wondered at its size, its desolation and, to my surprise, its different colours and textures. Evidently the great North African desert was by no means dunes from start to finish as shown in so many films.

I landed in Dakar at sunset. Warned that the Senegalese capital was a security nightmare, I spent half an hour in the airport preparing myself for walking its streets. I emptied the external pockets on my backpack, arranged my valuables firmly around my testicles and stuffed my trouser pockets with bog-roll. This last line of defence was beyond the quizzical amusement of the resident army of porters in the arrivals hall, so I involved them in a role-play to demonstrate how, when a pickpocket tried to make off with my money, he would find himself trailing a length of tissue between him and his victim. Good preparation often stops the worst from happening and I reached the Hotel Central with nothing more threatening than a few 'bonjours' from passers-by.

I knew immediately I was going to love Dakar. Though truly African, it has something of the charm of a southern French town, and some of their best patissiers. One was conveniently stationed below the Central. The roads, lined with palms painted white to waist height, were good tarmac and everything looked to be working, from the taxis to the payphones. In short, Dakar, unlike any pictures of African cities I had previously seen, looked as if it had been *finished*.

The small group I was to take, by train, to join Pete's trip in Bamako, Mali began to arrive at the airport. First was Sigrid, a jolly German who lived in Australia. We waited together for another plane containing Barry, Gary and Zoë. Not finding them immediately, I gave a uniformed man their names to search for them airside. They eventually appeared, the overtly British boys pasty white with matching side partings, and Zoë in tears. They complained that someone who knew their names had held them for half an hour until they parted with $50 each. Feigning ignorance, I taxied them all back to the Central. I would learn that uniforms could be picked up for $10 in the local supermarket.

Throughout the next day I taxied back and forth picking up the remainder of my group. First was Jacqueline, a Swiss Italian who carried a mirror in her money belt and moved with a gracefulness that belied the frenetic activity surrounding her. Before even greeting me, she quoted from a French poet and held out her bags for me to carry. Next was Urs. An extremely tall Swede, he towered above the already large Senegalese. "Hi. Urs. Call me Horse," were his first words. Not for any extreme physical gifts, he explained, just for ease of pronunciation. The last two were a Canadian couple. As self-proclaimed seasoned travellers, they refused to believe who I was until I showed my passport. I sensed trouble ahead.

We arranged to meet later and everyone arrived promptly, apart from the Canadians. Eventually, the hotel receptionist delivered the message that Kim and Jim had switched hotels. I had lost a quarter of my group on my first night as leader.

The following morning, after taxis, train tickets and rounding up my Canadian sheep lost in the posh, beach-side Sofitel, we were soon bouncing on the surprisingly comfortable seats in our First Class carriage and toasting the prompt start of our thirty-hour journey with open bananas. As joyous as a day spent peering out at the slowly changing scenes of West Africa can be, it's hard to keep it up after dark. We all fell asleep, and it was only the penetrating sound of prolonged silence which woke me at around 1am. We were going nowhere, and by 4am there was still no word to explain our lack of progress. Finally, when it got light outside and the town of Kayes revealed itself, a guard arrived. He explained that there had been a derailment ahead and we shouldn't expect to move for twelve hours. Kayes unfortunately has the dubious honour of being the hottest town in Africa, on some days reaching a scorching 50°C. The carriage started to cook.

We mostly kept our humour by buying fruit and sodas from the hawkers at the station. Barry, Gary and Zoë, becoming more and more adventurous in their wanderings from the train, found an hotelier who would rent them a shower. They came back sparkling clean. The Canadians were incensed. Why had they not been invited? Where was this hotel? What sort of leader was I if I couldn't sort a shower for everyone? It was turning into an unpleasant scene when suddenly, with a huge jolt, the train started inching its way towards our destination. Thankfully, the subjects of group cleanliness and poor leadership were brought to a swift close.

There was no bright orange truck idling outside the train station in Bamako as I had been promised, so I booked the group into the mean rooms of the inappropriately named Hotel Majestic, annoyed that Pete hadn't been there to meet us. As I was cooling down in the shower, someone knocked at the shutters.

"Hi, it's Pete. Is that Tim?"

"Yeah, I'll be out in a minute. Wait will you?"

Finishing up in a deliberately leisurely fashion, I found Pete lying on my bed fast asleep. His long, thin body was fully clothed and I noticed he had no hint of the healthy glow I had developed in only a week in Africa.

"You all right Pete?" I asked quietly.

"Huh?" he whispered. "Is that Tim?" Shaking himself awake, he swung his legs to the floor. I could see creases scored deep into his ashen-grey face and his short brown hair was tousled into irregular spikes like a cat's fur after rain.

"Are you all right?" I repeated, holding out my wet hand in greeting.

"Yeah, fine. Just a bit tired. Listen, sorry I didn't make it to the station. I've had a bit of trouble with the truck. Thanks for getting the group here – you can move down to the mission where we are tomorrow."

I asked which mission he meant.

"Oh yeah, sorry, the Lebanese mission. See you there later? I really need to sleep just now."

Looking grateful at my invitation to stay where he was on the bed, Pete was out cold again in seconds. I walked out of the gloomy hotel and back into the sunshine. Wandering through the town, I found the dust-blown streets full of people rather than cars, and everywhere music blared from ramshackle kiosks and shops. Obviously much poorer than Dakar, the permanent sound of music added a tangible vibrancy to Bamako's lively street-scene. Eventually, I came across the Lebanese Mission, where a boy opened the door onto a paved compound entirely shaded by one huge tree in the middle. I stepped across the threshold into a totally different atmosphere.

The overland group were very much in evidence. Stools were dotted about and cooking pots hung from the tree's branches. Teepee arrangements of tent poles held up mosquito nets covering army-issue camp beds. Rucksacks were spread on and between the beds, mostly open, with their contents spilled out. Washing hung everywhere that a net didn't. The Bedford, parked to one side, was balanced on a jack, tools, equipment and spare parts arranged neatly beside it. This was definitely a trip in progress. If I was a little shocked, I wondered what the new group would think when they saw it. I waved hello to three women who had looked up on my arrival.

"You must be Tim, have you found Pete?" said one, stopping sewing. Another placed a kettle on the gas stove and introduced herself as I walked over.

"Hi, I'm Tammy." She had a broad American accent. "We're in a bit of a mess here. Hey – it's been a difficult trip!" Tammy laughed in an easy manner and continued, "You're new to this job, I hear. I don't know if every expedition is like ours, but you sure gotta work your butt hard to get your fun out of the deal."

"What's wrong with the truck?" I asked.

"It's a lo-o-o-ong story," replied Tammy dramatically.

Tammy introduced the other two women. As Martje picked up her sewing and joined us, Sheila finished making the tea and slid a cup each across the table. Tammy cupped the beaker in her hands and started a lengthy explanation of their group's trip through Zaire.

A few days after crossing the border, Pete's engine had dropped a valve. With no equipment available to skim a scored cylinder head, Pete had hitched with the heavy block back to Kampala, Uganda, leaving the group at a campsite. He was gone for a week. Zaire's whole infrastructure has been pretty much abandoned since the Belgians left in the 60s, and crossing the country in a truck can take anything between ten and forty days, depending on the rains. After Pete had got back it had taken them another two weeks, during which time the repaired engine developed another major oil leak. Pete had to work every evening to keep the truck going, and to make matters worse, he and some of the group had contracted malaria. Even after they had left Zaire for the Central African Republic (CAR) the condition of the roads hadn't improved. Finally, the spare parts which had been arranged for delivery to Ouagadougou, Burkina Faso, had got lost in Paris. They had subsequently driven fourteen hours a day to get to Bamako on time. And I'd been annoyed that they hadn't been there to meet me at the station. *I have a lot to learn about this job*, I thought as I dealt myself an appropriate admonishment.

The Canadians were the first to leave Niamey. By the time I'd crawled out of my tent, bog-roll in hand and bound for my first khazi visit of the day, they were already packed and waiting for a taxi.

"I was going to get to you up earlier," Pete said, "but I've been a bit busy signing leaving forms."

"Are Kim and Jim really going?"

"Yep. They decided after last night's meeting. I had to be honest; I told them we'd be at least a week here sorting the truck, then I explained that the Touareg problem would mean further delays. They reckon they'll get a standby flight sometime today. A few more want to go too, but via Dakar. You'll be taking them by bus and train."

"What? Who else is leaving? I can't believe I slept through it all!"

"Just some of my old group who don't have time to wait. And the rest of us will get home Tim, but in Africa's own sweet time."

"How many have I got for Dakar?"

"Four."

"Have I still got time for a brief bout on the bog?"

"Well, OK then." The smile made a subliminal appearance. "But only because I need you here for a day. The bus leaves tonight at eleven."

At the Post Office, Pete telexed Graham with all the news. Hawkins insisted that drivers use telex wherever possible – 'It's instant, leaves a written record, and more to the point, concentrates the mind'. Graham replied over the open line:

```
Best we can expect under circumstances.  Agree to refund
those leaving so far.  Try to avoid any more.
Pete.  Essential you get local news on Touareg situation
before Tim leaves tonight.  We hear rebellion escalating.
Imperative you organise armed escort.
Tim.  When your group safe in Dakar Central Hotel, get
signed leaving forms and fly Niamey.
Pete, call in half an hour.  Will have decision on replace-
ment sleeves by then.
Safe trip Tim.  Happy camping Pete.
BiBi.
OK, BiBi, Pete typed, before closing the line.
```

As we waited with a dozen others next to the telephone operator's office, Pete explained the little he knew about the Touareg situation. We were, he told me, heading up to an undeclared war zone, albeit one largely unreported by the international media. It was much later that I found out the real details about the plight that had created our so-called 'bandits'.

The Touareg are a nomadic people living in the Sahara and the Sahel. What they see as their homelands were divided by European colonials between five African nation states born in the 1960s: Algeria, Libya, Niger, Mali and Burkina Faso. Their main areas are the Hoggar (around Tamanrasset in Algeria), Air (northern Niger near Agadez), Tassili-n-Ajjer (around Djanet in Algeria), and of course the fabled Timbuktu in Mali. As far back as the 1880s, the 'blue men of the Sahara' – masters of the desert and supervisors of the salt, gold and slave caravans that crossed it – have inspired awe. As distinctive as their bearing – they average over six feet in height – the blue actually comes from the veils the men wear, as the dye they use rubs off on to their skin. They differ significantly from the Arabs of North Africa in both looks and customs. For example, it is Touareg women who hold elevated positions in their society; they often own more than their husbands and are responsible for preserving tradition by maintaining highly developed poetry and music. They also wear no veil. Social prestige and economic survival is measured in livestock, mainly camels – also the source of meat, milk and transport.

Social changes and drought have had noticeable effects in recent times, however, and many Touareg have lost their herds and been forced into a more sedentary life, often living in tents on the edges of towns. Mysterious and majestic though they are, since the crisis known as the Touareg rebellion, they are now often referred to as terrorists.

In May 1990, the Niger military clashed with the increasingly rebellious Touareg and responded with firepower. That moment was regarded by the Touareg as the start of an armed insurrection against their perceived oppressors: post-colonial African governments. The Touareg were partly fighting for the right to be nomadic, and therefore borderless, but were also enraged by the fact that uranium and oil enriched the capitals of Algiers, Niamey, Tripoli and Bamako, while nothing was being done to help their desert communities through a succession of droughts that were destroying their livestock and way of life.

Rebellion and counter measures spread rapidly across the border to Mali. On both sides of the border, finding the rebels themselves untraceable, punitive military expeditions began to launch attacks on civilians. Hundreds of thousands of Touareg from the worst hit zones escaped to become exiles in refugee camps rapidly set up on the borders of Algeria, Mauritania and Burkina Faso. Those camps are now almost permanent, leaving a whole generation of nomads forced by oppression and drought to stay idly put in hopeless conditions.

In harnessing international support, for their plight, the Touareg have had a marketing problem. In terms of the modern nation-state model, they have no legitimate right to territory – they live within a cross-frontier zone and their strong community and identity are diluted in Western eyes because of their nomadic lifestyle. In demanding their rights, they are criticised as being the last breath of the world of customs as opposed to the world of law. Due to this perception, few of the attacks on civilians have attracted media attention despite the availability of first-hand reporting and film. When a people rebel against tyranny but have no claim on a specific territory, how can they be labelled? What can anyone write or protest about?

In their own eyes, the Touareg still have legitimate cause for resistance. Marginalised in the states they have ended up in, and not able to gain a footing in the new African order, many have become modern warriors mounted on Toyotas armed with Kalashnikovs. And they have a message, which in many ways shows great foresight in their thinking. They refer to the 'Africa of Nations' rather than the 'Africa of States'. They don't want to take power in Niamey or Algiers, but to be Touareg in the central Sahara, the bridge between Arab and black Africa. They think supra-nationally, criticising the model of the centralised state, a model that has led populations to war, social collapse and unprecedented economic misery – particularly in Africa. Perhaps the Touaregs' old-world wisdom holds the answer to some of the world's more intractable problems.

What better way of gaining money for their struggle, then, than robbing a group of wealthy Westerners on their sandy junket? Politely and nobly, of course.

Graham, calm and pragmatic, was back on the phone with a solution as promised. Collier was coming out. A trained mechanic, he was finally en route to deployment in Tanzania. With him he would carry three more cylinder sleeves and a dolly, a disk designed to spread the pressure equally across the top of the sleeve to aid insertion. He would arrive in five days' time.

"I'll believe it when I see it," Pete commented dryly. "Come on. Let's get into town and see what we can find out." He tucked the telex in the black briefcase that accompanied him whenever he was on 'non-truck business'. "You OK for a while? There's a toilet out the back."

"I know, I saw it. I think I'll give it a miss. And thanks for asking – yes, I feel much better today."

I caught the smile. "Good job. It's a fourteen-hour trip on the bus back to Bamako tonight."

It was our first visit to Niamey's city centre. A taxi dropped us in a dusty square surrounded by faded and tumbling buildings, obviously relics of Niamey's French colonial past. A busy scene was strangely muted by a lack of motorised vehicles; feet, hooves and cartwheels touched only soft sand. Outside the buildings, shopkeepers were stacking their wares, while men or donkeys pulling carts laden with everything from plastic jerrycans to piles of vegetables were making deliveries. Two trees in the centre of the square spread mercifully wide shade – it was already 25 ˚C. Tethered beneath them were several camels, standing patient and silent save an odd groan, their owners presumably lost among the busy people filling the crowded square.

Beyond the square lay the new town. We set off towards the consular district to make some appointments, walking past blocks towering over tarmac roads busy with vehicles. Incongruous with the earlier scene, still more so was the sight of Touareg or Hausa tribespeople in traditional dress mingling with office workers in western suits.

The address we had for the British consul existed, but a friendly man behind the desk explained that the position was honorary and the gentleman in question was away on business. He himself could tell us no more about the Touareg rebellion than could be read in the newspaper. We split up to interview the next two on our list – Pete the Canadians, me the French. Meeting again for lunch and a debrief, it became clear that here in the capital, no one was interested in the conflict in the Sahara, still less a missing twenty-year-old truck.

Thinking that perhaps the military would have more of an idea than the bureaucrats, I suggested I telephone the national military headquarters. I surprised us both by easily arranging an interview with a Commandant Malam for 4pm that afternoon. With three hours to kill, I recommended some exploration. Guessing that any more time I had in Niamey would be spent at the workshop or campsite, I wanted to see the river Niger.

Standing on the American-built Kennedy Bridge, we were dreamily staring at the vast river as it followed the winding route it had cut through the scrubby semi-desert on the southern edge of the city. Far on the opposite bank I could see the University, and behind me, a hill ran down from the city centre to the bridge. To my left I could see a tree-lined corniche following the curve of the great river.

Suddenly, a truck sped past us, a grinding noise rising above the clatter of traffic – worn brake shoes were scraping uselessly against a hot drum. Only metres past our viewpoint, the truck smashed through the railings and plunged into the river far below. With Pete, I rushed to the gap, the railings bent flat like a fallen five-bar gate.

The swirling brown water had already covered any evidence of mishap and we feared the worst. Presently, however, the crowd that had gathered around us let up a great cheer when two heads popped up further downstream. They swam to shore and climbed up the steep bank of the corniche. Not one to hide my curiosity, I led the pack of onlookers in sprinting to their aid, Pete puffing heavily just behind me, swapping the briefcase from hand to hand as he ran.

I found both men lying in the road hugging each other and laughing hysterically as if they had just pulled off their best ever gag. Stopping only when they were completely surrounded, they looked up sheepishly, then took to their heels.

As we walked further on down the corniche road, paying no attention to our surroundings, we reconstructed the story over and over again. Pete was laughing out loud for the first time since I'd met him, and I realised how much the pressures of the group, more than the truck, must have been getting to him.

All at once, he was jumped from behind. One man pushed him sharply in the back while a second grabbed for his case. Pete hung on grimly to the handle. The first man was unable to get good position to help the robbery along, so Pete and his assailant pushed and pulled in a ridiculous comedy routine. I heard a hideous sound and realised it was me screaming.

I ran at the man attached to one end of the case, ramming my head into the fleshy regions between his legs. Perhaps more shocked by the noise and technique than by the pain – it must have been like being attacked by an over-amorous labrador – he let go and fled, quickly joined by his accomplice. Still screaming, I watched them go, then turned to look at Pete. He was rolling around the road in what I took to be agony.

Oh no! – is he knifed? The gasps and sobs eventually slowed and turned into their more recognisable form. Pete was in stitches.

"What the hell was that?!" He couldn't continue.

"A low punch." I grinned. "But it worked eh?"

Pete eventually found some more breath. "Sorry to laugh. And thanks, I lost concentration there. I've been at this game long enough to know better than to end up in a place like this."

We looked around to take in our surroundings properly. Up the hill to our left I saw a collection of shacks. A dozen men, their skin hidden by a dirt blacker still, were burning what appeared to be offal, hooves and other inedible animal parts in pits. It was some kind of makeshift abattoir. Looking down the road, we could see that there was no one else around, and no vehicles. It struck me what we must look like: two white men, dressed for business meetings, one holding an expensive-looking leather bag, strolling along merrily in an obviously poor area. We had almost deserved to be robbed.

Over cold Cokes outside the military headquarters, Pete instructed me. "Now, Commandant Malam. I talk, you translate – don't say anything else. They like to talk to important people, and with a translator I look it, OK?" Any hint of humour had disappeared since the earlier incident.

On entering the modern block situated within a fenced compound, we were escorted by two armed soldiers down a corridor and into a large office. Behind a desk, flanked by two more guards, sat the Commandant. He smiled a greeting and turned his fan towards us, gesturing us to sit in two chairs arranged opposite him.

Pete broke a long silence. He put on a fantastic act, becoming almost unrecognisable from the man I had walked in with. Showing exaggerated respect and humility, but displaying such self-importance that they might have been of equal rank in different armies, he explained the problem and our reason for being there. Malam listened with intent until we stopped, then raised an eyebrow. We replied with further silence. Malam then rose, showing for the first time just how large a man he was. He rested his fingertips on the desk and spoke in a voice softer and kinder than his bearing would allude to, and in perfect English.

"My friends, there are no problems in Niger. As you see, we are a wealthy country. We treat all our people equally. If you have had problems, it is without doubt with Algerian bandits. When you go back to your country, tell them this. I will give you names of my district commanders in the desert region and of course a letter of introduction. I will also radio them so that they expect you. You will be welcome. But please remember this. There are no thieves in my country. If that is all, then bon voyage. Enjoy the beauty of the North."

Regaining his seat, the Commandant glanced at the two guards who had brought us in. Taking my cue from Pete, I bowed, then we backed away from the desk to avoid turning our backs him. In the corridor immediately outside, a uniformed secretary put down the phone, told us to stop and typed three lines on headed notepaper. He stamped it with four different brands, rushed into Malam's office and came out equally swiftly, pushing the signed note into my hands.

Once outside the compound I was itching to tell Pete how impressed I was: with the man, his speech and in particular the highly official, multi-stamped letter I was clutching. He spoke first though.

"What a waste of time! No thieves? We were nearly robbed only an hour ago." He took the letter and placed it carefully in the briefcase. "Come on. We're out of here."

Three days later I was back in Dakar with four of Pete's old group. They had insisted we travel Second Class in a carriage next to the bar. Populated by prostitutes and pimps plying their trade between towns en route, the regulars were as friendly as they were dodgy. The whole chaotic drinking scene was presided over by the enormous Zongo. Holding a fistful of cash, he sat atop his chest-freezer, moving only to retrieve bottles from within it or to stand up on it to quell any raucous behaviour edging towards violence.

Demob happy, the group had made me spend most of the ride drinking with them in Zongo's bar, dodging minor brawls and dancing with the regulars to the erratic rhythms of their improvised music. It was a fun place to be, and the group had no complaints about the train, the heat, the food or even the inevitable delays. I began to understand a little of why they'd come on a trans-Africa overland. They all had endless stories to tell and it became obvious that the expedition had given them incredible experiences and taught them to appreciate everything around them more. They were much more comfortable with the locals than my group fresh from Europe had been, and were happier to chat and eat the same food. They had also evidently lost the Western preoccupation with time and keeping busy, along with all expectations of a smooth journey and good service. As I filled out their leaving forms at the hotel, I reflected on my good fortune at having had that time with them to refresh the joy I'd felt when I'd first got my job.

By the time I got back to Niamey, Sigrid and Zoe had also bailed out. Leaving only Jacqueline and Urs from my first group, we were now only fourteen, including Pete and me.

"What's this?" Collier asked, holding up a package when I met him at the airport.

"It's a set of Bedford cylinder sleeves, and a dolly to aid their insertion," I replied, "what the hell do you think it is?!"

We caught up on workshop gossip. Two trainees had gone to South America and three others had done the Friday disappearance. Otherwise life in Northampton was just as it always was: hard work, long hours and freezing cold.

This time we removed the engine completely. Coupling each sleeve carefully with the dolly, Pete watched as they slid in easily under the controlled pressure of the hydraulic press. The engine was reassembled that day and on the Saturday, put back in the truck. After a test run we were able to drive into the campsite amid cheers from the remaining group. Collier flew straight off to Dar.

Louis, I suspected, had been waiting for his moment. Nothing bothered Louis. The life and soul of the group, he always offered help and a listening ear to anyone who wanted it.

"Look what I've got," he said, dragging a crate of spirits out of his tent. "Let's celebrate. No-one else needs to get back home, and I reckon it's a bargain – at least an extra month in Africa for nothing." His relaxed style was contagious. "Come on, let's chill out. And Pete, that includes you – give Tim here a break."

Tongue hanging out and panting like a dog, his plastic mug outstretched towards the proffered whisky, Pete signalled the start of a party. We carried on until dawn, the group now one tight community of travellers revelling in our shared adversity.

We headed out early the next afternoon. Packing up camp had been astonishingly swift. Pete had reorganised the diminished group, giving every person a job. Equipment that had seemed to fill half of the campsite was packed into lockers and previously unnoticed slots, or positioned under seats. Larger items were bolted to the sides of the truck and belongings were loaded into the trailer. It was like watching film of an explosion backwards. Done with tangible contentment, no one seemed at all perturbed that we were about to head towards an active, if undeclared, war zone. Looking around at the emptiness from my seat in the cab, it was easy to see why.

After two nights rough camping well off the main road, we reached Maradi where we stopped at the market to stock up on fresh vegetables, then just out of town we pulled over. Lunch was a fantastic display. With a renewed sense of teamwork, the standards had reached those I'd become accustomed to pre-Niamey. Salads, warm French loaves, three sorts of tinned meat and a heap of fruit covered the two long tables the truck was equipped with.

There is a well-developed system to overland cooking. Using a rota of pairs, one pair is in charge from lunch to breakfast the following day while the next pair act as their helpers. The group of four are given a generous sum – excellence in the cooktent is encouraged – and dropped daily at the market of any convenient town. The next day the helpers take over as chief cooks and acquire a new pair of helpers. In remote areas fresh food is bought in bulk at larger markets like Maradi, co-ordinated by a quartermaster. One of the jobs Pete had dealt out before we left, the QM's role also includes organising the efficient turnover of dry and tinned foods kept in lockers under the truck seats. Prodigious amounts of stores – from tea to tinned stew – are sent out on the truck from the workshop and restocked at major stops where such goods are available. Apart from daily staples such as rice, dried milk, pasta and coffee, the dry stores are used only if no fresh food is available. A humble tin of Spam, therefore, might well be out on the road for the two years it often takes for a truck to get back to the workshop. After eighteen months on Africa's harsh roads, MPP was very much ready for its biennial total overhaul, due at the end of its current journey. As indeed was the driver.

"Best give her a go then," said Pete, jumping up into the passenger seat after our delicious spread. I took the wheel of an overland truck for the first time.

Within an hour we had broken down twice, first shattering a wheel bearing, then running out of diesel. Pete was totally unfazed. "My fault, I forgot to swap tanks. Don't worry, it's like breaking in a horse – she'll get used to you."

The rest of the afternoon passed without incident. When the sun started to go down I drove some distance off the track and stopped behind some cacti. Without a word from Pete, who started chopping wood he took from a pile tied to the front bumper, the group made camp and prepared dinner. Done with the same impressive speed as ever, there was even time to play a game of boules with the melons we found growing along vine-like tendrils on the sand.

The next morning Pete stopped the truck outside Zinder Police Station. It was customary to present oneself in that area, and we also wanted to continue our Touareg investigation. The briefcase led us in and once again I translated Pete's questions. Had they heard of a truck going missing? Yes, they'd been radioed from Arlit, and had been visited by Chris and his group as they passed through on their way to Kano. What was the situation with the Touareg? As you see, very peaceful. What did they think of us arranging an armed escort? We should see the army.

The taxi driver, having taken us 10km out of town on the Agadez road, would not go within 500m of the army base. Pocketing his money, he hurried us out of his Peugeot and sped back in the direction of town, ignoring our pleas for him to wait for a return fare. We trudged disconsolately along the hot sand towards a walled compound, sweating in our long trousers and full shirts.

Suddenly I heard shouted orders and looked up to see uniformed men armed with automatic rifles appearing from inside the gates. They took up kneeling positions, guns pointing our way, audibly cocked.

Pete dropped the case and grabbed my arm, lifting it above my head with his. An officer stood, stepped out in front of his men and shouted for us to approach. That was not the option my brain was busy considering – all I wanted to do was drop to the ground and skirmish my way across to a nearby tree, there to feel it absorb the thud of bullets until they ran out of ammo. I moved only when Pete did.

In a Wild West scene I had the time to find amusing – coins jangled in my pocket for spurs – the two parties met in the middle after a long silent walk. Hands still aloft, Pete's tongue indicated a paper sticking out of his breast pocket. The officer took it and read it quickly. I'd already forgotten its very existence, but Commandant Malam's letter miraculously changed the scene. With his left hand, the officer signalled for the guns to be lowered, and after two men had run past us to retrieve the case, we were politely escorted into the compound to meet the commander.

Minutes later, we were outside again, standing under the same tree I had chosen for my earlier imagined dash for cover. It had been yet another fruitless interview and I was beginning to think Pete had been right when he'd joked about his own plan in the event of hijack. He reckoned he would be safer arming the team with crates of Coke to chuck at marauding Touareg, rather than have anything to do with the Niger army. The commander hadn't even heard of a group of tourists in trouble. On our mention of any Touareg insurgency, he had replied with the inevitable 'pas de probleme' and then offered the irresistible invitation to pay a visit to their colleagues further north in Arlit. When we had left the commander's office, the platoon of crack troops who'd confronted us minutes earlier were to be seen lolling on the steps or snoozing in outdoor bunks. As even a lift back to town had been deemed out of the question, it was by no means surprising that our suggestion of an armed vehicle to accompany our truck had been laughed at.

I flagged down the first vehicle passing south on the largely empty road, and we climbed into the back of a Telcom van, the driver only too keen to divert from official duties for a small sum. We rode home in the back, bouncing around with the tools of his trade: two reels of wire and one half of a pair of pliers.

From Zinder the road turns north towards Agadez and the Sahara. To experience life as one of the group I decided to spend the day in the back of the truck.

I found everyone dotted about quietly reading, much as if we were all on a National Express to Gateshead. Without a book to hand, I ended up indulging in the default pastime reserved for any lull in truck activity: watching the world appear from invisible wings onto my small square stage, I stared at the view out of the back.

It's quite fun actually. Donkeys, camels, trees and trucks even slower than ours – they all appear for their few seconds of fame before shrinking from view again. I started guessing which would come next and Rachel, a nurse from Hull, joined me. Soon arguing the point value of a correct guess, others began to put in their penny's worth. Before long, Louis had erected a cornflake box scoreboard, and rules and sanctions for cheating – sneaking a glance out of the side, for example – had been decided. Such is the inventiveness of groups stuck for days in the back of an overland truck. While it may sound childish, it is infinitely better than the common stresses of adult working life, an opportunity to experience much more simple pleasures.

We arrived in Agadez for Christmas Eve. We had more luck at the army base there as the commander informed us that a convoy was gathering up in Arlit.; on the 29th it would travel under military escort to the Algerian border at Assemaka. Asking around town for further information, I heard that there had been escalating clashes between rebels and military, but mainly far up on the border with Mauritania. With time on our hands, we chose to stay put in the beautiful surroundings of Agadez, rather than wait in the reputedly ugly Arlit.

For Christmas day itself, Pete called a work embargo, and in a scene typical of what I would encounter on countless occasions in the future, I found overlanders creating the familiar in totally unfamiliar surroundings.

We started work on Christmas dinner, for which preparations had begun as far back as Cameroon. Sheila – organised and frugal, the perfect quartermaster – had been collecting extra money from Pete and had bought whatever she'd come across that looked festive, squirreling it in her carefully guarded lockers. With the cooking rota suspended, almost everyone volunteered to help prepare the feast. And a feast it would be. In Sheila's stash were crisps and nuts from Nigeria, long-life cream from Burkina Faso, tinned whole chickens from Bamako (famine relief from Holland), and her piece de resistance, canned sprouts and chestnuts from Niamey. All this was to be accompanied by excellent fruit and vegetables from the local market.

Food preparation over, Sheila then produced coloured foil, card and sellotape, and showed Louis and me how to make Christmas crackers. Jacqueline, looking on in horror at our bungled attempts, took over the job and produced twelve beautiful specimens, even pasting small drawings of holly and reindeer on them. There was only one Christmas pudding, so Rolf and James decided to bake a cake in the overland oven.

Made from an oil-drum split into three parts, the oven carried aboard every overland truck is a marvellous contraption. One end becomes the base and with a 'door' cut in its side, it is upturned and placed over hot coals. The centre section, cut and welded to make a slightly smaller circumference, sits on the base to become the cooking compartment. The third section is placed on as a lid, with more hot coals shovelled onto it from the fire. Whetting our appetites for a memorable Christmas dinner, a wonderful aroma of baking, roasting and wood-smoke filled the desert air.

We rose early the day after Boxing Day and, having settled back into the trip routine, ate, packed and drove up to Arlit, the last major settlement in north Niger.

On our arrival the police told us to go to the campsite where the convoy was waiting. There, the drivers of four vehicles – three Landrovers and a VW Combi – gave us the same frosty reception overland groups always get from 'independents', and no useful information. Eventually an army Captain came to tell everyone there was a delay, and that his supply convoy would be leaving in thirty-six hours. Pete was as dubious as I about the benefits of waiting for them, but we were under orders from London, so we camped for the night.

The next evening, and twelve hours early, six armed vehicles flanking three huge trucks appeared out of the dust. The Captain, standing up in the lead Jeep, indicated imminent departure. Our camp wasn't the only one caught short. The independents followed our lead in frantically packing up equipment, dropping tents and gathering belongings. Within ten minutes we were all ready, and with the last of the daylight disappearing fast, the convoy set off in a tremendous roar.

"What's this? Wacky bleeding Races?!" shouted Pete, as we careered over unseen hazards on the desert piste.

We were at the back. The independents were keeping up, their smaller vehicles more able to maintain speed over rough terrain. Only minutes after leaving we could already only make out red tail-lights bouncing around in the distance.

"Oh sod this!" Pete exclaimed.

He came to a halt and went to see the group in the back. Pleased to hear he had pulled out of the race, they took the opportunity of a stop to nurse a few bruises. The situation was absurd. We had waited five days for a five-minute escort and now, deserted in our old jalopy, we were sitting ducks – if there were any lurking bandits our headlights could be seen for miles. As Pete settled himself once more into the driver's seat, I caught his eye and smiled. He shrugged, carefully engaged first gear and edged into the endless black hole of a Saharan night with no moon.

In the event nothing disturbed our slow progress to Assemaka. The tiny settlement was completely still when we arrived, a few administrative buildings and rude homes silhouetted in our headlamps. Late, we opted just to erect the cooktent to use as a dormitory.

We awoke to a violent sandstorm. Unlike the desert scenes we had seen so far in the trip, this was just like the films. The cooktent was threatening to take off in a wind that carried much of the desert with it; opening your mouth to talk was ill-advised as it quickly filled with dust, and outside it was bitterly cold. To walk was to be sandblasted. Looking across to the buildings I knew were less than fifty metres away, I couldn't make them out. Driving through the emptiness the night before had put me in mind of sailing an ocean. Now even more, the desert seemed as wild and powerful as the sea. We had been extraordinarily lucky that the storm hadn't begun earlier.

For those in charge of the border, business carried on as usual. An unfortunate posting – it must have been a miserable spot even in the brightest sunlight – it looked to me like a job manning the gates of hell. We sorted out the Niger formalities but after that there was nothing more we could do. Though it was only a 15km drive to the Algerian post, we would be lost in seconds if we tried.

It was New Year's Eve, but not even Louis could think of a way to cheer us up. Unable to read, or even eat, we sat silently in the cooktent all day, wrapped in sleeping bags, hawking up and spitting out gobs of dust. As night fell the storm was still in full force. Detecting someone shouting, I opened a chink in the tent zip; sand immediately poured in. Outside, a hooded figure pointed into the swirling gloom and I made out some of his words: "... le bar, c'est ouvert."

The barman led us in a human chain to a mud-brick shed no bigger than a garage. Shoulders pushing hard against the wind, we closed the door, sealing ourselves into a capsule with an atmosphere as bizarre as the bar in Star Wars 1. The occupants, crowded around three low tables in the dim light of paraffin lamps, were all dressed in Obe Knobe djolibas. Gnarled fingers gripped dusty bottles and all conversation took place in a low murmur. Resembling beings from yet another planet, we had doubled their number but were made far from welcome. Midnight, I felt certain, would be celebrated in our own corner of the shed.

Ordering beers, we discovered they were three times normal price. Given his circumstances, I could forgive the barman a bit of profiteering, but it further discouraged our desire to drink. We stopped by about 11pm and, with a wonderful disregard for our western sense of occasion, were thrown out shortly after our money stopped rolling in. We hummed our 'Auld Lang Syne' tight-lipped and prostrate on our beds.

The storm had largely abated by morning and with 500m visibility, we reached In Geuzzam without too much wandering from the route. Once in Algeria, we had a 400km run ahead of us to reach Tamanrasset, one of the two major towns in the Algerian part of the southern Sahara, a two-day drive away.

Only a quarter of the Sahara is actually made up of 'ergs' – the sand dune seas typified in movies – and on the Tamanrasset run I saw close up how much desert terrain could vary. First we drove along a rough track through 'hamada' – hilly rock-strewn areas – then the hills got larger, the track twisting up through them before it flattened out onto open sand. Here, tyre-tracks spread as far as the eye could see, creating a wide piste. Indicated by palms and soft sand, we saw the occasional 'guelta', a slight depression created by underground springs or streams. On the horizon we could see the dark brown rocky plateaux of the Tassili du Hoggar lifting out of the sand. High up behind the Tassili towered the jagged peaks of the Hoggar Massif itself, a forbidding range of black volcanic rock. Nestled at the foot of the Massif, Tam' is the region's main administrative centre.

Camping late in the afternoon at the Hotel Zeribas near the centre of town, I had an early night. It was still dark and cold when I got up and I was surprised to see Rolf standing on top of the truck, camera in hand in just his underpants. He explained that he was looking for a sunrise. I pointed out a roof terrace above the camp café that had a perfect view of the mountains and handed him some shorts.

We watched in silence as a beautiful scene unfolded in front of us. In myriad hues of pink, purple, orange and yellow, the Hoggar seemed to grow before our eyes. As the colours faded, a ball of sun rose over a lower peak to reveal the mountains' sheer sides and dramatic formations in detail. I knew the Sahara had once been fertile and I wondered what catastrophic event in the past had turned the land into the apocalyptic scene we saw before us.

After such a start, I went about my day's chores with a perfect serenity – we had serious preparations to make for our trip east out to Djanet, the remotest Saharan town accessible by vehicle. As we expected to be five days out of civilisation, we needed diesel, extra water and as much fresh food as we could carry. The truck of course needed another thorough checking over.

A day's drive from Tam' lies the Assekrem. At over 2500m, it is the tallest mountain in the Hoggar Massif and well known as the abode of Charles de Foucauld, a monk who built a hermitage there in 1905, inspired to get 'as close to God as I can get'. He was revered by local inhabitants but finally murdered in 1916.

On grades of up to twenty-five percent, Pete picked his way slowly up the rocky track to the top of the Assekrem. As we drove between enormous fingers of sculptured rock, we spent our time putting names to the formations: Vatican Rock, Mushroom Castle and Jelly Mould City were among the places we christened. Sunset, watched from the back of the truck, was as impressive as sunrise had been. As we looked back down to where we had driven from, the magnificent vista of volcanic plugs, extinct craters and dunes was slowly enveloped by darkness.

During two more days in the mountains we slowly descended from the Hoggar to Serouenout, before climbing again towards the Tassili N'Ajjer. Serouenout is one of the abandoned French foreign legion forts in the area. Looking at its surroundings – and knowing how difficult it had been to reach even in a vehicle – it was hard to imagine the lives of those who had manned it, or indeed what the French had hoped to achieve by doing so.

We soon came across one of the great sand seas, the Erg d'Admer, stretching out to the horizon. A true erg is nothing but dunes, Lawrence of Arabia style, and it occurred to me that it would be impossible to cross one even by camel, and that no one would ever think of trying. This conclusion was confirmed when we reached another fort nearby.

Strolling slowly in the fierce heat with forty or fifty camels in tow was a lone Touareg. Looking rather unmajestic in his dusty robes, he didn't even look up to watch our approach. We decided to have lunch at the fort and Pete asked if he would like to join us. The abundant table making no impression on him, he refused, but stayed to watch our efficient feeding system while we, in mutual curiosity, took photographs of him and his snorting entourage.

The Touareg could speak some French and explained that the journey from his settlement to Djanet's camel market would take him 'twenty-four moons'. On asking why he was skirting the dunes in a wide loop – adding at least ten moons to his journey by my reckoning – he frowned and wagged a blue finger at the distant sea. That was good enough for me. If the blue-men-of-the-Sahara wouldn't even cross a small erg like that one, then no one could. As we drove off, he waved cheerfully and continued his interminable plodding.

The piste turned to hideous corrugations. We had come across stretches of them before, but none this size, nor for such a distance. Corrugations start due to the bouncing of vehicle wheels; the wind then clears loose sand from between them and in a self-perpetuating spiral of degradation, further vehicles then make them bigger. I had seen smaller vehicles skimming over the top of them, almost planing, but Bedford suspension isn't up to that, so we bucked along miserably slowly.

Frequent temptations to drive off-piste onto the welcoming flat sand on either side always ended in a bogging. The choice therefore was bone-crunching judders or sandmatting the truck back to a hard surface, and sandmatting was definitely a job to be avoided. Removing the six heavy, metal sandmats padlocked to the side of the truck was a drag. Positioning them in front of both sets of wheels gave us a hard surface to drive on, but inevitably we would get bogged again, necessitating the procedure to start over again. At length I learnt to avoid some boggings by looking out for bushes ahead, generally a sign of underground rivers – wadis – where the sand was softest. As I experimented, Pete was a picture of patience. He obviously knew all the tricks of desert driving, but with good grace allowed me the time to work them out for myself.

As anticipated, our fifth day brought us to Djanet. Built along a wide gorge, it is a true oasis town. The sudden abundant greenery made us feel like we were entering the Promised Land, all the more so as we drove past the palm-shaded cafes of Djanet's pretty central square. Just off the square we pulled into another Hotel Zeribas to camp.

I led the group straight to the square for a mint tea. The other customers were almost all Touareg, and with few visitors to such a remote area, the local café society was keen to find out where we'd all come from. With the help of a dusty atlas found in a trunk used as a table, we pointed out the variety of countries that were our origin. Unlike many Africans I would share a map-moment with, Djanet's Touareg had no problem grasping how far we all were from home, and like the one who was still leading his camels to that very square, they too calculated the distances in moons. In fact it was we westerners who sat in wonder – not because of the incredible size of our world, but because it felt as if we were in a different one entirely.

Pete was in the cab doing his accounts when I arrived back at the Zeribas. Going into raptures about the delights of Algeria and its people, I detected a distinct lack of enthusiasm at his end of the conversation. I asked if anything was wrong.

"Get real," Pete replied. "When they're not being awkward they're being vindictive. You just haven't met enough yet."

In terms of Algerian officialdom, Pete was quickly proved right. In charge the following day, I needed to fill the truck with diesel – no simple task in Djanet, as you require a permit. The military police wouldn't supply one and sent me to the Gendarmes. Rather than help, the cops decided to take me back to the truck and search it.

They were looking for smuggled money. Dollars have to be declared on entry into Algeria and changed at the official rate, way below that available on the black market. Not finding our hiding-place amongst the spares under the seats, they demanded our passports. I had to scout around town for the group, then bring them back to the site to get their passports confiscated, a rather humiliating job.

"Delightful lot as you say, Tim," Pete commented coldly.

The Gendarmes reappeared an hour later and handed back our passports, but then spent a further two hours tallying up everyone's cash to their currency declaration forms. We had been as careful with our maths as with our hiding place, and they again found nothing to fault. By the time I got to the diesel station with my permit, it had closed.

Filling up first thing, I drove the group to the base of the Tassili N'Ajjer and, guided along the steep path ascending the cliff, we climbed up to the plateau to find the famous rock paintings. Up to seven thousand years old, they stretch along the cliff walls for hundreds of feet, forming a vivid depiction of Saharan life in prehistory. Along with pictures of domestic animals we saw sketches of game now found only in sub-Saharan Africa: elephants, giraffes, hippos, even crocodiles. Humans were usually depicted as hunters but also, strangely, as sailors in boats. All that time ago the area must have been teeming with life and human activity. Now only a few Touareg remain, eking out a living in extremely difficult circumstances.

I had found everything about Djanet unexpectedly fascinating and to leave it so soon seemed a tragedy of lost opportunity, especially as it was unlikely we would ever reach such a remote spot again. With five days to get there from Tam' and only two actually spent in town, it promised to take another week before we would see a proper town again. But such is the nature of overlanding. Part tourism proper, but predominantly an expedition, it is the journey itself that provides much of the entertainment. The events and excursions come as something of a bonus and in areas like the Sahara they are few and far between. The group seemed happy enough though. Bouncing around in the back of the truck they read, chatted, looked at the scenery or often just slept – 'Just passin' through' might well be the motto for travelling in this way. Overlanding serves a purpose, but quite what that purpose is, is hard to say.

Pete had instilled in us all an element of dread of the Fadnoun Plateau. Right again – but it was even worse than he'd described. Like driving along a dry riverbed, the truck lurched over beach-ball-sized rocks, the wheels spitting them out behind us as they fought for grip. After two days to do a measly 100km, I saw the shimmer of tarmac. I couldn't imagine why the Algerian government had built it, but the road stretched 40km south of the settlement of Illizi.

All tarmac now, we were covering a massive 500km a day. Even so, it took another four nights rough camping to get to Ghardaia, each time driving some distance off the road. Out of earshot of the huge oil tankers that plied the route, we could regain the magic of the desert each night – in whatever terrain it chose for the occasion.

One evening, camped between Bordj and Ourgla where the road cuts through a valley in the Grand Erg Oriental, I watched as the group split up and took individual paths into huge dunes. Nearly 700km across and stretching almost to the Mediterranean in Tunisia, the Grand Erg Oriental is the biggest sand-sea in the Sahara, the kind of landscape that seems to induce in people the desire to think. Alone.

Or perhaps more. Using the sandy peak of a dune as a pillow, I was staring out to 'sea', feeling the last of the day's sun on my face. The dunes, completely undisturbed by humanity, marched into the horizon, every one a different size and shape. The view made me feel insignificant, like an insect in a vast and silent natural wonder. There, time stops. You notice more: the patterns made by the wind on the surface of the sand, the different coloured grains being flicked from one side of a knife-edge ridge to another – the process which imperceptibly causes the whole enormous dune to move.

It wasn't until dinnertime that anyone noticed Jacqueline wasn't around. Quiet and independent, she often separated from the group to stretch or dance.

"I saw her walking towards the dunes earlier," I said, thinking it a helpful start to our enquiries.

"Then why the hell didn't you stop her?" Pete snapped.

I sensed Pete was more worried than angry, and I didn't think she'd have gone far, so I suggested blasting the truck's air-horn to indicate where we were. With the sound echoing around the camp, I made my way back up the dune in dim starlight. From the top I could see our fire far below. The second I went over the ridge, however, the sound of the horn disappeared.

Continuing down to a valley and up the next dune, I realised why Pete was so worried. If you didn't look at the stars before wandering off, you would quickly have no clue which way to go.

"She's nowhere to be seen," I told Pete when I got back.

"Shit."

He organised a controlled search. We walked directly into the erg in a straight line, keeping in sight of one another. Three or four dunes in there was no sign and the group, trudging in the steep soft sand, were getting tired. Pete called a halt.

"There's nothing more we can do 'til it's light," he said. "She'll be freezing cold, but if she stays put we'll find her in the morning."

I had one more idea. The first dune was by far the highest. I pointed this out to Pete, suggesting we build a beacon at the top. With aching legs, everyone carried a lump of wood to the top. There we stoked up a fire. Louis and I stayed there, throwing on cups of diesel to make it flare. After two hours there was still no sign, so we threw on the last of the wood and went back down to camp.

Now as worried as Pete, I couldn't sleep well, and it was still dark when I wandered over to the campfire. Nursing a cup of coffee and wrapped in a blanket was Jacqueline.

"Morning," she said jauntily. "Did you have a lot of fun last night? I saw your party on the dune. It must have been nice."

Unbelievably, Jacqueline had seen it all. In the early evening she had walked along the foot of the dunes until she'd felt completely alone. There, she had mediated and slept early. The horn woke her up and later, she saw the fire.

"It's impossible to get away from you all," she concluded with her captivating smile.

The Sahara became noticeably more fertile on the run up to Ghardaia. There, the Mozabites, a secretive group of ultra-puritanical Islamists, run the town. As well as alcohol, they reject music, smoking and, as was clear to see, decorative mosques. In fact the only decoration anywhere was a slogan – FIS – daubed on every wall.

We parked in the dry riverbed that serves as a truck park and the group split up to take in the town. Pete and I hadn't yet succeeded in telexing the office from Algeria; the facilities were available, but international lines had been down. At the Hotel Rostidemes overlooking town, we failed again but found out the reason – elections had just taken place. That explained the ubiquitous 'FIS' signs – the Front Islamique du Salut had unexpectedly won – but at that time, it wasn't at all clear why that should have caused cessation of communications with the outside world.

Snow in the Tellien Atlas gave us a sharp reminder that we had just driven into a European winter. But there was no room for wonder at the contrast with only days before – we were cold, wet and miserable. In recompense, we had also driven into a European quality of life. The next town we reached, Tlemcen, was a wonderful surprise. With a plethora of shops and well-built houses, the people of this working town were far too busy to take any notice of us. I gave the group two hours and they sprinted off in search of a chicken-and-chip shop one had spotted. Sitting outside a café in the wintry sunshine, Pete and I followed a chip-butty with splendid coffee and date pastries.

Save officialdom, I was still delighted by everything Algeria had to offer. The people were friendly and the whole country, from the harsh desert to the fertile mountains, was incredibly varied. It was also cheap, particularly with our black market Dinars, and there were enough treats to keep us sane: dates that melt in the mouth, the lovely pastries and coffee and, strangely, in Djanet, the best oranges I'd ever tasted. Yet Pete, even replete, wouldn't warm to the place.

"Still no sodding telex. Can't they sort this country out?"

We had tried to contact London from Tlemcen post office, again with no luck. Next on the list was the Hotel Zianide, a more attractive four-star hotel than its name would suggest. No line there either. But, having discovered that he'd changed too much money back in Tamanrasset, Pete decided to look at the Zianide's rooms. We found hot water, huge beds and televisions, and downstairs, a well-stocked bar – allowed by the government in international hotels. Two weeks without a beer and with money to burn, Pete booked us all in.

The group traipsed through the smoked-glass doors. As they gawped at the marble floor and chandeliers, the receptionists gawped at them. We had all become used to our appearance, but in truth we were disgustingly dirty. Later, at the bar, I gawped too – at the astonishing transformation of the group. Resplendent in clean jeans, trainers and shirts, they had suddenly mutated back into the nurses, teachers and office workers they had once been.

We left Algeria and crossed the border into Morocco. The hills of the Middle Atlas drop down to Fes and I felt incredibly lucky to be driving into this stunning place, perhaps the most famous medieval city in the world. I reflected that it was only a couple of months since I'd been scratching a living shifting van loads of possessions from one London house to another, and I winced at my old advertising slogan: 'Let Tim Drive You Round The Bend'. *Now*, I thought, *I can Drive Anyone Round the World.*

At the outer walls of the eighth century Medina, Kalam was selected from hundreds to guide us around. Walking through the gates into the labyrinth of alleyways truly feels as if you are stepping into an ancient world. Men and boys in robes work metal or leather in dark rooms below their tiny homes. Weavers spin cloth on wooden wheels and mosaic-makers chip at tiles by hand, placing tiny pieces into separate containers for assembly elsewhere. Delivery boys pull decorated handcarts past peddlers selling trinkets, food and water. As we weaved through the alleys in a dreamlike state, it became clear that without Kalam we would never find our way out.

We visited a tannery. In a dark passageway, where hides were piled up ready to send upstairs for processing, men worked in a sordid gloom, scraping off hair with sharp knives. The odour was unbearable and with relief we came out into the open and a view down to the tannery's dyeing-pools, where dozens more unfortunate workers, waist deep in smelly soup, were treading colour into the hides.

After the tannery tour, we were taken to the obligatory carpet shop. While we sat around drinking tea, a salesman described the manufacture of each carpet that his helper flung to the floor with a flourish. Works of art to some – certainly the 460,000 knots per square metre was an impressive figure – I couldn't muster any interest. I just sat there feeling sorry for the young girls the salesman described sitting in mountain villages tying all those knots by hand.

That evening we had a group meal. The traditional Moroccan food was an absolute feast. We started with pigeon pie, a very sweet, rich dish, and then ate a fantastic lamb Tagine – a slow-cooked stew served in earthenware pots that give the dish its name. We drank excellent Meknes red wine and danced to live music. Having such a good time, I began to think about when I would get to lead my own expedition. I was eager to put everything I'd learned into action and resolved to say as much to Pete the next day.

We reached Tangiers late the following afternoon. Sitting together in the cab at the ferry port, I waited until Pete had finished what he was writing before blurting out my thoughts.

"I wondered when you were going to say that," Pete said. "Read this. And by the way, you're staying here."

He handed over a report on me. In it, he recommended that I go back to the workshop, to learn, as he put it, 'company ways'. Nervously I asked him his reasons. I soon wished I hadn't.

"Nothing personal, Tim, but you act like a primadonna. You never expect anything bad to happen – but it does. Whether it's health, mechanics or security, things go wrong. And when they do, it's only you who's there to deal with them. Also, you've got to keep your distance from the group. I know you think you're ready to lead, but believe me Tim, you're not."

"So why am I staying here then?" I was still staring at the report; anything to avoid eye contact.

"I don't know," Pete replied coldly. "They haven't seen that yet."

Passing the papers back, I caught his weary-looking eyes. "Do you know how long I'll be here?" I asked.

"Tim. You don't get it, do you?" He looked utterly exasperated. "You'll be here as long as they need you here. Then you'll do whatever it is they want you to do next. It could be another year before you're leading a trip. And that's if you come up to the mark at all."

In light drizzle I watched as the truck drove away. Standing there with my pack at my feet trying to shake off the gloom, I caught sight of fortifications high up on the bluff overlooking the port. There, facing Europe like a shield protecting the exotic of Africa, was Tangiers' fabled Kasbah. The sight evoked in me such a strong sense of exhilaration that it pushed Pete's comments from my mind. Not even the incessant badgering from hoards of hustlers could break the spell as I strode purposefully up the hill.

I booked into the neighbouring hotel. Built directly in front of Tangiers' Medina, long before the ferry terminal had sprung up as the one minor blight on the view, the Continental is like a palace faded from past glory. The panelled lobby resembles an antique shop; full of grandfather clocks, beautifully crafted model ships, huge leather armchairs and old maps of Tangiers. Placing my hand on the polished hardwood banister, I ran my palm along it, following its smooth curve up to my room. There, I stepped through louver doors onto a wrought-iron balcony and as the sun set over the Straits of Gibraltar, I stared out in reverie. Beyond the harbour I could see the beach, the peninsula at the other end of the bay and Europe in the distance. Pete's words came back to mind, but I pushed them away. *Who cares?* I thought as darkness fell. *I'm still in Africa. It's fine – just as long as they don't send me back to Northampton.*

In the UK, a new moon has little significance – in fact it is rare that we even see it through our murky skies. Since I had been in North Africa, however, and in particular in the desert, the waxing and waning of the moon had become intrinsic pleasures. They were my soap operas; I knew exactly what was going to happen, but I still looked forward to seeing them.

That night was a special episode, though. As the new moon rose in the ninth month of the Islamic calendar, it signalled the beginning of Ramadan, when Muslims rigorously observe their abstention from food, drink, sex and smoking from dawn to dusk until the full moon a month later.

In the morning, there was no breakfast available at the Continental; in fact every café and restaurant in the whole town was closed. By the end of the day I was ravenous and on the lookout for food. With the sun setting, I took a seat next to a wiry-looking Moroccan outside a cafe in the Petit Socco, Tangiers' main square, made legendary by Paul Bowles.

Rachif, self-proclaimed King of the Socco, told me he was taking time out from hustling foreigners and seemed happy to share his thoughts on Ramadan. Nervously turning his cigarette packet from end to side to end again, he tapped out a rhythm as he explained why Muslims consider it the most important time of the year.

"How are you feeling though?" I enquired after the explanation.

"Terrible," Rachif answered. "I've got snakes chewing my belly and a lion in my head."

I could get the stomach part – I too felt queasy from lack of food – but I enquired as to the lion.

"It roars for cigarettes!" he cried in mock pain.

Rachif was surprised to hear that I too had spent a day marked by lack of indulgence.

"But you don't have to fast. You are a foreigner. For us Moroccans, the King himself would jail us if we even swallow our spit! But Allah is good, and Allah is right. We feel clean; we feel strong when the month has passed."

Certainly there could be no denying the detoxifying nature of the process.

"Look about you," Rachif continued. "Soon we will break the fast and celebrate. If it weren't for the lion this would be my favourite month in each year."

By now the square was full, the atmosphere one of tension. As he told me the downside of Ramadan, Rachif bubbled with laughter, displaying the heavy staining on his few remaining teeth.

"Don't travel in a car after four. The drivers fall asleep, or just go mad. In this month there are many deaths. Boom, boom. Pah!" As fist met hand to demonstrate the deadly collisions he could see in his mind, Rachif was further consumed by mirth. I didn't doubt his words. At the best of times, Moroccans appear to have something of a cavalier attitude towards the possibility of road-death. Long distance taxi drivers, I'd noticed, seemed particularly keen to meet their maker; overtaking not being an option until they can see a blind bend ahead. The rusty evidence that Allah sometimes chose to pluck a few believers from their earthly bondage is plain to see in ravines below any Atlas road.

The muezzins cranked up their amplifiers and the air filled with their cries. Lanterns lit up minarets all over the Medina and beyond and harira appeared unbidden in front of us. A thick bean-based soup, it is spicy and filling and makes the perfect meal for 'breaking the fast'. Eating it felt like a reward for a hard day's work. Milk and bowls of dates were also put on each table and Rachif took them around the square, offering them to the poor and elderly. The tension dissipated and I too felt an extraordinary glow. The overriding feeling was one of communal joy. All had shared the experience of minor sacrifice and now they wanted to give of themselves. Ramadan, even more than usual in Morocco, is a time of generosity and thanksgiving.

The entertainment started. Jugglers came between the tables, musicians found small spaces in the crowded square to perform and dancers gathered around them. Later, as the crowd began to thin out, I caught a glimpse of Rachif in front of a pair of percussionists who were skilfully keeping a pulsating rhythm on a darbuka and taarija – bass and treble drums. Surrounded by his hand-clapping subjects, the King was dancing wildly, kicking his gangly legs far out in front of him. On closer inspection, I noticed that Rachif was sucking hard on a cigarette stuck fast between his lips.

Mentally refreshed, I telexed Graham first thing the next morning. He asked me to call back in ten minutes.

He launched straight into business. "You two were lucky to get out of Algeria in one piece!"

Surprised, I asked if it had anything to do with the Touareg.

"No," he replied. "We've forgotten that problem. This is much worse. It's the Algerian election. The military have taken over and Algeria's closed. We'll need you and your French available for the next trip due to go through."

"What do you want me to do then?"

"Nothing yet. Just wait for orders. By the way, Pete's quit – the time always comes." Replacing the receiver, it occurred to me that Pete had, as usual, been absolutely correct. I wasn't going anywhere near the wheel of a truck. In fact, far from becoming the expedition leader I longed to be, I was about to forge a career as a mixture between errand boy and shipping agent. My only problem was that I hadn't thought to pack a tie.

By dragging a desk across my room's cool mosaic tile floor and out onto the balcony, I created an improvised office. There, I wrote up trip notes from the Sahara, kept my accounts and studied the papers for news of Algeria. Each day, I typed a short telex to Graham:

Tim here in Tangiers. Waiting for orders.

To which I always got the same reply:

OK, Bibi for now.

And nothing more.

What of Algeria? How had the military takeover happened? How relieved had Graham been, not about our clear run through Touareg territory, but by our successful crossing of Algeria itself, when we finally managed to telex from Morocco? And what current situation prompts the Foreign Office website to write the following?

"We advise against all holiday and other non-essential travel to Algeria, except to the Sahara Desert and mountainous regions in the south of the country, which are not normally subject to terrorist violence. The security situation in northern Algeria remains serious, especially outside the main cities."

After 132 years of intense French colonial control, Algeria became independent in 1962 under the Front de Liberation Nationale (FLN). The eight-year war had cost the country up to a million lives. It was a divided populace who had won, and the moment French forces left the country the leaders started fighting amongst themselves. With the first president already ousted by 1965, the new president, Boumedienne, created a one-party state, granting himself almost total power. Following a socialist doctrine, he nationalised private sector industries and used oil revenue to provide education and health for the masses. Algeria rapidly urbanised and industrialised, but by the late 1970s state planning in agriculture led to food shortages. Boumedienne's brutal response to protest began to alienate both the emerging middle class and crucially, organised Islamic groups. In 1979, he died.

The seeds of Chadlis Benjeded's problems were already sown, therefore, even as he came to power, but throughout the 1980s, oil money kept the majority passive. Yet when oil dropped from $30 a barrel to $10, his regime lurched into crisis. It was the youth – unemployed, living in overcrowded slums and disenfranchised from the power base – that rose up in October 1988. And it was Chadlis' military security that stepped in to keep order, killing hundreds of their own people.

The results of October 1988 were surprising. Re-elected, President Chadlis immediately held a referendum to adopt another constitution, one that created a new democracy; and by summer 1989, several new political associations had been authorised to operate, including the Front Islamique du Salut (FIS).

FIS quickly gathered momentum and soon formed a militia. In June 1990, local elections were announced and FIS won a resounding victory, taking nearly twice as many votes as FLN. They immediately demanded parliamentary elections, which were set for June 1991.

FIS saw through blatant government plans to rig the elections and, in an attempt to bring down the regime, called a general strike. Clearly the strongest political power, the strike may have succeeded but at this point the army stepped in. The military didn't want to run the country – they preferred to exert their influence from behind a democratically elected leader acceptable to international powers – so they pushed the government into announcing renewed elections, making it clear they expected FIS not to win.

While we had been enjoying Boxing Day in Agadez, Algeria was holding those elections. It took a week to announce the results, but on the day after we had entered Algeria, FIS learnt that they had won a massive majority in the first round.

The army stepped in again. By proclaiming that once in power, the Islamists might never allow democratic elections again, they won international backing. On January 4th the Assembly was dissolved; on the 11th, President Chadlis resigned, and on the 14th, an interim High Council of State was established, with Mohammed Boudiaf appointed by the army as President. On the day we had left Algeria, January 16th, the second round of elections was cancelled and the army mobilised to take control of all key installations, from the oilfields to the TV stations.

We had been fortunate that the political process had been effectively suspended for the three weeks we had trucked ignorantly through the country. Right up until the army mobilised, the expectation was that the FIS would win at least some part of a hastily cobbled-together government. While Algeria's citizens waited patiently for this announcement, we had slipped through.

The moment the tanks rolled, Algeria began to tear itself apart. In the last ten years, up to 200,000 people have been killed in clashes between armed Islamic groups and security forces. Branded terrorists, FIS obviously get little international sympathy, but they claim that "what the illegitimate ruling Junta have done in the past and is still engaged in pursuing, is an open war against Allah". If one looks strictly at the facts of the election, they certainly have a point. And more recently, despite fully documented evidence of government-sponsored murder, and accusations by Amnesty International of routine abuse of human rights, the US have allowed the Algerian government to sign up to their 'War on Terror'. Are theirs really the ideal credentials?

Algeria should be one of Africa's wealthiest countries, due not least to massive oil and gas fields, but also food and wine exports. However, the country I found so welcoming continues to decay in an endless spiral of violence.

A month on, I was just beginning to suspect I really was being punished for being a 'primadonna' when I received a longer reply to my daily telex:

Luke arrives Rabat March 18th **on Southbound Trans-Africa. He and group flying to Senegal same day.**
You to pick up truck at Rabat campsite and arrange immediate shipment from Casablanca port to Dakar port, Senegal. BiBi. Graham.

The truck was there as promised. Another bright orange Bedford, this one looked brand new. The lockers were crammed to the brim with food stores; all the tents, beds and cooking apparatus were clean and shiny, and even the equipment strapped to the sides was freshly painted black. I glanced at the registration number – MPP – and suddenly twigged that it was Pete's old truck, almost unrecognisable after its Northampton workshop turnaround.

As I drove to Casablanca, I realised that it had a new engine too. Indeed, everything that I'd got used to coping with had been fixed. The brakes were sharp, the steering responsive and the suspension much more comfortable. Even the old sagging seat – the one that arranged the driver's back into a concertina shape for maximum discomfort – had been replaced.

At the Comarine office at Casablanca port, I was told a ship was departing in two days' time – I had to work fast apparently. That day was spent on a merry-go-round of offices, meeting mysterious people whose only job, it appeared, was to extract a further sum of money in return for a heavily thumped stamp. My transitaire had provided me with two assistants in this endeavour, and BigMan and Bobblehat – their chosen names as translated from the French – babbled incomprehensible reasons for each hefty bribe. The reams of documentation generated were only rivalled by the paper trail of Dirham notes I left in my wake. By the end of the day, Big and Bobble had marked out an area in chalk only thirty metres from the correctly named ship.

I was already waiting at the port gates when they opened at 5am the next morning. I drove Luke's truck through and, unhindered, made my way to my rectangle. There, I found Big and Bobble lying dead centre, asleep under a canvas tarpaulin, dutifully guarding the sacred space. I made them a coffee, and we then strolled together to the Comarine office. We were told the ship would be loading some time that night.

At 3am, dazzling floodlights woke me up. Looking out of my cab window, the port looked like a prison camp after an escape. Dozens of porters were haggling over the cost of shifting loose goods, while uniformed supervisors waved orders to crane drivers who were moving containers overhead; customs men walked about, clipboards in hand, checking on both. Looking like the fugitives in question, Big and Bobble appeared out of the melee.

My truck was to be loaded last, but not before a certain amount of argument between all parties as to how it was to be achieved. Big eventually suggested The Net, to which a modicum of agreement was voiced. At a flurry of hand signals to a crane driver, almost invisible in his cockpit over eighty metres above us, the net appeared in seconds, the delicacy of movement from such an enormous machine beautiful to behold.

Once it had been unhooked and spread out across the tarmac I drove onto the metal-rope mesh, then got out to watch the lifting operation. The net's hooped corners were gathered above the truck, pushed into the crane's hook and without so much as a cursory tug to check safety, the truck was raised. As soon as it left the ground it lurched to one side as the front wheels turned with the transfer of weight.

"Down" I shouted. "Bring it down!"

It was Big once again who came up with the solution. His eyes indicated the cab and his hands a steering wheel. In reply, with a finger aimed at my chest, I indicated, 'Me?'

Gripping the knobbly wheel, I gave a nod to the supervisor who transferred the signal skywards. Suddenly, the dozens of faces smiling their encouragement disappeared, along with my stomach. The next thing I knew I was dangling high above the ship feeling like the baby under the stork's beak. Beneath me, the lights of the port looked like an inverted starlit sky.

With someone now captive in his normally lonesome orbit, and an admiring audience below, the crane driver evidently decided it was time for some fun. Travelling at a funfair type of angle, the truck swung in a full 360-degree circle over three towers of containers, the roofs of two goods-sheds and the upturned faces of the cheering port workers. My eyes had just begun to explain these blurred images to my mind when I came across my missing stomach still on its way up. The reunion was brief, however, as I was at the time being plummeted in a terrifying free-fall back towards the ship.

I landed, without so much as a bump, in a truck-sized space between two containers. With all my bits reassembled, I carefully manoeuvred the truck to get the net out, placed the loops onto the nodding hook, and watched as the trailer followed a similarly flamboyant trajectory across the skies of Casablanca.

I did buy the tie. I had to. And I got myself a Pete-style briefcase too. For the next four months, I dragged it between Morocco and Senegal, dealing with paperwork and loading and unloading vehicles. For now, true 'overlanding' was at an end and trips were being organised differently. Where possible, trucks were swapped between groups who overflew the Sahara. I met several drivers working their way up and down the continent, their groups and trucks in various states of disrepair. I didn't just deal with our company's drivers either; as the company made my burgeoning shipping skills available to anyone who heard of them, I organised whole convoys of vehicles, negotiating group rates for overlanders and independents alike as they gathered at either end of the watery route across Africa. Eventually, our company's trips began to be sold without the North Africa stage, groups beginning and ending their trips in Dakar or Bamako. As the work dried up, I remembered Pete's recommendation for my continued training, and slowly began to resign myself to going back to the workshop.

At least winter's passed, I thought.

Attn: Tim English. Hotel Central, Dakar.

Ray's Northbound group arriving Bamako 12/06.
Take train to Bamako and escort them back to Dakar.
Ray and truck staying in Mission for Southbound 20/06. Wait
for new group and escort from Dakar back to Bamako.
Pax lists to follow.
Bibi. Graham.

Three more train rides beckoned me yet, but I was so overjoyed that there was still no mention of the workshop that I resolved to make the most. After months of hotels and restaurants I was in severe need of some discomfort training, so I booked into Second Class – as far from the bar as possible.

In my carriage, an individual woman occupied each bank of four seats. Knowing by now the friendly nature of Africans on public transport, this arrangement struck me as odd, and when I was refused wherever I tried to sit down, I couldn't initially understand. All became clear immediately upon departure, when that whole section of the train turned into a mobile market, the traders representing yet another mini-nation inside this shifting world.

At each stop – some thirty in Senegal alone – a thronging mass of noise and colour appeared at the windows. The women inside bought buckets and sacks of various fruits and vegetables directly off the heads of those outside. The transactions were done in a desperate hurry, bids being shouted at tremendous volume across fruitily bedecked heads ten deep. When someone agreed terms, snapping up, for example, huge quantities of green-coloured oranges, there was a surge as the vendor was propelled to the front of the crowd. This went on right through the day and into the night, the produce piling higher and higher on each woman's commandeered seating area. I was genuinely in the way and was shooed from any perch I tentatively rested my behind on.

The compartment was brim full when we reached the Mali border at midnight, the women themselves barely visible behind their hoards. Customs officials came aboard on both sides of the border, and both times a shouting match took place. That the officials all went home laden with fruity goodies didn't surprise me; that they evidently re-enacted the same performance a total of four times each week without reaching amicable agreement did.

Once in Mali, the fruit and vegetables started their return journey back through the windows and into empty baskets crowning an even more colourful scene outside. As they were bartered for brightly coloured printed cottons, the carriage took on the appearance of a richly decorated period sitting-room. After my protest that I couldn't bruise cotton, and probably looking worryingly close to collapse, the women now allowed me to sit. Between stops only.

Despite exhaustion, I was, for the entire length of that journey, entranced. Whether drugged by the heady aroma in the carriage, barging through the fevered crowds at a stop to find a coffee or dozing momentarily whilst we moved on a few kilometres, it was a joy. Firm friends with most of the women by the end, I was almost sorry to reach Bamako.

It was a train-weary soul that gathered Ray's group together the next morning for another long hot rail journey back to Senegal. Meeting them, high on their trip stories, in the mission compound had reminded me that I'd been drifting around for over six months, picked up and put down anywhere on a vast sandy stage controlled by London. As I would only be responsible for them for thirty hours, I didn't feel like putting much effort into entertaining the group.

So, when pausing to look at my watch, only to find myself in my third hour of deep conversation with Kathy, I was amazed at how good I felt. We had covered African travelling tales, moved on to music and culture, lightly skimmed the difference between religion and spirituality and were by then discussing what West African tribal rituals might be able to teach people in the west. Kathy had so much to say that interested me and had drawn out of me thoughts that I couldn't even remember having crossed my mind before.

The face that looked over the seat in front of me, chin balanced on delicate hands, was to my mind perfectly sculpted. A dazzling smile and brown eyes shone from a clear skin, lightly freckled and pale despite three months in the African sun. Kathy's straight brown hair bounced with each emphatic movement of her head and her German accent was softened to an attractive lilt by her clear, deep voice. She was Swiss, but also spoke French and English with fluency. We conversed in both. At a low ebb, on a roasting hot train – and before lunch! ... *I couldn't be falling in love could I?*

Presently Kathy left the seat next to her sister, to sit next to me. Subconsciously, we adjusted ourselves to recreate the permanent gaze we had been enjoying. With only a few interruptions from curious members of the group, we continued to talk and laugh for the rest of the day. At a few stops we got off the train to wander over to the Second Class section where the traders were clamouring. I waved to the women furiously making their deals, feeling very pleased with myself when one momentarily paused to wave back.

After nightfall, I took Kathy up to Zongo's bar He arranged for us to share dinner with the train guards and took us two carriages back, to the rear of the train. I hadn't got that far before and was delighted to see a little balcony behind their eating area. We sat on the floor with the guards and ate goatmeat stew and rice with our hands out of an enamel bowl the size of a dogbath. I had brought beers, which were also shared around.

Before heading back to work the guards unlocked the door to the balcony. There, as if we were crossing a new world in another century, we watched the moonlit bush saunter past on either side of the rails, bending slightly as if to acknowledge us. At the border, during the two-hour wait in the middle of the night for our passports to be processed, Kathy and I sat at one of the hundreds of little refreshment stalls. Planks balanced across beer crates for benches, each had a kerosene lamp to highlight their food or drink speciality. We selected coffee, Nescafe and sweetened condensed milk – there was no choice in how you took it. Tea was next door, fruit juice the stall after that; no one trod on neighbouring toes by serving the whole selection. And still we were talking, exploring each other's motivations, aspirations, fears and joys. Nothing even approaching this had ever happened to me before.

"When will I see you again?" I whispered in Kathy's ear, lying behind her, my hand caressing the curve of her slim waist.

With an extraordinary frankness, Kathy had asked for a double room on our arrival at the Central in Dakar. When she'd announced it in front of the whole group, I was slightly flustered, but a marked lack of comment indicated that they had expected it after our intensive courting marathon. We had gone straight to our room and, apart from a meal each evening, had barely left for three days. We'd lived on coffee and pastries I fetched from the patisserie below, cigarettes and wine that Kathy got from the market.

That afternoon, as it had been every afternoon, the bed was bathed in sunlight, white cotton curtains billowing in the warm breeze. As well as being engrossed in each other's minds, we were now also entwined in each other's bodies. One subject of conversation always met with silence however; it was the only unmentionable – Us – and I had just brought it up once again.

Kathy turned her face towards me and fixed her eyes on mine. I flicked a twist of her hair to one side that tickled my nose. Looking at her familiar gaze, I felt a perfect intimacy. But I was silent. I was waiting for an answer.

"Tim," she said with an almost cheeky smile. "You won't see me again."

Her expression would normally have accompanied one of the playful, mocking comments she excelled at, so I remained silent, expecting to hear the peal of laughter I was used to. Then Kathy spoke again, her features taking on a more serious aspect this time.

"This is too good, Tim – it cannot last. We are lost in our hearts. It is because it is Africa. I told you I wanted with all my soul to be here, and I saved for many years. You and I have met now like a beautiful end to my dream. Tomorrow, the dream ends. Your group arrives and I go home. If you are as similar to me as I think you are, you will understand." Her brown eyes stared with emphatic intensity.

I wasn't the first to have heard such words snuffing the life out of a relationship they thought would stay like it was forever. My mind seemed to be struggling to put everything back into shape again – just as it had been only seconds before. The emptiness in my stomach told me it wasn't possible.

Kathy's smile returned, and she leant up on one elbow, stretching to kiss me tenderly on my dry lips. "It is a present, Tim. I'm being generous. You will one day thank me." Betraying, perhaps, another aspect of her emotions, one tear escaped her eye.

I fell back to the pillow and looked up to the ceiling, focusing on the fan turning lazily above us. Taking in a final mental snapshot of my surroundings, I was a long time silent. Eventually, the meditation took effect and order came back to my scrambled head, my mind regaining a flimsy reality: this was one more thing I was going to agree with Kathy about.

From the moment I'd met her I had been entranced by her otherworldliness and her wisdom. And here again she was right, streets ahead of my perception. Europe, jobs in offices, a cold apartment, struggling to decide between paying a mortgage and saving for two-week package holidays – none of it could ever fit with our experience together there in Senegal, and she knew we would be foolish even to try. It *was* a gift, Kathy's final lesson, taught with only a few words in her beautiful French.

But it sure as hell doesn't feel like it.

Kathy wouldn't let me take her to the airport, nor even wave from the window. "It's already too much like a shit American movie," she insisted.

At the door to our room, I took her in my arms. We hugged until our muscles ached. I could feel her shoulders jumping as she sobbed silently, but I couldn't let my own tears go while she was still with me. One kiss, one look and she was gone, the door closed carefully behind her.

I sat on the bed, gripping a corner of the sheet, staring at all I seemed to have in my life: a backpack. And finally they came. I cried for Kathy, but sneaking in there too while the going was good, I cried for the wretched loneliness of my job.

The gathering of another group in Dakar, the beery meals there and in Bamako, and the train journey that linked the two passed by in something of a daze, but at the conscious level at least, my recovery was as swift as the five-day-love-affair itself. Two things helped me achieve such a quick resumption of normal duties inside my head. The first was my mind. Finding the relationship so surreal and closed with such ruthless finality, it had chosen to label it 'apparition' and filed it accordingly. The second was Graham's next telex.

Fly immediately to Kampala. You to join Al Casey on north-bound trans-Africa.
And congratulations from all in London. See fax for details.
Telex on arrival in Kampala.
BiBi. Graham.

As the fax slowly edged out of the machine, a brief internal battle concluded that the sheer joy of expectation would conquer the sharp tug of regret. What I was reading, upside down, was a copy of a letter Graham had sent to Al. In it, he explained that I was to be considered his co-driver. From June 26th, my traineeship would end. I still wouldn't have my own truck – London considered it prudent to first give me a proper trip across the hardest terrain Africa could produce – but I had nonetheless graduated to driver.

And my wages were on the brink of spiralling. Shortly I would be raking it in – nearly sixty quid a week!

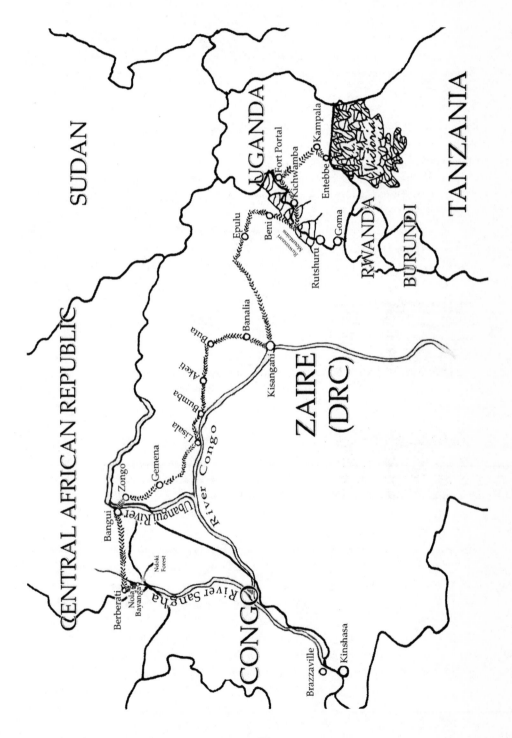

It took four flights to cover the 5000km to English-speaking East Africa, and my first step onto the tarmac at Entebbe airport was greeted by an immense thunderstorm. It stopped as quickly as it had started, evaporating with visible speed from steaming puddles and leaving behind a heady aroma of wet grass and exotic fruit.

On the bus to Kampala I was instantly entranced by the great contrast with North Africa. Where I had been used to sand and scrub, I saw palms, flame-tree acacias and huge mango trees spreading shade across shambas – smallholder farms – situated between endless banana plantations. And here, there were masses of people, the roadside bustling like a busy high street. Wearing shorts, T-shirts and flip-flops, everyone moved purposefully, some pushing trolleys laden with goods, others carrying tools – mattocks or spades – slung across a shoulder, but most carrying nothing more than a handful of bananas or a few mangoes.

The bus drove on, past the ubiquitous adverts for Coca-Cola, Blue Band, Close Up or Omo, and into the succession of shanty towns that follow the highway out of the city, the buildings now brick-built shacks, a few 4x2s holding up their rusted tin roofs. Many were shops, indicated by hand-written signs hung at jaunty angles: Maji Ubongo, The Old Entebbe Butcher, Safe Sham Enterprises and The Seven Sisters Beauty Shop. I couldn't see what was inside the intriguingly named 'Goodlove Shop', but names didn't necessarily describe wares: 'Banana, Banana, Banana' proudly displayed a selection of brown velveteen chairs and settees – not a bent yellow fruit in sight.

The hills and red-tile roofed houses of Kampala appeared in the distance. Every time the bus stopped to drop someone off, we were surrounded by hawkers, each sweating face desperate to sell some piffling object to the stony-faced travellers. In a similarity to West Africa, each hawker concentrated on a single product: bars of Imperial Leather soap, loaves of sliced bread, a handful of plastic wallets, a stack of cashewnuts, an open packet of cigarettes, boiled eggs or water in plastic bags. The most enterprising carried a box displaying a range of products, but still in one line only – haircare or electrical items, perhaps – while the most hopeful, I thought, was a gentleman armed with a dozen pink and green nylon feather dusters. He poked one through the bus window and tickled my nose.

I never saw more than a few coins change hands. Looking around me at the fevered attempts to drum up business, I could only wonder at the brand of 'lazy' that stigmatises people in this part of the world – they work hard all day for money that a westerner would barely bother to pick up if he dropped it. Their problem isn't lack of energy, but lack of opportunity.

On the streets of Kampala, the first thing that struck me was the colour. There were no Arab features in sight and none of their sombre robes and shrouds. The second was the business of the streets. There were more cars than I was used to; half-cars and clown cars, all vying for a patch of broken tarmac. Hot competition came from matatus, the minibuses that provide city transport, their names emblazoned in gawdy signwriting: Death or Glory, Break the Limit, Hell for Leather – none too tempting for those desirous of a safe journey. Personally, I would have chosen Kiss my Bust had it been going in my direction. Dangerously darting between all these vehicles were the average working Ugandan's prime means of personal transport – bicycles. Many done up like a Mod's Vespa – frames festooned with mirrors, bottle caps in the spokes – they were evidently also a means of showing flair, pride and relative wealth.

Nowhere had I been so visually assaulted by activity. Released from a terrible era of war, repression and civil slaughter, Uganda had attracted massive investment from the west under President Musoveni, and it was evidently being put to good use. Every other plot in the centre was a building-site of multi-storey concrete crawling with workmen, the floors propped up by mangrove scaffolding, the madly bent branches so freshly cut the building looked as if it was actually growing. With such a tangible buzz in the air, I really felt that I was going to enjoy the fresh atmosphere of sub-Saharan Africa.

The next day I waited for Al at our rendezvous, the Sheraton Hotel. He was a long time coming, so I browsed the small hotel shopping arcade. It was depressingly empty and I bought what there was – a newspaper and nineteen bars of Cadbury's (I hadn't seen that for months) – and then went out to the carpark. Eating a slice of fresh pineapple, I was just contemplating a small pile of ant-filled mango skins at my feet when the orange truck appeared, easing down the ramp before skilfully performing a five-point turn – not easy with a short trailer.

The door opened. I climbed into the cab to meet my new mentor, Al. He couldn't have been any more different from Pete.

"What have you been doing?" shouted Al over some Madness blaring from a quality stereo. "You look like you've got pussy juice running down your chin."

"Erm, I'm just finishing my breakfast."

"She sounds like a bag of nails in a tumble drier," he pronounced, crunching into first gear, "and I hear you're no help. Can't spin a spanner, right?"

"Well, if it's on the list of things I've done you'll be all right, if not, you're on your own. But if you're stuck for ordering a part in French, then I'm your man."

Al reached the top of the ramp, threw the truck into second with another painful grind and deftly turned the wheel with his left palm while reaching his right hand over the top to shake mine.

"Al. Just pulling your scrotum." Reaching third without any noise, he turned One Step Beyond down to a bearable pitch. "It's just first, second and reverse. Dunno what it is, but I try not to use them. If I do, I just turn the music up. Didn't hear a thing, did you?"

Al turned to me with a questioning expression. This broke into a smile and a wink, demanding my complicity in his denial of any possible wrong. Good humour oozed from Al's every pore. I was laughing already and I knew straight away we were going to get on.

Al wore enormously flared, fluorescent yellow shorts topped by a t-shirt proclaiming MUZUNGU ('Whitey'); a vicious crew-cut of his blond hair made him look bald. His long, thin body sprouted what looked like a strap-on gut, further accentuated as his seat was pushed forward, forcing his knees up at a wild angle. On the straight out of town, I realised why. Al liked to use them to hold the wheel while studying his map, or sometimes – accompanied by a satisfied sigh – while diligently rearranging his balls.

I certainly wasn't going to have any problem with my own tendency to accumulate cab flotsam, nor would we be quietly seething over each other's music choice – Al enjoyed swapping tapes as erratically as I did, and his taste was as eclectic as my own: ska, punk, classical, funk and industrial rap, anything went. In fact, conversations about drivers we knew, complaints about the London office – overland drivers' stock in trade – weren't even mentioned as we scrabbled furiously in his box of tapes, plucking jewels from the chaos of plastic.

Heading towards the Ruwenzori Mountains on a quiet road, we stopped for lunch. As the group made the usual preparations – putting up the tables and balancing washing-up tubs on sandmats and stools – we were slowly surrounded by people. Initially, children formed a dense circle around us, then some men arrived and stood with them. There didn't seem to be any contact between them and us, so I asked one of the group what was happening.

Helen, a sylph-like English girl of about twenty, explained that it happened everywhere they went. Even way out in the bush, she said, people would turn up from somewhere. Her travelling companion, Wendy, joined her and expressed surprise that I hadn't come across it before. I explained that what driving I had done had mainly been in the desert. While it unnerved me to be scrutinised so closely, the group seemed totally comfortable with it.

Over a typically high-quality lunch, I met the group properly. Becky, an American psychologist in her thirties, had that entertaining way of talking, common to New Yorkers, which made even the smallest observation interesting. Dan, a ponytailed blond Canadian, had happily left a crew running his construction company and seemed in no hurry to get back. He appeared to have become good friends with Nick, a water engineer who normally looked after Burnley sewage works. The two swapped banter and flirted with the women, especially Lesley and Pauline.

Lesley was a tall, thin, very pale British midwife. Her serious expression belied a sharp wit as she skilfully offered ripostes to the lads' remarks. Pauline, a chunky, loud Australian lawyer, helped her out but, instead of clever sparring, just produced excellent abuse from an unwashed-out mouth.

With chiselled features and a square-cut jaw that matched his hairline, Robert, another Australian, looked tough, but when he donned an apron to help with washing-up, the image was shattered. From what I could make out there were four couples: Tom, a bearded, bookish man was being waited on hand and foot by Rachel, taller than him and, strangely, nearly as bearded. Another Tom, a fit-looking New Zealander who worked in an outback mine in Australia, was apparently hooked up with Jean, judging by the running of hands across legs as she walked by. She was an artist from London and was wearing a red and blue kanga as a wrap.

Chisiko was Hong Kong Chinese. Her heavily accented English was punctuated by frequent laughter, at what it was hard to determine. Perhaps she shared some telepathy with Chris, who sat so close to her it looked as if he was her bodyguard, an image reinforced by his shorn hair and sunglasses that never left his face throughout lunch. Hector was an enormous man. An Argentinian from the Falklands, he spoke only a little English and stayed apart from the rest of the group, with his wife Isabel. Dangerously thin in comparison to her husband, Isabel was dressed well but looked nervous. She spoke good English, translating for Hector as he issued gruff remarks.

Finally, completing the group of seventeen, there was Charlotte, an Australian who worked in tourism. She looked like she might be thirty, particularly as she seemed to be the matriarch of the group, but could also easily pass for twenty. She had a natural presence and was permanently on the move, ushering people to finish up, chivvying them to use the disinfectant, and was the first to start packing away. Yet such was her positive and personable nature, she achieved it without obviously irritating anyone.

I wondered what had brought them all there. Were they running away from something? It was too soon to tell. Were they adventurous? Well, if they were about to go into Zaire voluntarily, they must be. So why were they not travelling alone, particularly the couples? They probably wanted the companionship and also, if you travel on public transport you are never out in the bush, the jungles, the deserts; you go where the buses go and never stop in between. And 'in between' is where real people live real lives. But then they weren't really living it with them, permanently on the move as they were. Maybe they thought it was safer – particularly the single women. Maybe they thought they would score – particularly the single men. Or maybe they came just because it was cheap – overland companies don't exist for the profits, that's for sure. Most likely everyone had a different story, and at last I would have time enough with a group to find out.

Al had checked over the truck during lunch. Once back in the cab, I asked if he was with Charlotte.

"Nah, Tim. She's the one, eh? But I reckon she's into the girls. Still, they're all convertibles, and I'm still trying. Why – you on for a bet?"

51

"Give us a chance. I haven't even spoken to her yet."

"Well, you must be gagging for a plug. If I'd spent five months on my own in Arabland, I'd be ready to root a boot." I laughed again – I was getting more used to Al's turn of phrase. "Truth is, my friend, they're all mine. There's only four available, and with Charlotte out of the game there's not enough for us both." As Al paused to reflect, his caricature looks told me he didn't take himself too seriously.

"Hold on!" Al shouted, looking delighted with an offer that had just sprung to mind. "You can have Pauline – she just gave me the elbow. Friends, mind – 'an underperformer of the highest order', she said." I was still laughing, so Al continued, "You got a bird at home? Not into offshore drilling? You'll be a first on the road."

The sudden shift to my own situation cut my laughter dead. "No, no-one at home. And we'll see what happens – there's plenty of time." I made for the tape box.

"Now Charlotte…" Al was no longer listening. In a trance-like state he finished the conversation with himself. "…why I'm attracted to that sort of girl, I dunno … Yes I do, I'm a wanker … And – mmmm – I bet she's got a well-appointed beaver."

Hearing my renewed chuckling, Al turned, as if shocked I was there. "What are you looking at?"

"You. How can anyone wearing shorts like those think he's got a chance with someone like that?"

"Ah now, there you'd be wrong. My ridiculous wardrobe is one of my secret weapons. Revolt them. It works every time."

With that he gave me a wink and asked me to dig out his Kajagoogoo tape. 'Too Shy' bellowed out three times before we moved on to the next 'revolting tune', now the theme for the afternoon.

That night we camped on a beautiful hilltop in Kishwambe near Fort Portal, Mount Ruwenzori hidden behind thick clouds. Overlanders often stop at the Mporo Family Project* – an amazing achievement by Morence, the owner. He set up an orphanage on his own land and runs it as a self-sufficient farm with basic tourist accommodation. We looked around the farm – they had cows, goats, a fish farm, maize, coffee, matoke and vegetables – then we played football with the children until it was dark.

The following morning, the lush green sides and dark brown peaks of the mountains were in full view as we watched the children set off on their 10km hike

---

* I recently visited Morence again. The project continues. He has 22 resident children and supports another 86 in the local school. He is hoping to raise funds to build a local school for his children and the local community, complete with solar lighting so they can study at night. His greatest success, he said, is that one of the first children he took care of is now at university – no mean feat in Uganda.

to school. Heading south again, we skirted the massif and pulled into the Queen Elizabeth National Park airstrip.

"Last chance saloon. Best give London a bell-end." Al leafed through his paperwork while I held out my diary with all the essential numbers written on the inside back cover. Spotting it, he took it.

"Ta. Mr Organised eh? Bet you don't know how long it takes to cross Zaire."

"No idea, you?"

"Yep. Anywhere between ten and thirty days. The rule is, the day before going in we call London with a best estimate. And that's what I say every time. Once we're in there they won't know a thing till we're out. But they like to pretend they've got a handle on it." He disappeared into a small building where presumably there was a phone. The place looked completely deserted to me.

"Sorted," he said with satisfaction as he slumped back into the driver's seat and slotted in a 'Best of Chilli Peppers' tape.

We were aiming for the border at Katwe, but didn't seem to be racing to get there. Al explained that he wasn't even going to attempt it until the morning. Apparently, from there until Mali, borders were generally manned by corrupt officials. Assuming a typically western attitude towards waiting, officials would stretch out arguments over visas and vehicle documents if you arrived in the afternoon, hoping to make the driver part with cash as closing time approached. Such was Al's ruse anyhow, and he'd been through several times, although not at that border.

Normally, the trip went via Goma further south – between there and Rutshuru are the reserves that attempt to protect Silverback Gorillas. But London had issued a strong warning to avoid the area, as there had recently been a violent robbery at the Rutshuru Falls. An overland group had been badly beaten by people claiming to be Rwandan Freedom Fighters, but London suspected it was simply the Zairian Army. Al had promised the group he would find some gorillas elsewhere if he could.

We camped early in the Ruwenzori foothills. As night approached, Tom and Jean prepared dinner while Lesley and Pauline, not on duty but keen participants in camp life, volunteered to bake a chocolate cake. Dan, something of a salesman when it came to the bar he was in charge of, kept us all plied with beers. It wasn't quite a party, but the mellow evening gave me an opportunity to socialise a bit more with everyone. It felt strange that they would be my travelling companions for the next few months. And stranger still that I felt so relaxed in the company of another driver.

I ended up sitting around the fire with the last few people. The couples, all of whom I had guessed correctly, had gone to their tents and the rest of the group were sitting in the truck reading or writing under the lights.

After getting all his paperwork impeccably prepared for the border, Al appeared in a fresh pair of shorts – bright pink with black swordfish printed on the backside. He sat down next to Lesley.

"So, Lesley, Pauline told you what a crap shag I am?"

"Yeah, but I'm not sure I believe her." It sounded odd coming from such a prim woman.

Pauline, evidently quite happy with the situation, used it as an opportunity to compete with Al for crudeness.

"Mate, those fish'll give you more of a prick than he ever could!" she shrieked, before breaking into a manly laugh at her own joke.

"Listen, Pauline," said Al, "I was doing you a favour. Don't be ungracious – you never know when you'll next get some."

"I can get it whenever I want, matey. And in bigger portions than you can provide."

It occurred to me how well Al and Pauline were in fact suited.

The three-way spat continued, keeping the rest of us in a state of amused incredulity until we started chatting amongst ourselves again. It wasn't more than an hour before Lesley and Al got up, said an unabashed goodnight and disappeared into her tent, Pauline hollering after them, "If you catch anything, it wasn't me. I'm clean – or I was anyway."

The next morning I checked over the truck while Al sat beside Lesley eating a fried breakfast, Pauline happily sitting to the other side of him. We set off with me at the wheel – my first time in a while – crunching through first and second. Al turned the music to full and shouted, "She judders a bit, but she'll set off in third on the flat."

Presently, with Richard Clayderman diminished again, he said, "Well, aren't you going to ask?"

"What, how far to the border?"

"No – what's Lesley like?"

"I'm not that interested in the whereabouts of your cock, Al."

"Oh? Well, for your info, it's right here," he announced, reaching down for his first rummage of the day. "But you must want to know what happened?"

"I've a feeling you're going to tell me."

"I might not."

"Thanks."

Al looked at me, his expressive features inventing a new word somewhere between 'baffled' and 'disappointed' at my lack of interest.

"OK then," he murmured. "It's not far to the border. And when we get there, drive up nice and slow with the biggest grin your ugly face can muster."

Before long, a few tin-roofed wooden sheds came into view behind a scaffolding pole for a barrier. "This side won't be a problem," Al advised, "but you wait till you meet those Zairies along the way. It's the Belgians, you know. Corrupted the lot of them. These ex-Brits are perfectly civilised." Slowly but correctly, the Ugandans dealt with our paperwork and waved us through in just over an hour.

Not far down the road, a significantly less maintained one, we came across another barrier marking the Zaire side of the border. Sloppily uniformed, armed soldiers lounged in wicker chairs, smoking cigarettes. On seeing our approach, unsmiling faces, mostly hidden behind mirror sunglasses, turned in our direction. This was the first display of a macho and threatening approach to officialdom that I was going to have to get used to.

Pulling up slowly as advised, I waited for one of the soldiers to either move the barrier or approach us. Nothing happened. Eventually, I hopped down and explained in French that we wanted to present our documentation to the border officials beyond the barrier. One rose from his seat and kicked a colleague in the thigh, who then also got up. Ignoring me completely, they passed together along the side of the truck, leering up at the group, then both climbed up onto the trailer hitch to look in the back. Following them, I saw they were blatantly staring at the women. It was an uncomfortable minute, though I sensed that to interrupt would cause more problems than to leave them be.

They eventually jumped down. Swapping a joke in their language, they called their colleagues over. Four more men took their turn on the hitch to look the group over, making comments to each other to roars of approving laughter. After about five minutes of this mild intimidation, they spoke their first word to me: 'Marlboro'.

"Je fume pas," I lied. The commander replied by gesturing with his chin towards the back of the truck. Now taking my turn on the hitch, I felt embarrassed as I asked Tom to lend me a few of his Marlboro. I had definitely lost round one.

Relinquishing three cigarettes from Tom's packet, I passed them to the commander who shared them with his men. While they smoked I repeated my request to get through to the border proper, which was again ignored. Instead the commander turned to the trailer he had been leaning on and gave it a sharp slap with the palm of his hand. "Ouvrez!" I explained that it was just luggage. He looked straight through me.

Two rounds down.

Opening the trailer is a laborious job, hence usually only done in the morning and evening, the group keeping what they need for the day in daypacks. I undid the tarpaulin, pulled it back and removed the padlock. Lifting off the metal cover, I revealed one side of the trailer brim full of backpacks. Once again I explained that it was all personal luggage. The commander and his men gathered around, poked a few of the bags and decided not, as I had feared, to have us empty them all out.

"Ça va. Allez-y," the commander ordered, having already turned his back on me. Round three to me. Well, sort of.

I got back in the cab and fired the engine. The soldiers had taken up position in their seats by the barrier again. Laughing and joking once more, they ignored us completely. I really didn't know what to do. To sound the airhorn would no doubt anger them, but to go back and disturb them would probably mean they'd start the whole process again.

"Just wait," Al said, sensing my impatience. "It's a game. They're playing with you. Just don't forget one thing. These poor bastards haven't got a thing, and this pole is the only thing they'll ever control. We, mate, will sooner or later be off up the road leading our privileged lives once again."

It was perhaps the best advice I would ever be given on the road. All we had to do was smile and wait. There was no competition, no rounds one to fifteen. They would hold us up for those few minutes, and then our paths would separate. Al was right. Sadly but indisputably, it is a fact of Third World travel, in whatever form it is undertaken, that the surface is barely dented. We can never live what we see and in that situation could, at best, only hope to walk away with some understanding of their motivation. Duly, after another ten minutes, the commander looked up, and then gestured towards the barrier. One of his men slipped it back and we were through.

Customs, Police and Immigration all tried similarly to wind me up into some sort of showdown, one they would surely have won. But following Al's advice, I calmly handed over the truck carnet, a stack of nineteen passports with completed cards and a copy of the pax list. When asked, I politely answered their questions, led them around the truck, into the back, and helped them when they asked to look inside the padlocked lockers. It was long, it was dull, but we eventually entered Zaire' three hours later without any raised tempers.

"Nice one," Al said, looking up from his book when I climbed into the cab. "And if you don't mind one more bit of advice from an old lag, keep the fluent français to yourself. The less you say the better." I nodded, sure that he was right there too.

---

* The fabled country of Zaire, nee Belgian Congo, now the DRC (Democratic Republic of Congo), as opposed to the neighbouring country of Congo. Both countries lie on the river Congo or, depending which map you read, the river Zaire. Congo's capital, Brazzaville, is situated directly across the river Zaire from the Democratic Republic of Congo's capital Kinshasa, nee Leopoldville. Confused? For this reason I will refer to the current DRC as Zaire, as it was at the time, and the river as the Congo. No offence to the citizens, or indeed President Kabila, intended. Now that's not Laurent Kabila, recently shot, but his son and replacement, Joseph Kabila – odd for a democracy, but then look at the family Bush.

The road deteriorated even more after the border and everything began to look poorer. Passing roadside villages, I noticed a startling contrast to rural Uganda. There, I had seen a huge effort to work, trade and enjoy. They grew tea, coffee and endless matoke, and signs outside freshly painted buildings indicated schools, pubs and clinics. Trees shaded cottage-industries: bicycle workshops, outdoor welders, brick manufacturers or timber merchants, and bado-bados – more bicycles – carried people and produce between all this activity.

In Zaire, people sat outside dilapidated mud houses and watched us pass; the odd chicken ran out in front of the truck, seemingly deliberately playing dare. The children, naked or semi-clothed in rags, ran to the side of the road, put out their hands and shouted 'cadeau' one and all. All the way to Beni I didn't see one sign, one little shop or workshop. The scene was one of utter dereliction, poverty and hopelessness. This country, it appeared, had simply ceased to function – in the western understanding of the word. The things you would expect in a town such as Beni just didn't exist – no service station, post office or bus station; no running water, phone lines or electricity. The only buildings that were in any way similar in standard to Uganda's were the churches, presumably erected by the same happy band of missionaries on both sides of the border. Even though the trip-notes I'd read had warned me, it felt incredible that on our intended route via Kisangani to Bangui in CAR, we would cross only the northeastern tip of the country. OK, not an inch of the road would be paved, I'd thought, *but could it really take thirty days?* Perhaps it could.

As the road descended towards the Ituri forest, we could see the tops of trees stretching away into eternity like fields of broccoli. When we dropped under the treeline the light dimmed and all we saw ahead was a tunnel.

"Wave goodbye to the view," Al commented with surprisingly good cheer. "Apart from by the river, that's about the last time you'll see any distance for a month."

With a lack of sunlight the road immediately turned wet. Ahead of me I could see a final steep descent and at the bottom, a concrete bridge the width of the truck with no railings. I had never driven on mud before and with only a hundred metres to go to the bridge, I touched on the brakes. We skidded to one side. I tried again with the same result. The bridge was approaching fast and I didn't have control over the truck.

Al turned and solemnly pronounced his judgement: "Ditch it." I had no other choice, so did literally that, driving straight into the drainage channel running along the side of the road. The truck slammed against a wall of mud. When we finally came to a halt, at an angle of some thirty degrees, leaves were sticking through my window as if poking fun at me.

"Fuck it!" I shouted, hitting the steering wheel with both hands. "Fuck it, fuck it!"

"Language, Tim. At least we're not at the bottom of the river. That would've hurt." Al was all smiles as he addressed me, his face inches from mine. "This is nice. But I've got two questions for my esteemed co-driver. One – what music would you like, and two – what are you going to do now?"

I climbed over him, jumped a long way down to the road and ran to the back. "Is everyone OK?" I called.

"Yeah, yeah – fine," I heard someone say, "I just wasn't expecting to be snogging Becky this time of the day." It was Nick, who was peeling himself off Becky's voluptuous frame where he had landed in a bear hug.

"What the hell happened?" shouted Chris as he picked Chisiko up off the floor, where she lay in a heap with her legs on Hector's lap.

"Sorry, I skidded off the road. Listen, I need to make sure you're all all right. If you can, please get off the truck."

Miraculously, there weren't even any cuts. When Al next appeared, he started undoing the padlocks on the side of the truck to release the sandmats, spades and mattock. I noticed the jaunty theme tune to English Test Cricket playing in the background.

"Best start digging, I reckon, unless we want to camp at an odd angle tonight. Where shall I start, boss?" There was nothing patronising in his voice. Al was simply giving me the opportunity to redeem myself in the eyes of the group, to show some leadership.

I climbed under the truck with a jack, and from there directed the group in filling the ditch with wood and digging into the road to lessen the incline out. When the front of the truck reached a near-horizontal position, I slid out to arrange the sandmats along the group's excavations. As I got into the cab I noticed that the group were excited – Chisiko was even taking photographs. I was nervous, but Al gave me a surreptitious thumbs-up, which I took to mean that he considered my preparations adequate.

As I let the clutch up, the wheels bit and I immediately moved forward. I pushed hard on the accelerator and the truck dragged itself up the incline, spitting the mats out behind it. Seconds later we were out, and only then did I register the cheering from the group. Embarrassed as I was, I realised that the incident had actually been yet another lesson, as evidently the initial shock and anger had been forgotten in the group's effort and involvement.

Staying in first gear I gingerly descended the last few metres to the bridge and crossed over. Below us gaped a ten-metre deep muddy gully. "Ditch it," I muttered to myself.

"What?" shouted Al, boogying in his seat to Level 42.

"Nothing, mate. Just said 'thanks' really." Al didn't say a word, and carried on playing an air bass-guitar just below his chin.

As evening approached, I noticed that the thick forest precluded pulling off the road. Anticipating having to stop in a village, thereby subjecting ourselves to the close scrutiny of hundreds, I asked Al where we would camp.

"Just keep on driving, compadre. There'll be a gravel pit up ahead."

In Zaire, the roads are made of orange crystallised mud – laterite – from the forests. Every thirty to fifty kilometres, the original road builders had cleared a large area which doubled as worker-camp and gravel collection zone. To overlanders these gravel pits are the stuff of Zaire sleeping life. Twenty kilometres out of Beni we found our first, which actually looked like a first-class camping ground – large, flat and relatively dry.

There was still a buzz of excitement following the accident, and with Dan making several rounds with the bar sales ledger – a school exercise book – the group was soon fairly well oiled. Al, still in dancing mood, positioned his speakers on the truck roof and cranked up the stereo. Not satisfied with that, he rigged up flashing Christmas lights between four tentpoles to create an instant dancefloor. As darkness fell he was to be found gyrating madly to one of his mix tapes. Alone.

It took everyone else a few more visits from Dan to reach Al's natural stage of merriment, but soon Tom and Jean had daubed a tarpaulin with mud and hung it between the truck wing mirror and a tent pole. PIT PARTY it proclaimed. Dinner was taken on the hoof, much of it spilling onto the dancefloor.

Al danced with the women, who seemed happy to drip from his sides as if he were the archetypal playboy. He had put on a pair of 'Produit de Zaire' floursack trousers for the occasion and, otherwise topless, was slinging his prodigious gut from side to side, trying to slap it against his hangers-on. Even the couples were roused to action by the atmosphere, Hector and Isabel reserving their corner of the dancefloor for some skilled Samba, her tiny frame rolling across various lumps of his hefty body. I soon found myself in some sort of waltz with Charlotte, and after a while we moved to one side to talk properly for the first time. We got on well, but eventually we were tempted back into the throng, packed tight by the psychological barrier of the Christmas lights. It struck me that I was enjoying my first full-on party since Niamey.

"Right up the arse by Friday." Al broke the morning silence by calling his verdict across the cab. We had woken late, cleared up a dreadful mess of dusty cups and dirty plates and set off after a quiet, hungover breakfast.

"Righto – you just found your dildo then?" His filth was catching.

"No, but I borrowed Lesley's. And she borrowed it off Pauline." Al would always be one step ahead mind.

Briefly silence returned, but Al wasn't having any. "You mate. You'll slither in there by the end of the week. Guaranteed. I'm glad you never took me up on that bet." Al lifted himself from the seat and thrust both hands down his shorts, managing to make it look as if he was hoisting some impossible weight into position.

Keen to change the subject, I offered Al some chocolate.

"Aw, you never talk dirty. Hey – are you some kind of ponce?" He looked me over. Then, as he finally heard my offer in his own mind, continued, "Chocolate? You said chocolate? Where? Have you got some? C'mon, gimme, gimme." Whining like a dog, Al pawed at my shoulder. "Where did you get it? I finished all my Nairobi stash."

"At the Kampala Sheraton, while I was waiting for you."

"Well why didn't you tell me they had chocolate?"

"Coz I bought the whole bloody lot."

Al turned to me, and in a conspiratorial whisper asked, "How many?"

"Nineteen."

"Nine – bloody – teen!" He gasped. "Go on. Peel one open, pal. And don't let anyone see. We'll have one a day between us and we'll aim to get the fuck out of this shithole country in nineteen days."

It took three days to reach Epulu. Though only 250km, it was impossibly slow going due to the roads. Without regular grading – not forthcoming in Zaire – large holes appear anywhere water is left standing on a mud road. Although I had developed quite some respect for the truck's ability to power through mud, the trailer was doing its best to hold us up. On two occasions we had unhitched it, driven the truck through a bog-hole, then attached it to a long hawser to pull it through separately. On convex camber it had a tendency to head sideways, as contrary as a horse. Only a quick turn and a burst of power would stop it from dragging the truck with it wherever it was going. So far we had avoided a full bogging, but up ahead I knew we would find Zaire's notorious truck-depth bog-holes.

Epulu is a Zairian jungle paradise, which we took advantage of for two complete days. Al gave the group strenuous warnings not to mess about at the beautiful falls. The gruesome photo-display at the entrance showed the results of those who had; the police had photographed bloated white bodies, found days down river. I marvelled at the stupidity of anyone going over. One overland driver, for a bet, had done so on a lilo. He now featured on the board. Only a hundred metres upstream from the falls it was entirely safe, and wonderful for swimming. That, coupled with the lovely lawns stretching down from our camp to the riverbank, made for an idyllic spot.

As much as in our approach to women, Al and I differed markedly in the mechanics department. Where I would have been perfectly happy just to give every nipple a squirt from the greasegun, and every nut I could lay my hands on a tweak of the spanner, he was an inveterate fiddler. Spring bushes, brake shoes, endless unidentifiable bits and bobs from the rest of the brake system; all were subject to a good stripping down, a thorough check over and a replacement if he could find a spare. The whole thing left me cold, but all day I laboured and sweated regardless, assuming that by so doing I must be learning something useful for the future. What I couldn't understand though, I wasn't about to say anything about – in case I gave Al any ideas about tackling the dodgy gearbox.

At sunset we downed tools. Thereupon, sporting another pair from his endless collection of shorts, Al transformed back into camp entertainer and consummate letch. Meanwhile, I found myself gravitating towards Charlotte, and between her sudden disappearances to arrange, cajole or tidy we spent that evening together happily chatting.

I still hadn't managed to see any game in Africa. Before I had joined them, however, the group had been treated to several East African gameparks, and Charlotte was an expert. With a clear passion she explained everything there was to know about the spoor, gestation periods and the eating, sleeping, mating and hunting habits of most of the animals I had heard of. It was fascinating. Slipping off from under the truck for an hour on the second afternoon, I joined her in hiring a guide to show us the Okapi; Epulu is a research station for these strange beasts. Only found in the dense forests of northwest Zaire, the Okapi looks extremely odd, like a mixture between a zebra and a mule. Actually a member of the giraffe family, it is referred to as a 'living fossil', an animal whose nearest relatives are long since extinct. Hunted by forest pygmies for food, Epulu exists as a safe haven for these rare ruminants.

That evening, I countered Al's detailed questioning and colourful references with enough suggestion to cover my tracks and put him off the scent. Keen to relate details as lurid as his shorts about his own progress, he explained how he and Lesley had reached a series of new highs in sexual exploration. The animal cries that later accompanied them verified his boasts, and I wouldn't have been surprised had the Okapi come with their own guides to view the strange goings-on in their tent.

Our next stop would be Kisangani. That's the way overlanding goes, particularly in Zaire. There's simply not the time to stop between towns or attractions – except to shop. Unfortunately, we could find nothing more than pineapples and tomatoes for sale – not even an egg, even though Zaire's suicidal chickens still rushed us at every opportunity. With dried foods, pasta, rice and tinned meats from the stores, the cook teams still turned out imaginative food, and baking became a nightly exercise. I don't know which I was more impressed by – the effort and expertise of the group, the foresight in stocking the truck so well at the outset, or the frugal tendencies of several previous quartermasters who had saved food for us who now needed it.

Apart from checking over the truck, Al and I had developed one more routine in the day; we shared our chocolate bars with increasing fetish and still counted our days in them. At Epulu we had reviewed the map and had made a new rule to compensate for the huge distance still staring at us. The eleven o'clock sharp unwrapping – always to the Bolero – was to take place 'on the road' only. Shortly after our third bar since that decision, we saw signs of increased roadside habitation.

As the population increased, so too did the number of army personnel. These finely tuned fighting machines had all, it appeared, been through the same training school. To pass out they had evidently needed to: A) get a beret; B) wear it in an original manner with at least one piece of regulation fatigues (but a Hawaiian shirt or jeans would do for the other part); C) find an enormous pair of shades, preferably mirrored; D) procure as big a gun as possible; and E) set up a roadblock and slouch around with half a dozen mates smoking, drinking and shaking down passers-by for funds to buy more of the above. From Epulu to Kisangani outskirts: roadblocks x 4. From outskirts to centre Kisangani: roadblocks x 5. And every time we employed the same tactic: we smiled, waited patiently and kept quiet. It was intensely dull, worse even than hand-riveting a new brake pad to the shoe – a labour Al had recently introduced me to. But both had to be done. As the villages linked up they turned to shanties, then the shanties eventually opened out into a town.

Of sorts.

The reason for the army's presence in such numbers became clearer as we drove through Kisangani town centre. There had recently been yet more fighting there, and everything that hadn't been destroyed was boarded up. Trading, what there was of it, was carried out on mats outside the shuttered shopfronts; almost no one walked the streets, even fewer drove. Suddenly however, as if seeing ourselves in a mirror, we met our match coming the other way. It was Ray.

"You got here fast!" I hollered as both trucks pulled up.

"I've been going hell for leather to beat the rains," Ray replied. "You'll be in trouble though. There'll be some nice bog-holes up there by now."

Frosty greetings then passed between Al and Ray, halting any further conversational gambits on my part. To break the awkward silence Ray muttered, "See you at the Olympic", rolled up his window and drove off. As we too moved off, Al wouldn't say a word, so I sat back to take in the view of the first war ravaged town I'd ever been in.

The Olympic Hotel is right in Kisangani's town centre. On our arrival, watchmen opened the tall gates and we drove through a passageway into a large compound behind the hotel buildings. Like the town, it was a mess. Broken concrete filled huge puddles, rubbish was piled high and everywhere damp washing dripped on criss-crossing lines.

The group set up camp between Ray's group's ten tents, struggling to knock in their pegs. I went to reception and found a charming African woman in traditional dress behind the desk.

"You've just missed your friends," she offered helpfully. "But they're coming back."

"Yes, thanks. I've just seen Ray."

"Good. Mr.Ray, a nice man. Mr. Al – he's a very good man too. How are you? How many nights?" I told her we would stay at least two nights, and then asked if I could change some money.

Along with the rest of the infrastructure outside of the capital Kinshasa, banks in Zaire are non-existent. There is no way to change dollars except unofficially. We had changed some money on the border and I had been amazed at the size of the banknotes we'd got in return. At 3.5 million to a dollar, the man had dealt out our Zairies in hundred thousand notes. I had asked Al if 3.5 million was a good rate. "No idea," he'd replied jovially. "I was here six months ago and it was a million." Hyperinflation had obviously hit Zaire big time.

Mama Olympic offered me six million to the dollar. I changed $300 with her and was presented with nearly two billion Zairies. Splitting four huge bricks of notes into two plastic bags, she handed them over. I felt like a bank robber.

"Can the group change with you too?" I asked.

"As much as they like, but only for cash dollars." *No wonder*, I thought. The country's banknotes were as good as useless. There was next to nothing to buy and to hold on to them meant losing their value – over five hundred percent in six months at a conservative estimate. To keep any profit, therefore, a trader's income has to be spent, and it is this lack of saving that contributes to the vicious circle of hyperinflation. Mobutu, the incumbent president at the time, would have been too busy buying Jumbo-jets and beachside homes on the Cote d'Azur to worry about such economic trifles. Besides, he worked entirely in dollars himself, and only in billions at a time, a situation I was going to have to get used to myself, albeit in his country's banana money.

Outside, Al already had the truck on a jack and the front wheel off. Shaking my head as I strolled towards his prone, protruding torso, I kicked him.

"Come on. You're coming for a beer. She's got a gas powered fridge."

"I know," he snapped. "I've been here before, you know."

What could be wrong? Al still hadn't spoken since we had met Ray. I had begun to rely on his permanent high and was determined he should get it off his chest.

"Cold Primus – the best in Zaire." Under the circumstances, it was my best possible offer.

"I know that too. It's the only beer in Zaire," Al said, looking up at me. From upside-down, his face looked even more expressive. It broke into a grin. "But it's bloody good."

Downing a socket wrench, Al slipped himself out from under the truck and jumped into a crouch. He then took my hand and frog-hopped all the way to the bar. "Ripput, Primus. Ripput, Primus," he croaked. He stayed that way as we passed Mama Olympic, and like the group she didn't bat an eyelid. Al, I imagined, was well remembered wherever he went.

Primus is the only product distributed efficiently in Zaire. No matter where we went we saw signs, crates both full and empty and the delivery trucks themselves, swimming through the shit like the rest of us. It was a masterful operation, one that Mobutu would have done well to emulate with his infrastructure. We drank our first, then some more, keeping it cold by sharing each bottle. Al told me the story.

"So you shagged Ray's woman," I said in conclusion. "No wonder he looked a bit miffed."

"Miffed bollocks. He was up for a scrap there at the gamepark. I had to flee for the hills. Anyway, she shagged me."

"Good point, when do we ever get to make the decision? What happened to her after that?"

"She carried on with his trip and I've never heard from her. Good job too, Lesley would kill me." Al was grinning now between swigs.

"Hardly, she nicked you off Pauline herself."

"Well that's different. She's a woman."

I couldn't get to grips with how Al thought about women. His fabulously crude comments seemed to hide a sense of his being a victim; that whatever happened was out of his control.

Hey – but what do I know? I was only glad that my own attitude didn't get me into such scrapes, and gladder still that Al was back in his habitual good frame of mind. Just then Ray came in. He joined us, sitting opposite Al, and ordered more beers. Al surprised me.

"Ray. I've got to tell you mate, I'm sorry. I was pissed. Sophie came to my hut while you were out rattling on about animals to the group. It just happened, all right? You know how it is on the road." Al finished his semi-apology by holding up his beer bottle. Hesitantly, Ray raised his bottle too. No chink, but a swig each in unison.

"One thing, Al," Ray growled. "I've been with Sue since Bamako. Touch her, and this very bottle cracks your head open."

"Wooooooooooh," Al cooed mockingly. "What's she like? I'll have to check her out first."

"Al," I interjected. "I think an agreement is in order." This time the bottles clinked and Ray launched straight into an on-the-road story: "...four-hundred litres of diesel, lost in a bog-hole ..." I left them to it.

Outside, I gave the group a rundown on money changing, told them what little I knew about the town and warned them to stay together and be back before dark. According to Mama Olympic there was still a curfew in place. Some wandered off to town in twos and threes and some went back to intense Zaire conversations with their opposite numbers from Ray's truck.

"Tim, there's a cafe in town. Well, it's the bakery actually, the only functioning shop. But they serve some sugary nonsense and hot mud they call coffee. Fancy it?" Charlotte had already done her washing and checked out the town. No doubt she had already spoken to every one of Ray's group too.

"Sure, I'll just tell Al," I answered.

"OK. Wendy and Helen are coming too. See you outside."

"Right." Suddenly, crap cupcake and sweet grit didn't sound quite so attractive.

That night turned into quite a party. Wanting, I guess, to keep the illusion that they have Africa to themselves while they're there, groups from different trucks – especially different operating companies – sometimes ignore each other completely when they meet. Some, however, like Ray's and our groups, can't wait for the next cross-truck party; a chance to swap stories, find those coincidences of mutual friends – so common it belies the size of the world – or if possible grab a partner for the night. Drivers, on the other hand, regardless of which company they work for, would go days out of their way for the chance of a night talking rubbish over a beer with one of their own. Apart from getting route advice or borrowing tools, for example, drivers are at work, and like all workers they need to let off steam with their colleagues. Factory moans, office moans or overlanding moans – they're all the same.

In the morning, Ray's group were up and ready to go by 7am; late, but it had been a long night. Ray and I had caught up on our respective few weeks since I had waved him off from Bamako, and now I wished him good luck for the rest of his trip. As he drove across the compound Al crawled out of his tent. I noticed Lesley leaning on her elbows, smiling benignly as Al, stark naked, stood and waved. As the gates were swung open he ran after the truck blowing kisses. The gates shut in his face. He turned around to see us all looking at him. "What are you staring at, eh? Want some of this do you?" He came charging back waving his dick around, scattering us all in a panic of screaming.

Back on form.

Something was missing. It wasn't much, but losing a stool and a washing-up bowl was annoying as they were difficult to replace. Wendy had also lost some underwear from the line. Robbery is endemic in Africa; the poorer the country the more likely it is to happen and the more trifling the pickings. Like all drivers, I judged it our responsibility to keep everything locked up. We were a travelling jamboree of useful goods and incredibly valuable items – from cameras to the boots on our feet. If we didn't look after it we could expect it to walk.

That, much more than personal safety, is what is referred to as 'truck security', and drivers take it as a matter of personal pride to keep all the truck's equipment safe. Pete had even given someone the job of tent-peg counter – they had checked each bag for the correct number before leaving camp. There was a constant call from driver to group – and driver to himself – of 'Keep it locked up!'

Even within a locked compound we had lost gear, and Al was livid. Speaking to the group over breakfast, he went back over old ground. They listened quietly, each no doubt dying to get up and check all their own belongings were safe. I stopped Al stomping into Mama Olympic's office. Approaching her myself, the reply was predictable: a shrug and an instruction I had heard somewhere before: "Lock it up."

"The washing?" I asked.

"I'll talk to the boy. He will bring it back." No mention of sanctions or apology – it was expected, he would admit it and the bloomers would return. It was a timely reminder that we would have to increase our vigilance.

I got back to find Al under the truck. Donning my overalls I slid along the gravel to join him. "I'm just switching over the bearings, I reckon they're knackered. I heard them grinding all the way here, and did you feel the heat on the hub?"

No, no and no, but I wrestled with nuts, casings and hubs regardless, the therapeutic value of a quick tinker beginning to rub off on me too as I worked.

By lunchtime we had finished and I decided to go into town. I wanted to order a whole batch of bread to take with us the following morning. Explaining for the third time the huge number of loaves we needed, I noticed an enormous white car pull up outside the bakery. Blinking in disbelief, I saw that it was an immaculate Rolls Royce coupe. I'd have been less surprised had a flying saucer just landed on Kisangani's empty streets.

Instead of a gaggle of green aliens, a short elderly white man stepped out of the back, the door held open by a uniformed chauffeur. The man walked into the shop, said a cheery "Bonjour tout le monde" and bowed, doffing his white hat.

He sniffed the air. "Ahhh, du pain. Pour moi, c'est la vie," he said to no one in particular, though it caused a beautiful smile to spread across the assistant's face, one that hadn't appeared for me. "Une belle journée comme d'habitude," the man continued, now talking directly to me.

"Oui, oui, très belle," I replied, still taken aback by his stylish entrance. It was as if I'd been transported to 1950s' Paris.

"Vous prenez un café avec moi," he demanded, simultaneously holding out his left hand into which a baguette was placed. No money changed hands.

"Certainement." We sat at a grubby table.

"Vous venez d'où?" he asked me.

"Angleterre. Et vous?"

"Ah, England," he replied, ignoring my question completely. "I am English too. That is when I am not a Frenchman."

Uh?

François, as he introduced himself, had all the hallmarks of an ex-filmstar: charming, handsome even in his seventies, a purveyor of eloquent and amusing anecdotes and the confidence to talk about only what he wished to talk about. I wasn't complaining though. I had just met a jewel in the ex-colonial crown, every bit the character of the old Africa-hand. It turned out that apart from being a wealthy businessman – he had the largest palm-oil factory in Zaire just outside town – he was also the Honorary Consul for the British there in Kisangani.

Ah ha!

François was apt to ask a question then change the subject, or vice versa, abruptly moving from a topic that went beyond his interest by asking a question. He was fascinating though. Lubumba, the assassinated first president of independent Congo, had been a personal friend. He also knew Mobutu, had an adventure story for every day of his forty years in Africa and liked a good yarn on the subject of women. For the latter, I wished Al had been there. He would have given better than he got.

François' main passion was cars. The Roller outside was just one of his collection of pre-1950's classics, he told me. As soon as I expressed interest he jumped up. "Well then, Mr English, we must go and see them."

I stepped into the back of his car with him, skidding across the shiny red leather seats. As the driver shut the door, François glanced out of the window and implored, "Who is that beautiful girl there? You know her?" Walking towards the café were Charlotte and Robert. She was still on duty, looking after the quiet ones.

"Yes, she's on my trip."

"Well, she must come too. And her boyfriend, although he looks too ugly for such a woman." Smiling at his frankness, I stepped back out of the car and explained what they were being invited to do.

François' house was a huge, rambling bungalow set behind a large, white wall in what would once have been Kisangani's wealthy suburb. The garden was a magical place: trees, bushes and blazing flowers provided covered walkways and shade throughout the compound. A long veranda, full of hardwood furniture and African carvings, and cooled by six noisy overhead fans, overlooked a swimming pool at the back of the house.

"Swim. Swim my friends. I have coverings. I am afraid I shall not join you." François clicked his fingers and two young male servants appeared.

We got out to find iced limejuice set on a circular teak table, the legs carved into the shape of three elephant trunks complete with tusks. François had already polished off half a bottle of French red wine. After drinking, we ventured further down the garden to a large concrete lockup where twenty beautiful cars gleamed under electric lights, the air-conditioning keeping his Mercedes, Porches, Jaguars and a Bugati, amongst others, in perfect condition.

Wandering around like schoolchildren, we ran our hands down the lines; lines envisaged by designers before computers applied aerodynamics and economy to their art. François turned over the engine of each one as we passed it. "I do this every day, just to remind me I am still alive," he mused, edging the atmosphere ever closer to the celestial. The scene seemed too incredible for such a place and I was glad Charlotte and Robert were there or no one would have believed me.

Back on the veranda we listened once more as François held court. Mentioning Epulu, he explained that it was he, fed up of travelling there to deal with European corpses, who had arranged for the police to erect the sign with the grisly photographs. Thus far, apart from the driver-on-the-lilo incident, it had been successful. He then gave the full amusing details of a story I had heard part of before on the overlanding grapevine.

Buta, which would be our next stop after Kisangani, had one of the three bridges between there and Bumba that were structurally sound but had no plank base. An overland driver had driven off the bridge while crossing it. He was uninjured, but the truck had sunk without trace, leaving the group stuck in Zaire with nothing as all their belongings floated off towards surprised villagers downriver. Buta itself – 'in the middle of Bumfuck Nowhere' as Al would have had it – like every town in Zaire, also had nothing. They were cashless, foodless and without passports. Word got out to Kisangani and François hired a twin-prop plane to pick them up.

He found the miserable bunch waiting for him by the airstrip. They were tired, hungry and above all thirsty. In the style I could now envisage, François produced three crates of cold Primus – no food or water. The group erupted into joyous applause and drinking commenced. During take-off one of the engines failed. Too late to abort, the pilot shouted for everyone to put their heads between their knees. Many did so, but François was to be seen standing upright at the front of the plane holding up a glass of red wine while the plane narrowly skimmed above the trees at the end of the runway. Safely aloft, François finished his toast, 'Salut, et beinvenue en civilisation encore.'

Each story was told in such a way that I felt like applauding at the end, but as François began to tire a little, I sensed it was time to leave. Just then, however, Badi appeared. A true African gent, not quite as old as François but equally entertaining, Badi spoke excellent English in the same charming accent. They were very old friends and had obviously shared many adventures together, the like of which we could barely imagine, such had Africa changed in their time.

François and Badi bantered about women. Hearing that Robert was not with Charlotte, they suggested that she and I should get together forthwith. She happily joined in the fun, and for their benefit flirted with me. François, re-energised, turned to me and shouted, "You must try the Rugunga!" before emptying the last of the wine into his glass. "Badi, tell our guests about the Rugunga."

We were told how Rwandan women excel at this bizarre sexual practice. They begin by bashing their partner's penis against the floor until it is bruised, bloodied and numb. That done, the man's penetration is reputed to last the whole night, giving both of them extraordinary pleasure… "But you must be careful. Too often and you will die of a heart attack." That was the second good reason I had heard to avoid such experimentation.

With his usual abruptness, François declared, "I am tired. You should go now. Henri will drive you home."

We offered profuse thanks, but he waved them away, suddenly bored of our company. We left. As we stepped past the veranda, I looked back and saw him and Badi settling into another bottle of wine. Old friends are always the best, even if you are a lonely man in Africa.[*]

Having picked our way through increasingly atrocious road conditions and endured several more army roadblocks, we reached the first baseless bridge at Banalia, two days out of Kisangani. Banalia Bridge was guarded as if it were a national monument. The officers were surprisingly friendly and it turned out that they had planks to rent to help us cross it. They looked remarkably like they may have been the originals. Moods swung when we produced the mats and extra planks Al had brought along specifically for the job, and it took several more Marlboros than usual to get the pole raised. The two hundred metre long, iron bridge had railings, but only a treacherous framework for a base. Al had tackled it before but even knowing what he was doing, he approached the task with great caution. First rule – group off. For safety, obviously, but besides, it was a whole team operation to get the truck across.

The rectangular holes were wider and longer than the wheels, and to fall in would mean damaging the brake and steering mechanism, not to mention a long jacking job. Al signalled me onto the bridge, making sure that the wheels were centered on mats and planks lined up in front of me. I drove tentatively. It was strange to be able to see straight down into the rushing river many metres below.

---

*   I recently met François again. He was in Tanzania having been chased out of Kisangani by Laurent Kabila's troops advancing across the country to take Kinshasa and topple Mobutu. Badi was with him. François narrowly escaped with his life; his house was ransacked and his driver, Henri, killed. He does not know whether the cars survive.

Easy enough to get the front wheels right, it was harder to place the mats correctly at the rear. Then there was the trailer to worry about – especially as it had a different axle width. As I drove, the group replenished the front with planks from the back and I just trusted Al's signalling. There wasn't much room for error, as I found out when one plank, caught at an angle, shot out from under a rear wheel. Fortunately, the wheel dropped harmlessly onto a strut. The plank we lost to the river. It made clear the advantage of double rear wheels, an arrangement I had already noticed every African truck had.

The customary cheer went up when I reached the road. I had been tense, and Al too was sweating with a combination of heat and intense concentration. The group had worked brilliantly, doing all the lifting, keeping an eye out at each wheel and calling Al if they saw me veering off course. Without doubt the best times for any overland group are when they are most involved with the trip. Hawkins' theory of providing an 'expedition' was well founded. Had only one leader been there it might have taken longer, but the group would have felt more valuable still.

"They're fucking sore nipples I've got," Al observed, peeling off his t-shirt. He ran a finger around both, checking for the source of pain. To me, they were hard to distinguish from his mosquito bites. "Ya bastard that hurts. How are your nips, old boy?"

"I use suntan cream – it works."

"Poof."

Al was of the rough school of overlanding. He wore thongs instead of boots and stayed in shorts at night. I had seen what Pete looked like after his malaria, so despite the heat, I was fanatical about covering up and smearing exposed skin with Deet. At least Al always used a net, either on the front of his tent or, when he and Lesley took a well-deserved night off, over his campbed. Other problems we all suffered from were the jiggers in our feet, leeches on our legs and, in my own case, giant but painless chest-zits. Being permanently drenched with sweat night and day was something every overlander gets used to. It would be unimaginable in London, say, to get that hot and dirty and not have a shower. But there we would have to go days, even weeks, without a proper wash. Unless specifically told it was OK, we steered clear of water as there was the constant threat of bilharzia. Exciting as it is, Zaire truly is a hellhole.

Countering Al's comment on my sexuality, I launched into some unsolicited advice. "If you don't cover up, you'll get malaria."

"I've already had it. It hurt, but I survived. I'm building up resistance. I can't be doing with all those drugs." Al didn't take the prophylaxis the company provided either, but insisted on the group doing so and was equally insistent that they cover up. He didn't set an example, but they seemed to accept that he was somehow able to get away with it.

"Bollocks to resistance, you need to be born here," I replied, getting slightly heated. "And I'm not talking about taking anti-malarials. Just try not to get bitten."

"Too late. They've had half my brain away already."

With that, Al climbed over the gearshift and sat on my lap. I was still driving and there was Al pulling grotesque faces inches from my own and howling like a lunatic.

"Get the hell off. I can't see a thing!" I shouted through my laughter.

"Then put the bloody brakes on, Nobcheese!" He fought his way down between me and the door, edging me off the driver's seat. Grabbing the wheel, he kicked my feet off the pedals. "My turn. Test Cricket please."

It was a favourite at the times when his lunacy peaked, and in the jungle the frequency was increasing. It was only lunchtime before I got to watch the next episode.

We weren't far from Buta when the heavens opened. It poured down, outpacing the windscreen wipers and blocking visibility, making Al drive still slower. Fifteen minutes later the rain stopped. We pulled over for lunch and started eating our increasingly dull fare.

A few pale yellow butterflies landed amongst us. Followed by a few more. Then, in an extraordinary phenomenon of nature, came a deluge. It must have had something to do with the rain; indeed I expected David Attenborough to pop out of the trees at any second to explain it. In seconds, the delicate insects coated everything around us and applied a new yellowy surface to the road. Once they'd landed however, that appeared to be it – no more effort required; they wouldn't fly one more foot, but crawled over one another, flapping their wings for an extra surge of power only if a particularly steep pile of fellow yellow merited it. Enchanting as it was, I felt a touch guilty at the multiple murder every time I moved; to step anywhere meant squashing dozens at a time.

"And lo" – I saw Al up on the cab – "the Lord sent down manna from heaven. May we all give thanks."

Off again.

In a pastor's voice Al boomed down to the group, "Now gather them up. We shall have butterfly stirfry tonight." No one moved. "Come on. It's a gift from the Lord to those hungry for meat. We *must* eat meat." Still nothing. "Well, *I* must eat meat…" The voice was trailing off. "…please?"

Becky was first to say it. "No way, ya crazy muthafucka. I ain't chewin' on n-o-o-o-o-o insects."

Dan took up the objection, adding some sound advice. "Al, I think you'll find it's flying ants you can eat, not butterflies." Dan dangled a flapping bug by the wing. "Try one – I bet they taste like shit."

"That I shall." Al scraped up a handful of butterflies from the cab roof and stuffed them into his mouth. Like a child with candyfloss, wings and antennae poked out between his lips as he chewed. His smug expression quickly changed.

"Pppphhlaaaarrgh!" He spat them out. "They're revolting! You're right Dan – they taste like earwax. Cancel the last supper everybody, I shall call upon the ants." His arms in the air one more, Al lifted his face to the sky as he exhorted the heavens to rain down an alternative insect.

"Fly to me ants, fly."

Using the same careful procedure as before, we crossed the bridge into Buta. Although it had no railings it seemed hard to imagine what, apart from impatience, could have caused a truck to go over the edge. Immediately after the bridge we saw a pleasant open area by the river. We normally avoided towns, but seeing a Primus truck pull away clinched a decision the sight of a wooden bar at the water's edge had presented – we would camp there.

That night, having been lulled to sleep by the calming sound of running water, I was woken by a woman screaming; not in pain but in horror. That was followed by a man's voice swearing in Spanish. Coming to, I realised it was Hector and Isabel.

I turned over and chuckled to myself, thinking they must have found one of my favourite giant flying beetles in their tent. The size of a tennis ball, they take off like a helicopter if disturbed, making a similar racket. Like bees, it seems impossible that they can fly – only in their case, they really can't. Once up, they fall out of the sky, revving their engines each time they near the ground to make another short-lived ascent. For such a scary-looking beast, it always seemed such an ignominious departure.

The din didn't diminish though, so I crawled out from under my net, grabbed my torch and put on my boots. I found Hector and Isabel rummaging around inside their tent, frantically lifting up their sleeping bags, clothes and other – rather excessive – paraphernalia. Seeing my torchlight, Hector peered out. Standing there in my boxer shorts and hiking boots, I must have looked an unlikely saviour. I could feel myself being bitten and wanted to get whatever it was over and done with sharpish.

"What's the matter?" Isabel had stopped screaming, but now I could hear her sobbing.

"Bandidos," Hector blurted in a mean voice. "They have robbed us." Between the vocab' and his general demeanour, he wouldn't have gone amiss accompanying Clint in the spaghetti deserts.

"Are you sure? What did they take?"

"Todos. Every fuckin' 'ting Tim." Hector looked as if he could kill.

"Everything what?"

"Our bag. And in it our money, camera, our passaports…"

"You said your passports?!"

"Yes, our passa-bladdy-ports. They were in Isabella's Gucci bag."

"Holy Shit!"

I was awake now, and thinking quickly. There could be little worse that they could have had stolen, and no worse a place than in Zaire – the only embassies were an impossible distance away in Kinshasa. Then I realised something else. Hector was on an Argentinean passport. The flight-to-Kinshasa option was already out – no embassy.

"Have you checked everywhere? On the truck? In the trailer?"

"No. They were here, I know it."

My mind was screaming at him – *why did you have your passa-bladdy-ports in your bladdy daypack?* But I knew there was no point in saying it – he was already furious with himself, as much as with whoever had taken them.

I ran through more options. Travelling without papers is a serious issue in Africa; hell to pay at every army checkpoint and to try and leave Zaire without a passport, let alone enter CAR, a country apparently just as plagued with corruption, would be financial suicide. *Perhaps François could help?* I wondered. But we were a three-day drive from Kisangani – a week there and back – and had no other way of contacting him.

"Well, Hector, we'll just have to find them," I said in a voice more confident than I felt. "The money'll be gone, but your passports will turn up."

Hector made to get out of the tent. With a hand on his shoulder, I stopped him.

"It's pitch black out here. First thing in the morning, we'll go to the police." He nodded, suddenly looking like a little lost boy, and disappeared inside.

"Tonto in pants and boots," I muttered to myself as I walked back to my bed slapping my shoulders and ankles. "The Loan Ranger's going to love this."

Fitful sleep saw images of Gucci bags bobbing off downriver together, or hitching across Zaire in the cab of a Primus truck visiting remote jungle bars. At the first sign of light I got up. Hector and Isabel were up too, looking around our camp and beyond. I went over to Al's tent where I could hear contented breath in stereo.

Here goes.

"Ground control to Major Tom," I said in a loud whisper, trying, weakly, to inject a little humour into the situation.

"The circuit's dead, there's something wrong," Al croaked, surprisingly tunefully. "But what the cock do you want, Control? It's still dark."

"You'd best get up, Major. Like you said, there's something wrong."

"I can't get up now, I'm supporting thousands of mosquitoes," – I didn't doubt it – "not to mention the whole tent with my morning glory. Or is that it? You want a look?"

With bag-rustling indicating that he was already preparing to give me an eyeful of erection, I launched straight into the problem.

"Hector and Isabel have had their passports nicked."

Silence. Then: "Is that it? Is that what the kerfuffle was about last night? I thought it was serious. LIKE SOMEONE HAD DIED OR FUCKING SOME-THING!" The yell nearly made the tent billow. Then he was out, tucking a flaccid dick into his shorts as he pulled them on. He looked angrier than I'd ever seen him.

"Well, I'll check your pockets and you check mine," he said with a sudden smile. "Then we'll all line up and check each other's. Then, with a bit of luck, it'll end up as one mass shagging session by the river and the passports will be discovered up someone's arse. Whaddya reckon?"

Calm – as always – in a crisis.

"It's a start mate." I smiled now too. "Bend over."

Finding nothing near the camp, Al and I went to the police station, a collection of wooden sheds on the edge of town. Beyond the windowless hatch of the largest we could see two part-uniformed men asleep on the bare floor.

"Wakey wakey!" Al called, sticking his head through the hole. "Twenty wazungu have got a case for you to solve. Oi, monsieur le detective, up we get." They stirred, then one got up and opened the door at the side of the shed.

"Bonjour. Entrez." He beckoned us in, rubbing his eyes.

I explained the situation and got the stock reply – "Pas de problème."

"Yes, but what are you going to do?" I asked.

"Find the passports."

I couldn't coax any more out of him. He explained the problem to his colleague and then looked back at us.

"Cadeau?" he asked. I told him that there was money in the bag. We didn't want to see that, just the passports – and cameras if possible. He told us to come back that night.

Back at camp the atmosphere was predictably low, and lower still once Al had told everyone we would be staying put until the passports appeared. Needless to say, Al went straight to his toolkit, brushing Hector off when he came to talk to him. I told Hector everything that had been said at the police station, halfway through which Isabel arrived. When I had finished, she blessed herself with the sign of the cross. "Every little helps," I noted wryly, for which I got a glare.

As opposed to the action-packed, get-through-with-a-team-spirit bogging type of disaster, this was more of the engine-stuffed-in-Niamey variety, the kind that saps group morale. No one can do anything, and waiting interminably for a solution entirely out of everyone's hands is hard to handle. Having seen it before,

I chose the Pete angle – keep everyone informed, but avoid them as much as possible. I joined Al under the truck. The group, having carefully packed away everything that could move, donned daypacks and headed off as one to the bar.

Perhaps Al had been waiting for such a serious occasion to tackle the big job. He had the prop shaft off already and was finding the right spanner to start on the gearbox. "Must be the clutchplate if it only crunches in reverse, first and second."

"I'll take your word for it."

"Bet you two pineapples and a tomato."

"Done, even though I agree with you. Does this count as an on-the-road day or an in-town day?"

"Neither, it's just a chocky day," Al said decisively. "We can hide under here. I'll get Les on the Bolero and kettle at eleven."

Charlotte beat her to it, having come back from the bar. "I thought you might like some tea," she said, kneeling on the ground holding two mugs out to us under the truck, her elbows keeping her balanced. Her breasts were clearly visible in that position and I feasted my eyes on their firm form for a moment.

"Charlotte. I can see your tits from here" – reliable old Al – "they're gorgeous. Let's have a hold."

"I think your hands are full with Lesley's," Charlotte laughed flirtatiously.

"Fried eggs, mate. Yours are much better. Don't suppose you'd like a bang up the brown bonzer as well, would you?"

"I'm fond of any new experience," she replied, giving her breasts a jiggle before they disappeared from view.

"I don't believe it," I spluttered. "There you are, sprawled on the dust, covered in oil and still trying it on. What's more, it's bloody working."

"Dipshit. All that was for your benefit, you know. She's yours, Tim. You've done it your own way, mate."

"I dunno, Al. It's too late I reckon. I've told her everything – she's my conscience."

"Your conscience? How can she be your conscience? You're a bloke. Blokes don't have a conscience!"

That evening we went back to the police station. The truck was still in bits and Al was taking no more chances – he had asked one of the group to guard the pile of parts. In the event, we were in no danger of having to effect a quick reassembly in the morning as the passports hadn't been recovered. But something else had been found as part of the investigation.

Behind the wooden bars of a neighbouring hut sat a woman with a baby at her breast. The policemen proudly revealed their plan. In front of us was the suspected thief's family. Effectively, they were being held hostage as ransom for him to give himself up. The policemen seemed quite sure of who was responsible and were waiting for word to reach him in the forest that his wife and child were being held prisoner.

The stench from the hut was appalling and the woman was waving a limp hand in front of her baby's face. Between each weak waft busy flies settled back onto its eyelids and lips. Momentarily I looked back at the woman as she stared directly at me, and found no expression to discern her feelings. Guilt? Probably not. Fear? I presumed so. But what I imagined she felt was an absolute hatred.

I turned away and walked past the smiling policemen to stand next to Al, who had already left. With his back to the hut and his face turned upwards, he was breathing in deeply. Whether he was controlling his anger or filling his lungs with fresher air I didn't know, but if he felt anything like me he was feeling sick to his stomach. Between us, we had achieved a repeat example of King Leopold's 19th century methods of subjugation; methods that I later read about in *King Leopold's Ghost* by Adam Hochschild[*]

In 1879, King Leopold II of Belgium funded Stanley's third expedition to the Congo. By May 1885, when the flag of the new Congo Free State had been raised, Leopold's personal colony covered millions of square miles of equatorial Africa. For the next two decades he extracted vast quantities of rubber, by force, enslaving and murdering to do so. In that time, his Belgian officers developed a technique to replace those they killed or dismembered during the work effort – they would capture the women and children from villages and hold them hostage until runaway men returned from the forests to claim them. They were then set to work.

Like every other European capital, most of Brussels' beautiful architecture was built on the blood of the indigenous peoples in the colonies: in their case the Congo. Little of the horrific methods employed in gaining such wealth made it to the public eye, however, until E.D. Morel began his work as the world's first human rights campaigner.

A master of harnessing the power of the media, Morel was the first to make proper use of photography to show that people had died as a direct result of Leopold's rule. Murder is now estimated to have accounted for many hundreds of thousands of deaths; at that time there existed the belief that for the smallest considered slight it was justifiable to kill an entire village. Other factors caused many times more deaths – exhaustion and starvation killed millions of rubber workers; disease, including European imports such as smallpox, killed millions more.

In 1904, Morel, while speaking about the Congo in America, met James Twain. Twain took to the cause and brought it up with President Roosevelt, before publishing a damning poem about what was going on in the rubber plantations. En-

[*] Publisher: Houghton Mifflin Co;, October 1999

titled 'King Leopold's Soliloquy', it was an imaginary monologue by Leopold that brought the cruel facts of his colonisation to a worldwide audience.

In 1908, the Belgian state was forced to buy Leopold's personal colony from him. Slave labour and blatant murder was halted, but forced labour and brutality continued. This really just brought the Belgians into line with the standards of British, French and German colonial administrators. Indeed, rich countries were all guilty of mass murder; only Leopold had chosen a bigger target and reduced the population of his state from twenty million to ten million in just twenty-five years.

Our situation was hardly in the same league, but the detail was uncomfortably similar. The woman's husband was quite possibly the guilty party, and to continue on our convivial junket we needed those passports. So we needed her to make him come back. But it is pertinent to ask: what on earth were we doing there in the first place? Overlanders do take back great lessons in life – an understanding of the perverse imbalance of wealth distribution across the world, for example – and once home we could make of that what we wished. But it is harder to identify what we gave back. When I thought of the truck trundling across plain, jungle and desert, I thought only how ridiculous we must have looked; how detached, as we flounced along, stopping to drink beer around our campfire at night. It could easily be viewed as an obscene parade of our wealth and freedom.

So what did Al and I do after standing there together, quelling our nausea? We went back to the truck; Al to his gearbox, me to my notebook. To our credit, we did ask the policemen not to harm the woman and child, and gave them some money to buy them food and water.

The next day we did what people like us do in situations like that. I fell into a melancholic mood and Al was silent, ignoring everyone, except to glare at Hector. Charlotte kept up a ready supply of tea and tits to our self-imposed incarceration under the truck and the rest of the group, intensely disappointed by the lack of food in Buta – pineapples only, not even tomatoes – began to squabble. It really was turning into a Niamey, only with increased speed, as there was absolutely *no* distraction from our predicament. Our western misery had set in, and neither Al nor I were in any mood to do anything about it.

Going back to the police station as arranged at 4pm, we found one change. The policemen still beamed with pride at the continuing success of their immaculate investigation and the prison hut still stank, but this time the woman and child were sitting on the step outside it. Her expression didn't change, however, as we held out what we had brought: some bread and fruit, a small tin of powdered milk and two big bottles of water. She refused to take our offerings directly, so we put them beside her on the step. In contrast, the policemen were effervescent in their promises of a successful recovery by the same time the next day.

Things didn't improve much for the Congolese after Leopold. Fifty more years of an exploitative foreign ruler brought further misery – until independence fever eventually created signs of unrest. Frightened by the prospect of open rebellion, Belgium granted a hasty independence to the Congolese in 1959.

Patrice Lubumba, a popular maverick leader, was elected President in 1960, immediately taking an anti-western stance. This incensed the US and struck fear into the hearts of Belgian settlers. Provoked in part by US policies that had undermined Lubumba's presidency, the Congo fell into civil war. A high-ranking military man, Mobutu Sese Seko, had Lubumba put under arrest, but he escaped. He was recaptured and subsequently killed by 'hostile tribesmen'. There are many theories about who killed him, including one that he was abducted and killed by the CIA, the agents then driving around with the body in the boot of his car looking for a suitable place to dump it. I had asked François about this story. He entirely rejected its authenticity, declaring passionately that the secessionist Katanga tribe had murdered his friend.

Mobutu seized power in a coup in 1961 and declared himself president. There he was to remain until 1997, presiding over one of the most corrupt governments the world has ever known. Almost until the very end of his tyrannical reign, France and the US supported him politically and financially. The same was true of most first world governments, and the reason never changes – profit. While Mobutu plundered his country, so too did the world's largest mining companies and other western businesses.

In 1991, when Mobutu cancelled promised multiparty elections and renewed his term of office, the country fell into further looting, rioting and arson. The results of those riots explained the devastation we had seen in Kisangani, not to mention the outrageous exchange rate.

Mobutu clung to power through further crises until 1997, when Laurent Kabila swept with his forces across the country, taking Kinshasa in months. Hailed as a saviour by the west – they had suddenly begun to voice concern over Mobutu's twenty-six year reign as if they had just noticed – no one delved too deeply into Kabila's shady past. He had in fact been involved in gangsterism, prostitution rackets, a failed coup attempt and had amassed millions through diamond smuggling. Zaire's new president, Laurent Kabila, was by all accounts an opportunist crook. Once in power he continued in a similar vein to Mobutu, creaming what little was left in the pockets of his long-suffering people into offshore bank accounts. The rape of the country's resources for the benefit of the few – western business still included – continued unabated.

In a dramatic shootout at the presidential palace, Laurent Kabila was killed 'by persons unknown' in January 2001. His son, Joseph Kabila – the world's youngest president – took over. Western governments now queued up to pour scorn on his father, before quickly arranging new business deals. They weren't the only ones. At the time of Laurent Kabila's death, the forces of five neighbouring countries were occupying the forests of his renamed Democratic Republic of Congo (DRC). No doubt their agendas were different, but the results of their presence on the population were always the same: fear, death and abject poverty, brought on by total economic collapse.

In camp that evening, with my nose in my notebook, I was pondering further whether the theft had a rational explanation. I was trying to work out who was ultimately responsible. What if we had never come, I wrote, or had never left the bag – so tempting to a man trying to achieve the basic dignity of feeding his family – unguarded outside a tent at night? I couldn't answer at the time, but once again, though much later, Hochschild helped. At the end of his book, he quotes a 14th century philosopher, Ibn Khaldun, when he writes: "Those who are conquered always want to imitate the conqueror in his main characteristics."

When Mobutu died from cancer in the same year he was ousted, he was one of the world's richest men with a personal fortune of $4bn, all of it gained at the expense of his country's people.

Perhaps our missing bag *did* have a rational explanation. By creating conditions where he had total power, giving his trusted men unfettered control over every level of society and extracting every last cent from the country's production for his personal use, Mobutu had followed in Leopold's footsteps; was like him 'in his main characteristics'. His men were corrupt beyond imagination – stealing anything from the school budget and public sector salaries to international aid. Conditions for ordinary people like our thief had long ago reached what could only be described as desperate. I find it hard to imagine how a country can sink so far and still survive, but that survival is testament to the ingenuity of its people. One of them, probably hungry, steals a bag. The wrong bag, because it had passports in it, and now his wife and daughter are locked up in the shit, piss, vomit and blood of the previous inhabitants of Buta prison.

The woman wasn't on the step when we went back the following night. The policemen beckoned us into their hut and one of them, reaching into his drawer, pulled out a Gucci bag. Opening it with a flourish, he produced two cameras and two Argentinean passports. He then turned it over and tipped out the remaining items; tissue paper, a couple of biros, make-up and a few coins. The money, he told us with his largest smile so far, had not been recovered, but he was pleased to have been of service. Nothing was owed for their efforts and success.

I felt no overwhelming joy as I put the passports back into the bag along with the other items. Slinging it over my shoulder I muttered "Let's go" to Al. We stepped outside, but the policemen ran out to block our path.

"Come. Please. You must see the man who did it."

I was in fact vaguely curious to put a face to my three-day imaginings of the 'poor man of Africa', so I followed them. Al stayed put. Perhaps he already knew what I was about to see.

A second was enough. Being nursed by his wife with a damp rag, her child now slung with a kanga across her back, was a prone man. I should say body. His face was criss-crossed by the shadow of the bars but was otherwise bathed in sunlight. It was totally disfigured, smashed to a pulp; purple with swollen bruises and bloody from cuts above his eyes. He had been beaten violently about his head, obviously with more than fists.

Thankfully, for the moment I was there, the woman hadn't looked up – the man couldn't have done. Turning away quickly, I saw one of the policemen standing a few feet from me. With a big grin on his face that begged me to give him my heartfelt congratulations, he was tapping a truncheon against the palm of his hand.

The rains started. Every afternoon, clouds that had spent the morning congregating gleefully tipped their bulging contents over Equatorial Africa. As a result, the already unroadworthy road deteriorated into a quagmire. Even Al was surprised. Our route across Zaire was officially part of the Trans-African Highway, a project dreamt up by the Organisation of African Unity to link Lagos with Mombasa, two major ports on each side of the continent. Now, with the track in ruins, and only the width of the truck, it seemed to me a ridiculous notion.

The crux of the problem was that in theory that part of the road didn't need to exist. From Kisangani east, ferries were supposed to ply the river, transporting cargo, people, even trucks to Bumba and beyond. Unfortunately they had all ground to a halt and this road was still at the bottom of a long list for the few Zairians on grader duty. Within a few kilometres we encountered our first truck-sized bog-hole. Deep, half-full of water, this one had whole branches jammed into the mud at the bottom. Fortunately Al was driving, so I could get a few hints as to the required technique. Not too difficult, in fact. He waded through it once, moving branches to make sure none could puncture a fuel tank, burnt two leeches off his left calf, climbed back behind the wheel and gunned it. After talking with those on Ray's truck, the group had been waiting for it and like me were exhilarated as we crashed down into the hole, bucked through it and crawled back out in one violent manoeuvre.

Slithering around on wet mud we slowly made our way to the next bog-hole, which was considerably longer. We were now in permanent four-wheel-drive, but even so, halfway through after a flying start we got completely bogged. Al seemed unperturbed. He got the group out and unhitched the trailer. With the help of the keener members of the group, those who had probably suffered most during the thumb-twiddling session in Buta, we dug out mud from under all four wheels – difficult as we were digging underwater and getting sucked dry by leeches. When he was satisfied that the wheels were unhindered by clinging mud, Al put a mat under each and with the remainder made a track for the rear wheels to follow.

The clutchplate had been renewed just in time, as first gear was a necessity. The truck bit on the mats, gaining enough momentum to keep moving to the next set. The front wheels climbed out of the hole to where they too could gain more purchase. Then, skidding and jolting, the truck pulled itself clear like a body being pulled from quicksand. I untied the hawser from the front of the truck while the group collected the mats and laid them out for rebending. Tying the hawser to the hitch of the truck, I got the group to stand clear while Al hauled the trailer out too. He then drove over the mats to straighten them out. A neat operation; it took less than half an hour.

Thereafter we went through many more bog-holes, some requiring a similar operation. By the end of the day we had covered only 30km. I wondered how some of the local trucks got through as they were woefully ill equipped and too overloaded to tackle mud. Soon all became clear.

In the bottom of the first hole we came across the following morning – we were now getting up in the dark and leaving at first light – was a big, local truck. The drivers were sitting by the roadside, each sporting a large leaf on his head for shade. They were doing nothing.

"Here we go," Al shrugged wearily. "Overland AA to the rescue. Turn around when you can, Tim, and back up to the hole."

I could see what was coming. I unhitched the trailer and backed up. The drivers had by now got into their cab. They hadn't said anything, but were giving me the thumbs-up as I hitched our hawser to their truck. With the help of some screaming from the group and the Zairians revving their own engine, I pulled them clear of the hole and set them on their way. Such was the mutual expectation of your average trucker on the Trans-Africa Highway. Like many systems African, it worked. If slowly.

Our next destination would signify two thirds of our journey complete. By missing the rains, Ray had reached Kisangani in only eight days, yet we had already been in Zaire for two weeks. With only 50km under our belt that day, I estimated it would take another week to reach Bumba. Nonetheless, with memories of Buta fading under the constant work, the group seemed to be loving it. Without exception they had abandoned themselves to the filth and leeches – though, like me, they all wore boots. Al was still in thongs, which allowed his feet to become filled with jiggers. These he picked out each time he got back into the cab. His legs and arms too were covered in scabs from tropical sores – the result of infected mosquito bites. In contrast, I was relatively unscathed, apart from my bulging chest-zits which had now spread to my shoulders and were multiplying in an attempted assault on my back. I had learnt not to nag Al about covering up, however; Lesley did that now. And Al ignored her too.

During the next two days Rachel and New Zealand Tom started complaining of headaches. Soon they both had a fever. In the morning they were both extremely tired and had to be helped out of their tent and put on the truck, where they promptly fell asleep again. Rachel woke up halfway through our breakfast, complaining that she felt cold. She was shivering, so Isabel found her a sleeping bag and placed it around her.

I was worried. Inside our truck medical kit – replete with enough drugs and equipment to open a pharmacy or perform a small operation – was a book describing tropical diseases, their identification and treatment. Al had voiced his confidence that it was malaria, but I wanted to be sure.

The symptoms matched, and the book advised *'treat with course of fansidar, quinine or chloroquin. Do not use if previously taken prophylactically. Chloroquin can also be used to reduce fever.'* We had the lot on board. Many of our drugs fell within the realms of prescription-only and with the aid of our trusty manual, and any local or on-truck knowledge, it was the leader's responsibility to administer them and record having done so. That sounded like a sure-fire way of being sued to me, so whatever I chose to give Tom and Rachel was going to be a clandestine affair as far as London was concerned.

Al saw me studying the manual. "That's all rubbish, mate. Give them the new wonder drug. Has you up and about in a few days. They'll be boogying at the next pit party before you know it." He certainly wasn't worried, and there were seemingly plenty of packets of Wonderdrug. We set off once again. Isabel – at last finding herself a role – became nurse, and when they woke up she gave our patients the first two of their six tablets.

We had been free of holes requiring mats for a couple of hours. But it couldn't last. Just after a bridge made of six huge tree trunks we saw it. The hole stretched way up the road, perhaps half a kilometre. Wallowing in the bog like so many hippos were a total of eight trucks spread across the entire distance. Al stopped and switched off the engine. There was silence; no spinning of wheels, splashing of spades in muddy water or straining of engines.

"Swallow my knob!" Al exclaimed. "Will you look at that shit? How are we going to get through there?" With the engine off the group had begun to get out, gathering around the cab in some excitement. Those with cameras took it in turns to climb on the cab to get a clearer picture.

"You'll have plenty of time for photos, guys," Al called out of the window.

"In fact, the artists among you have my full permission to set up an easel upstairs."

The extent of the problem was dawning on them as it was on me. We could tow the first truck out, but there was no way of getting to the second or any of the others.

"Why the hell did they all drive in?" I said, as much to myself as to anyone else.

"Heard of lemmings?" Al replied. "Well here you have their closest relatives." He was sweeping his hand at the grim scene in front of him. "They seem to think that if they get in there, someone else'll get them out. But in this instance, my esteemed colleague, I believe they are sadly mistaken."

"I think, Professor Casey, you are correct in your hypothesis," I replied. "And if I too am not greatly mistaken, we will be awaiting their extraction before further commencement."

"Too bloody right."

Al called out of the window to the group, "We're camping here for the foreseeable future. And you don't have to get back in. Right here will do."

Evidently there was no danger of passing road traffic – save any long-distance cyclists – so the road itself would be our campground.

Tom and Rachel groaned in pain when I asked how they were. Stretched out across the bench seats in the back of the truck, her sleeping bag under her head acting as a pillow, Rachel told me she felt hot again. Erecting the cooktent in a shaded area the group had already cleared, we guided our patients into its slightly cooler air. Al, myself, Charlotte, Nick and Dan then walked along the side of the hole to survey the damage. In the worst cases only the trucks' cab roofs and loads were visible from the road. We came across the drivers. Gathered together in a clearing of their own, they waved on our approach and offered us pineapple. What else!

I chatted with them a while and heard a conclusion as predictable as the fare on offer. There was 'pas de probleme' and a grader was on its way to pull everyone through. They also explained that if they weren't already in the hole when it arrived, they would have to pay to get dragged through.

Ah ha. Financial lemmings. We decided to risk the payment rather than sink everything we owned three metres deep in mud.

Continuing up, we found the inevitable Primus truck at the far end of the hole. Even in the bowels of God's earth we could buy beer.

The grader didn't show up that day, nor the day after. Tom and Rachel had begun to regain a little strength and had taken their first tentative mouthfuls of our ever-duller food: rice and tomatoes, pasta and tomatoes, pineapple for pudding. Whatever wood we could gather was so wet that it had to be doused in litres of diesel to get it burning, then furiously flapped by teams wielding pan lids. It was horribly smoky and the minute flames made little impression on our aluminium pots. There was no chance of a pineapple upside-down cake, as we couldn't create sufficient coals to heat the oildrum-oven. To boil water we used gas. Like our water supplies, that too was running low, so we implemented drinking-only rations.

With Tom and Rachel's partial recovery came the next victims of our parasitical friends. Helen, Nick and Jean all started complaining of headaches, then fever and muscle pain. A day later, Chisiko suddenly keeled over. Al found her lying on the ground, shaking and moaning. Tiny as she was she had always been a hardy soul, and perhaps due to her tougher culture had made no previous complaints. I was down to three packs of Wonderdrug already and we had six people asleep in the cooktent most of the day.

On the morning of Bog-hole Day Five, Al was spectacularly grumpy. He had gone to the drivers' camp to ask about the grader and had come back furious. "They're full of shit, those boys. They'd sit there through three new governments before they did anything useful."

I felt like pointing out that we weren't exactly a virtuoso display of useful behaviour ourselves, but thought better of it. He continued to stomp around, picking things up and throwing them down, snapping at people for using too much water when they weren't, and picking faults in the standards of washing-up and food preparation. I had already suspected something was wrong, as he hadn't opened the toolbox for two days, and later I saw him behind the truck swallowing some tablets.

"Anything wrong, Al?" I enquired gently.

"My bonce is throbbing like a good'un. I must be dehydrated."

In severe denial more like, was what I thought – what I said was "Righto, let me know if I can do anything. I'm just going to check the MASH-tent." In matters of manliness, Al was best left undisturbed.

It was Becky who had christened the MASH-tent, an apt moniker. While the patients slept in their two-man tents on the road each night, during the day our nurses, Isabel and her new assistant Rachel – now back on her feet – tended to them in the cooktent. There was much mopping of fevered brows and feeding of water to pursed lips. Charlotte, of course, was Florence Nightingale, keeping a note of how much each patient drank and when they had taken their drugs. The drugs generally lived up to Al's description, but worryingly Tom had still to get himself up properly even though he'd finished his course three days previously.

Those remaining upright, and not in possession of the nursing-gene or a spare sponge to dab with, filled their days as best they could. Over-the-truck tennis, using branches fashioned into rackets, was a favourite. A Frisbee could often be seen taking a similar trajectory. Dan and New Zealand Tom went running in the mornings and did muscle-enriching – though sweat-inducing – exercises at other times. Chris had taken Al seriously. When he wasn't checking on Chisiko in the MASH-tent he was to be found painting. At 2pm on the dot all outdoor activities ceased when the rain came. At that point everyone climbed into the back of the truck. There, letter and diary writing – a difficult task given our circumstances, unless there was much to catch up on – and the usual activities of song and joke creation filled the afternoons. The evenings were especially dull. Despite our proximity to a mobile bar, beer drinking was a rarity as no one felt like being too cheerful around the MASH-tent dwellers.

Throughout all this it was Robert who was having the most fun. While in Buta he had bought four live chickens. Allegedly, when in a dark place chickens will always sleep – certainly that was Robert's justification for keeping them in what I thought made a meagre home: the oildrum-oven. Every morning and evening he had let them out to fatten up their scrawny bodies on our leftover food. But since they proved somewhat difficult to catch at bedtime, he had attached a long piece of string to each. A problem solved often creates a new one. Even with leads he had still lost two and the others, while pecking around for food, would get themselves tied up in horrible knots and then lie blinking up at us in supplication for release. Only Robert could be bothered to unravel them. With a continued and ridiculous fondness for the stupid creatures, he was now frequently to be seen heading off down the road with his two chickens, Judge and Pickles, strutting and clucking on their leads to either side of him.

That evening, I found Al asleep in the cab, his head lolling out of the passenger window. I called Lesley over.

"I told him to cover up," she admonished. "He's had malaria twice before, and I don't think those drugs'll work again."

That was something I hadn't thought of. Consulting the blurb that came with the tablets, I couldn't really decide if they would or wouldn't work a third time. Les woke him up gently and Al made the decision for us.

"Don't give me that shit. Save it for the others. I haven't even got malaria."

"At least let us get you to your tent then," I urged.

"I can get there myself." Al opened the door and fell straight out. "Bollocks – that hurt."

He reached out to Lesley and me, and we pulled him up. His knees visibly wobbling, he finally acknowledged that he needed our help, "OK, Les, I want Wonderdrugs and your best blowjob in the tent right now. Come on. Chop chop." Walking like the drunken front row of a rugby team, we staggered together to his quarters.

To my relief, Tom was up and about when I got up the next morning. He put on the kettle for coffee and the early heat of the day brought out the zombies, helped from their tents by their nurses. They staggered into the cooler MASH-tent. A line of four trucks had accumulated behind our camp and I saw a number of their drivers coming towards us. I met the deputation who explained that the grader was parked behind them. It had arrived in the night and could soon begin its work.

Al was in a bad way. He hardly woke up as Lesley and I half-carried him the short distance from his tent to the MASH-tent. With all the small tents removed from the road the grader came by, a shiny new Japanese monster. With remarkable ease, it dragged the first truck clear of the mud and the encrusted vehicle squeezed past our camp to head off on its way. By the end of the day the grader was working on the Primus truck, dragging it slowly towards us from its distant berth. The hole clear, we would be first through the next day, we were assured.

I hadn't thought quickly enough. On Bog-hole day seven, I saw that the queue from the other end had taken up position along the length of the hole – I should have taken the plunge the night before to assert the rightful turn of the queue at our end.

The first few rescues had been fun to watch but by the afternoon all interest was long gone. Finally, our turn came. Our truck did pretty well, travelling some 200m before getting stuck. The grader towed us the rest of the way. An hour after it had descended, our truck finally popped out of the Bog-hole from Hell, our home in Zaire for a week.

A long uphill stretch at the other end was totally washed out by a mass of deep rivulets, random like a Norfolk marsh. However slowly I drove I couldn't avoid the violent jolts as one wheel after another lurched into the holes. The fit were walking but the patients, Al included, must have really suffered in the back of the truck.

As dusk approached we camped, pressed tight between the trees and the edge of the road. Depressingly, we were still in view of the Bog-hole. During that day, both Helen and Nick had pretty much recovered, but were replaced by Dan and Charlotte. And I only had one pack of Wonderdrugs left.

Completing the ascent in the morning we then had to fit everyone on board – the patients now had to doze with their heads on other people's shoulders. Al was propped up in the cab against the window. Despite a towel for a pillow his head knocked against the glass with every bump, but he slept on regardless. The road had improved slightly, but before we could reach Aketi we had one more baseless bridge – and the obligatory army roadblocks – to negotiate.

Aketi Bridge is actually a road and a rail bridge in one, and very long. During our crossing, however, I was far from worried about being mown down by a speeding express. Nothing else worked in Zaire, so I imagined the rail network had gone the same way to rack and ruin.

In the ghost town of Aketi we eventually found water. As the puny trickle from the hose indicated, tank filling would be a long job, so some of the group went in search of food. Tom and Rachel arrived back accompanied by two locals, all four wearing a fetching green barnet of bananas on their heads. They looked like a coven of Medusas. The appearance of a long-forgotten taste brought great excitement and we all feasted on the succulent, sweet flesh. Even the patients revived an interest in food, nibbling a little each, apart from Al, who waved my offering away.

That night, after further reasonable progress, I went to visit the four patients still lying in the back of the truck. Dispensing with tents as the heat was insufferable, we had moved them and their mosquito nets into the truck to sleep. The fifth – Al – was in the cab.

Charlotte was awake, so I sat and told her about the events of the day. We ended up laughing but she stopped herself, squeezing her head between her hands to stifle the ache. I reached under her net and gave her temples a massage. Relaxing, she began breathing contentedly and then fell asleep. Pulling the net down, I checked that everyone else was sleeping too and then joined the group around the smoky fire.

Halfway through a beer, Rachel interrupted my thoughts, tapping me on the shoulder and asking to speak to me privately. She led me away from the group before facing me. Her lips were quivering slightly.

"I saw you, you know," she said quickly.

Puzzled, I asked her what she had seen. She gulped audibly before speaking again.

"You, with Charlotte. In the truck."

"I'm sorry, I don't get you."

"I was ill too, you know, so are lots of other people." Her voice had found strength now. "But you didn't go round massaging anyone else."

I looked at her. I couldn't even conceive that I had done anything wrong; yet here was my accuser staring me in the face. Rachel was deeply upset. My emotions wavered. Guilt crept over me as I rewound my mind and saw she was completely correct. Then I started to feel annoyed. I had had other worries: food, water, diesel, driving, and truck maintenance – not to mention Al. I had checked everyone on the truck that evening and only Charlotte had been awake. True, I wouldn't have massaged anyone else, but we were close friends, and besides, I hadn't seen Rachel tipping up with cups of tea while we worked. Rachel broke the silence.

"In your job, you shouldn't show favouritism. There are some people on this trip you and Al don't even speak to. You've got your own little gang, and you can't be bothered with the rest of us." The tears now appeared.

I wanted to stop the conversation. I wanted to gather everyone around and ask if they agreed with her complaint. I wanted Rachel to stop crying. But even though I had so many thoughts, I didn't want to share one of them with her. We were coming from completely different directions and to discuss would be to argue.

"I'm sorry, Rachel. I'll bear that in mind. Thank you."

I walked back to the fire and picked up my beer. Rachel arrived shortly afterwards, wiping her eyes as she sat next to Tom. She crossed her arms and legs, bouncing one foot rhythmically up and down – no doubt my words had been an unsatisfactory conclusion for her. As I drank, I thought. I had long ago decided that my primary role as driver was to ensure safety and health and even under our outrageous circumstances I was doing the best I could, with help from everyone on board.

But what was at issue were my personal relationships. I had a very busy job and when I was 'off duty' surely it was up to me who I chose to speak with. I couldn't pretend to find everybody fascinating. Like everyone else, I had settled into a small social circle within the wider community. That wasn't favouritism. This was overlanding – not regular tourism. We spent months together; it wasn't a guided tour of a few highlights. To me it was up to the group to look after themselves while I provided the means to do so. That was my baseline, and if I reached that I could then choose my own enjoyment. I couldn't be responsible for how each individual fitted into the group, any more than I could divide myself up into seventeen parts, dispensing conversation – and massages – as if I was sharing a bag of sweets. No, Rachel and the other members of the group with whom I had nothing in common could create their own friendships, like I had. In terms of sociability, I concluded, my contribution was no more important than anyone else's.

Theft struck Rachel two days later. She always insisted on taking a spade into the bush at piss-stops, thoughtfully saving the endless rainforests of Zaire from her litter. Coming back from her chosen spot way up ahead of the truck as we drove towards Bumba, she stopped by the cab and told me someone had nicked the shovel while she squatted. An opportunist if ever there was one. We could well have done without the loss, but I still had to laugh at her close brush with a wily villager. Poor Tom was made to accompany her from that day forth.

Al was the last to recover from malaria. He had been asleep, slumped in the cab, for five days. I had been on the verge of giving him the last of our drugs and had found it difficult to keep my worries from the group. He came to just in time to point out a bit of a shrine to overlanding, one that trucks had taken to stopping at for a moment or two in respect. On a rise overlooking the Congo just outside

Bumba are the graves of two overlanders, victims of malaria. If it goes wrong in Zaire, there is no getting out.

"I thought you might be burying me here with these guys," Al said, the nearest he had got to humour for a long time.

"So did I, mate. But I couldn't have anyway. Rachel lost the spade." I told him the story and he laughed weakly, clearly lacking the energy to get annoyed at further equipment loss.

"Nice spot," he whispered dreamily. "But I'd rather be in Paris with Jim Morrison, not out here in Bumfuck." He was gazing across the river, perhaps two kilometres wide and moving with grace and power on its long journey to the Atlantic.

"See up by those cranes?" Al pointed out two decrepit, rusting iron towers a short distance upriver by the quay fronting the town. "That's where we camp. There's a warehouse with a big yard. Not a thing in it, but it's got a bloody big door. Did you hear what happened to Craig Hutchinson here?"

Craig was a company legend – but I couldn't think of any Zaire stories about him.

"Cracking story. The dozy sod was having his truck craned on when we used to take the ferry from here down to Kisangani. He must have pissed the driver off somehow though, coz when the boat moved for some reason, the driver lowered the truck anyway. Whoosh; one Bedford straight to the bottom of the Congo. Next thing he saw were the seats floating downriver and a load of pirogues paddling after them."

"Shit – how did he get it out?"

"Cool customer Craig. He took the controls, hoisted the truck back out and put it on the ferry himself. Then spent five days on the ferry stripping it down and putting it all back together again. Apart from a battery he had to borrow off a bloke with a Morris Minor, he was able to drive off at the other end like nothing had happened."

We had all learnt to laugh at these disasters and such stories were passed down from driver to driver like tribal legends.

"What did he do, make new seats out of floursacks and palm thatch?"

"He even got those back. The fisherman sold him his own seats for five dollars apiece. Even the passports dried out OK, but he had to fill in the date on a few visas."

Craig wasn't known as The Golden Boy for nothing.

Al eased himself back into the job with a spot of light tinkering the next morning. I had tightened up a few nuts that had rattled loose and had kept everything well greased, but he decided it was time to change the fuel filters. In Bumba town we found a reliable tap but few new varieties of goods, so the group shopped for the usual plus bananas – now in abundance as well. An air of calm had spread among the group, as if we had won the battle, though now that everyone was relatively healthy again, they definitely needed something to cheer them up.

A shower helped. Dan found it in a toilet in the unlocked warehouse and spent half a day filling the overhead tank with buckets of water. There was enough for a few minutes for everyone. But better was to come.

Towards the middle of the afternoon, people started turning up at the quay. Some had baskets of fruit, others had plastic bags of belongings; all sat looking upriver. More and more people arrived until they numbered at least a hundred. I went to find out what was happening and heard that the ferry was due in. It had left Kisangani a week ago, the first one in seven months. If we had known, we could have missed the horrendous drive we had just completed, and the Bog-hole from Hell. Neither of us had even thought to ask.

The ferry was definitely going as far as the next town, Lisala. Beyond that no-one knew, but Lisala was on our route. On hearing the news, some of the group expressed more than a passing interest in going by boat up the Congo. They were keen for the chance for a new experience, and I was inclined to agree with them.

To my suggestion that we took the ferry, Al replied, "I wouldn't trust my truck to that rusty crap up there even if I was giving the driver a blowjob while he put it on the boat."

I tried a new tack. "We could split up though."

"You can go with them if you want. I'm not. I get seasick."

"Al, it's a bloody river."

"It's still wet, mate."

I soon had it set up. The ferry was leaving that evening after unloading and the cost would be negligible. Once the idea had spread all but New Zealand Tom, Rachel and Helen decided they wanted to go, and Al was happy to tackle the road with only a skeleton crew on board. We packed up the equipment we would need and joined the multiplying crowd on the quay.

The arrival was quite an event. The first I saw of the boat was a plume of black smoke rising above the opposite shoreline, and then it appeared around the bend in the river. The crowd, now about two hundred strong, started shuffling forwards with their bags, jostling for position near what I took to be the gangway – a small wooden platform lined with tyres. What had looked like an insignificant spot on the great river loomed large as it docked at the quay.

The turnaround was surprisingly efficient. Passengers disembarked with loads rather similar to the ones the embarkees had with them, pushing their way through the crowd who refused to budge from their positions by the platform. Quite what the motive was in transporting exactly the same produce to a town that was just about to export its own surplus elsewhere I couldn't fathom. They were well laden though.

Not nearly enough people got off, certainly not as many as were getting on, and the ferry looked packed past any capacity limit already. Passengers lined every inch of the two decks – the first had no railings, the second no cover.

Leading our group on after everyone else, it became even more apparent that we were going to have to search for space. I had expected a long delay for the usual no-apparent-reason, but the boat set sail immediately. Splitting up, Lesley, Charlotte and I went straight down a set of iron steps into the hull. It was like stepping off the world into hell.

In a cavernous room, poorly lit by the few remaining lights, people were sitting and lying everywhere, their belongings stacked around them. We had been given a choice of tickets and I had chosen the most expensive, still only a fraction of a dollar each. Presumably, below deck were the cheap seats. It was hot, noisy and smelly but we wanted to explore.

We found the ferry restaurant. Equally full of people, though smaller and darker, it looked as I imagine the staff quarters in a medieval castle would. The clientele were lined up along three great narrow tables, each eating from a tin plate that rattled against that of their opposite number. What the gruel was they were eating became clear as we edged over to where the cooks laboured at the far end.

Two sweating men were equipped with a grill, a spit roast and two oil drums. Peering into the first one I saw a writhing mass of black worms. When someone ordered, a hand reached in, scooped some up and threw them into a frying pan on the grill. The length of a frankfurter, the worms were fat and very juicy – evident once they were bubbling away in the pan, oozing and slowly squirming in the heat.

The chef, smiling at my expression of disgust, held one out to me. Refusing it, he then dangled it in front of Lesley. Another fast rebuttal. It was Charlotte who grabbed it and took a large bite without any hesitation.

"Don't tell me," I said. "It tastes like chicken."

"More like pork actually," she replied, still chewing. "But squidgier. Try it." I shook my head.

The second drum, standing on a charcoal burner, was half full of brown lumpy bubbling liquid. Next to it stood the spit roast. A skewered animal was being turned by hand over the flames, and I could see a set of teeth gleaming white from the otherwise charred flesh. On closer inspection it turned out to be a monkey. Behind the spit-roast I spotted a third chef. He was chopping a fully cooked specimen into pieces and adding chunks of flesh and bone to the oil drum. *Monkey stew – yum*. In the gloom by the hull itself there were two women washing up. Through a porthole, water was hauled straight out of the river with a bucket, and sloshed into a tub of tin plates. Charlotte declined a portion of stew.

We reached a second set of stairs. Heaven beamed a few rays of sunlight our way, but Charlotte and I had to wait while Lesley gambled on the Ladies. She reappeared, twitching her shoulders as if she'd just eaten a bag of lemons. Rats, she explained, were crawling in and out of the cistern. Enough was enough.

Back on the upper deck we scoured the area for white faces. It was hard to find anyone as hammocks were slung everywhere, passengers sitting below them for shade. Someone grabbed my ankle and I turned to see Wendy. She had managed to rent five hammocks between us, offering a good price for some people to vacate them. Becky and Tom were guarding a pile of bags and our two jerries of water.

The sun was not far from setting, so I climbed into a hammock to watch. Charlotte climbed in after me. The great orange ball grew bigger as it lowered itself gently to the horizon, a long reflection creeping towards us across the water. The ball grew red, and then disappeared. In darkness, the group slowly reassembled. Those who had been to the restaurant described it to the others, and a popular decision was made to skip dinner. Soon, everyone had sorted out their sleeping arrangements, either two up on a hammock or stretched out underneath. Charlotte and I stayed where we were, talking quietly until we fell asleep, the slight swaying of the ferry wonderfully soporific.

I awoke having realised that we were no longer moving. The night was cool and, as we were far from the bank, free of mosquitoes. I looked at Charlotte as she slept and wondered what she thought about us. We seemed to have slipped into a relationship of sorts but unfortunately had altogether missed out the sex angle and gone straight to happy companions. We behaved like a pair of pensioners after forty years of marriage. It was a conversation we needed to have at some point but now wasn't the time or place, surrounded as we were by the rest of the group, and at very close quarters.

I got up to investigate our lack of movement. From the deck below I could hear soft wailing. I couldn't get down as the stairs were packed with people, so I asked if there was a problem. There was – an hour previously a toddler had fallen off the boat; there were no railings to stop her. The wailing was coming from a group of women, presumably amongst them the poor mother. Apparently, as soon as the alarm was raised we had stopped, turned about and gone back. At our railings on the upper-deck I looked down into the dark water. Men in pirogues were paddling about in a totally futile search for the body.

Presently we started moving again. In the morning I was amazed at how coolly our group, myself included, had taken the tragic news. Had we been on a train in Europe and a child had fallen from a door, we would surely have been devastated to be witnesses. Here in Zaire it seemed almost inevitable. I had never come across death back at home and my life had been mercifully free of tragedy or causes of grief. Yet in less than a year in Africa, I had been brought much closer to our ultimate fate and had even seen a body for the first time – that of a little girl, run over in Mali. Though I couldn't forget the actual sight, I had found myself curiously detached. And selfishly I had decided one thing: I didn't want my own death to be there. It would be so impersonal, and so far from anyone who really cared for me. I had no intention of ending up in a grave on a pretty riverside hillock in central Africa.

Bananas, bananas, bananas: our fare for two more days on board. They were delivered by tradesmen on pirogues who paddled out from riverside villages to meet the ferry. They had to get the timing right as the ferry didn't slow down for them. While one man paddled furiously in the bow waves, another would hoist their baskets of bananas up onto the lower deck, receiving a few notes in return. Live monkeys and fresh worms were also delivered in this way. Transaction complete, the pirogue would peel away, the occupants' heads dropping to count the money. Sometimes they would look up, holding out the notes in their hands and shouting as if they had been ripped off. But there was no catching us back up.

Perhaps because it had been seven months since the last ferry, there were often quite a few eager salesmen. The longer they stayed in the bow wave, the more unstable it was for them. One unfortunate pair tipped over. They fell in, separated from both their pirogue and their bananas. It didn't look like they could swim, which is very common in Africa even amongst fishermen. The boat ploughed on while they floundered five hundred metres from the riverbank. Perhaps I had just witnessed yet another death, though I didn't stay to watch.

Even before we reached Lisala I could see the truck on the quay. I was very glad to see that they had made it through OK. Getting closer, we could see Al on the roof of the cab. With his baggy, green florescent shorts flapping in the wind, he looked as ridiculous as ever. He was obviously back in good health though. As we drew up to the quay, he gave us a full moon – to the delight of well over a thousand people. Trumping his anal display with a loud Tarzan cry, he was beating his chest to create the authentic tones. His belly, halved in size after a week without eating, was still large enough to wobble in time with the rhythm of his fists.

To get to Lisala campsite, we climbed a long rutted track, Al surfing the cab roof until he had to take over driving after I unexpectedly dropped a front wheel into a hole. The steering wheel had spun violently, wrenching my wrist when I didn't let go quickly enough.

Lisala campsite was beautiful. Having seen trucks coming through for years, an entrepreneurial farmer had turned a section of his banana plantation over to camping. Word had spread and he was now on the circuit, a beneficiary of the overlanders' grapevine. On a bluff overlooking the river in one direction and the forest in the other, the terrace of his banana-leaf thatched bar provided us with our first full view of Zairian countryside for a month. It looked slightly wealthier here. Cultivated fields spread around groups of thatched huts, pathways meandering between them. The sounds of the occupants' daily lives floated up on the smoke of their fires. I was suddenly aware that all my senses had been dulled for a month. Along with the uniform view of red road dividing green-tree sea, and the tastebud implosion, I had also heard so little variety – overland chitchat, a ceaselessly clattering diesel engine and Al's tapes in repetitive rotation. Now I could hear hens, dogs, a turkey, goats, children laughing and the women calling to each other in the fields. The clanking of iron pots interrupted the steady rhythm of a mortar and pestle. I almost fancied I could hear the beating of the butterflies' wings that fluttered around me. I felt an extraordinary peace.

Later, lying under the truck, a warm Primus in my bandaged right hand, Al joined me in checking that the steering mechanism hadn't rearranged itself. The group were packing up the truck apart from what we needed for the night. Taking quick advantage of the abundant supply of water, they had given it a well-deserved spring clean. And the availability of water held other attractions. An orderly queue of washbags had formed outside the single and currently engaged grass-hut shower. The view from there and the adjacent toilet was as gorgeous as from the bar; but it would be a long wait till my go.

"Shagging on a hammock for the benefit of thousands, eh, Tim? What are you, an aspiring porn star?" With road and ferry conditions adequately covered, Al was keen to get on to more serious business.

"Not shagging, Al, chatting. Charlotte and I are just good friends."

"I don't believe you. She's choking on her own horn that one, gagging for a stuffing."

"Al, you wouldn't understand the concept of friendship with a woman. For you it's just yes or no."

"Yeah, and a 'no' hurts like getting yer cock stuck under the bog-seat."

"No 'nos' lately eh? I hear you succumbed to the temptations of youthful flesh."

Word had quickly spread that he and Helen had shacked up during his three-day separation from Lesley.

Now entirely free from malaria, the whole group's mood lifted with our quickening pace, the result of a smoother road surface. Not only had the road started to look more like a highway (in a fit of donor enthusiasm and no doubt to show off the capabilities of their road-building equipment, the Japanese had built embankments over valleys and cut-outs through the tops of hills) but a grader had also been through; our drive to Gemena took only a day and a half. On the outskirts of town one of Mobutu's many monstrous palaces was visible behind high, fortified walls; a huge construction. Furnished no doubt with European goods, it would have cost millions of dollars. Apparently, he had stayed there no more than three nights.

From Gemena onwards, there was a perceptible increase in both population and animosity. We had to instigate a shift system to guard the camp at night, but could do nothing to stop young abusive men from hanging about, sometimes provocatively helping themselves to a stool by the fire and in one case pissing on the floor in our cooktent. To remove them would have meant manhandling them. To do this would have caused a fight, such was their belligerent attitude. Two long nervous nights later, we reached the border town of Zongo.

Clearly of the same disposition as other local dwellers, the immigration official was intent on stripping us of cash. He arrived at our campsite just out of town in a Mercedes with three other men. All wore stock issue mirror sunglasses even though it was dark. The provenance of his wildly expensive vehicle became apparent when he demanded $100 each for our exit stamps – nearly $2,000, and without even the pretence of a reason. Al simply said that he would see him tomorrow in his office and asked him to leave.

I hadn't got involved in the short conversation. At sunset, I had put on a pair of floursack trousers I'd had made outside a Kisangani tailor's. Still religiously covering up despite sweaty, humid conditions, I had proudly donned them for the first time, but had soon noticed a slimy sensation. Now, while Al talked tough, I was concentrating on washing a thick flour-paste from my legs which had stuck to my skin like good render. Al sauntered over.

"Forget to wash your new pants, mate? Or just trying to stiffen up your unused dick with concrete?" He laughed at my messy ablutions. "You can deal with that fella tomorrow. I've met him before, and could end up in Zongo nick if I have to deal with him again. Remember, play dumb and no French."

I didn't in fact need to play dumb. A cold had been threatening for a while which I had chosen to ignore, judging it an impossibility in that heat. In the morning, however, my throat was so sore I could barely speak. In frustration with my croaking and clear lack of comprehension, the official allowed his hapless victims through for the still extortionate sum of ten bucks a head.

"Nice one – it's normally three hundred all up," Al enthused as I sat snivelling and sneezing in the cab while we crossed the Ubangui River by ferry. "He's the only one I cough up to on the whole trip." A song called 'The Ubangui Stomp' was blasting from Al's stereo and faces peered at us from the elevated passenger platforms on left and right. But we were out. Crossing a corner of northeastern of Zaire had taken a mere thirty-seven days.

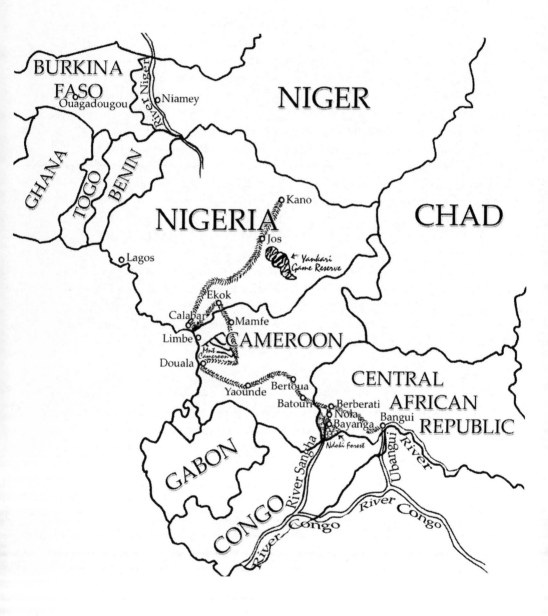

The officials in CAR were perhaps even more ungracious than their Zairie counterparts. Blatantly trying to provoke us into insolence, they kept toying with the group's passports before turning to other matters, making great play of ignoring us completely. They got nowhere though, as Al was on full form, out-ignoring them by regaling me with stories of Mick who he expected to meet in Bangui.

As it is a town in which visas have to be acquired whether going North or South, Bangui is traditionally a long stopover. We hadn't seen Mick's truck on the road, so Al presumed his group would be in town. He drove for another company, but having crossed Africa in convoy the previous year, they kept each other informed of their whereabouts on the overland grapevine. While Al was excited at the thought of seeing his friend, I was looking forward to meeting another group.

It was amazing to be in town. Once we had finally got entry stamps, we drove straight to a riverside hotel for coffee and croissants, before driving through town to the Post Office. Though it was by no means beautiful, the mere sight of tall buildings, cars and the now resumed frenzy of African street commerce caused us all to gawk. I could see arms pointing out of the truck as the group excitedly spotted each sign of relatively normal life, attractions we had been long deprived of.

At the Post Office, Al armed two people with tent poles and left them to guard the truck until replacements returned clutching mail from the Post Restante. There were letters for me and I devoured them as eagerly as everyone else. We also telexed London, who sent congratulations on our safe crossing of Zaire, though they had been worried by our exceptionally long silence. They also told us we had $20,000 dollars waiting at the bank.

The campsite was way out of the city at PK12; Bangui's satellite towns are imaginatively named after the number of kilometres they are from the centre. We passed PK5 market on the way; so big that it had spread across the road onto nearby playing fields, it was as well known for opportunist robberies as the city centre. Even with the continued vigilance of the pole-wielding group, we lost the long bungy rope that secured the cover for the trailer. The group had actually seen the culprits, but couldn't reach them. One had jumped into the slow-moving trailer and slashed the bungy while another held the valuable elastic as it pulled through the eyelets like a woolly jumper caught on a nail.

I asked Al if he wanted to stop at PK5 to get food. He looked at me incredulously. "A) I can't be bothered. B) You might as well give them everything we own and C) Erm … I can't be bothered again. They can go in by taxi with sticks and a few coins, it's the only way."

Mick's big grey truck was there. Nicknamed the Popemobile due to the massive perspex viewing-platform above the cab, it was a real monster. Inevitably

Mick was underneath it, his legs poking out, to be quickly joined as if by some contortionist's trick by his bearded but otherwise bald head. A toothy grin spread across his face as he saw Al driving towards him with one leg and one arm out of the window, a boot waving in time with an enthusiastic hand.

Parking a short distance away, Al got out and stood hands on hips in a matador pose. Mick mirrored him by his own truck. Putting index fingers to temples, they each snorted, pawed the dust with their feet, then charged, emitting bestial bellows. At a seemingly pre-decided spot their arms moved in front of them to form a cross at the wrists. The yelling reached a crescendo as they met, taking each other's necks in a backhand hold and lolling tongues with fake throttling.

"Wankaaaaaaaaaaaaah!" screamed Al.

"You're the wankaaaaaaah!" shouted Mick in return. They fought until Al collapsed, Mick pinning his shoulders to the ground.

"One, two, three – out! Ya Bastard." Mick stood up, his right foot on Al's heaving chest. "Give in?"

"Never." A practised hand took a hold of Mick's entire tackle, causing a scream of genuine agony.

"A draw. It's a fuckin' draw!" yelped Mick as I winced in sympathy.

"Done," replied Al coolly as he stood and led Mick by the balls to the bar. "Primus, mate?"

Bangui lived up to its reputation as a hellhole. Apart from visiting the Poste Restante, no one would have chosen to stay any longer than it would take to chew on a croissant, but to continue into Cameroon and Nigeria a stay was necessary. Even carrying sticks in defence, the groups of four shoppers would return from PK5 market either traumatised or elated, depending chiefly on their attitude to random violence. And it was incredibly expensive. On a drivers' night out with Mick at a pizza house, our bill totalled $90 each, admittedly including several bottles of imported French wine.

On the way to the restaurant we had gone past the aftermath of an horrific accident. An open truck, full of people, had evidently split in two. The sides had fallen onto the road, spilling some fifty people onto a busy highway. We saw two bodies on the side of the road covered in banana leaves, and the injured were still being attended to by ambulancemen when we passed. They would be destined for the Bangui Central Hospital, which Mick described to us; he had just evacuated a group member rather than chance their recovery from malaria there. It sounded as if a long repose under fruity foliage would be preferable to that cruel fate.

To pick up London's promised dollars from the bank, Al and I planned as if we were robbers ourselves. On both the Thursday and Friday, staff had refused to hand over anything but CFA (Central African Francs), while we argued that our money had been wired over in dollars. It was the normal way of things apparently, and required the usual degree of patience to resolve itself. On the Monday, when the dollars were suddenly forthcoming, we now found out we needed passports, which were still at the Nigerian embassy. Finally, with our visaed passports returned on the Tuesday afternoon, our plan sprang into action.

At the bottom of a long flight of steps, lined with dozens of the same languishing, local youth that had seen us coming and going for days, stood our getaway car, a rusting taxi. Inside the bank, hiding behind a pillar, I put our brick of dollars down my pants while Al stuffed an empty box down his. If it came to it we would split – a 50:50 chance. Preparations complete, Al opened the main door through which I sprinted, charging down the steps past (in my imagination) the lynch mob, closely followed by Al. The taxi driver flung open the door as planned. We piled in, slamming the door behind us and locking it – we had earlier checked that his door-locks worked. "Go – Go – GO!" we cried. The engine was already running.

As soon as the driver put his foot down, we careened straight into the bank's perimeter wall. "Poncture," the driver said without surprise. His own cameo role now over, he was entirely unmoved by our perceived plight. While the mob on the steps looked on in nothing but amused curiosity, we sat slowly frying in the back of the taxi. Windows firmly up, sweat oozing onto the notes in generous quantities, we sat feeling extremely foolish as the driver changed the wheel with excruciating slowness.

Diesel was at a premium in CAR, just as it had been in Zaire. As we were planning a long detour from the main route in search of the promised gorillas, we had to search for sufficient fuel on the black market. A 'helper' at the campsite, Pierre, said he had found some illicit barrels at the bargain price of $4 a litre.

Pedalling through the PK12 backstreets on the campsite bicycle, Pierre on the carrier behind me, I felt like a Belfast Catholic on the wrong side of the wire; malevolent eyes slithered in my direction – without Pierre I would have been mugged within seconds. At a compound fenced with corrugated iron, a guard with a bow-and-arrow opened a padlock and let us into the yard. Dozens of empty drums were stacked on one side and four stood separately on the other. I opened two up, checked them for water, which would have settled on the top, then tasted it. Disgusting – but it was diesel OK. I handed over a depressingly huge sum and found a pickup to deliver us, the two drums and the bike back to the site, checking them on and staying with them all the way as if in charge of gold bullion.

Siphoning the diesel into both tanks was a long and messy job, and by the end I had swallowed several mouthfuls. Complaining about the taste, I convinced Al that only wine would remove it, so we organised another pizza night. We agreed to contribute $5 a head to the meal, the cost of a reasonable dinner at the campsite, so it was not surprising that only four people came out with us – Charlotte, Dan, Nick and Pauline. Lesley was still refusing to speak to Al, and Helen was keeping a low profile; their illicit liaison, conducted in contrived 'secrecy', was common knowledge.

At almost exactly the same point as we had seen the accident, it suddenly went dark outside the windows of our taxi. It was nearly dusk, but this nightfall came unnaturally fast. The taxi driver stopped and gestured at us to raise our windows. Al's call for flying ants had finally been answered. An even more extraordinary sight than the butterflies, the cloud of insects plunged us into total darkness, the car windows a frenzy of millions of moving legs and wings like a garage carwash come alive. Al was thundering more biblical exhortations but his words were drowned out by the noise. Then, with the abruptness of an African rainstorm, the deluge of insects suddenly ceased.

Our driver, like the rest of us, immediately jumped out of the cab – we to take in the post-apocalyptic scene that confronted us, he to gather up the struggling insects. Rummaging in his boot, he produced a cardboard box and a plastic binliner and raced to stuff each full. All around us drivers and their passengers did the same, while on the side of the road passers-by made swift progress in grabbing their own piece of the action. I couldn't see the rush – a two-inch coating of ant jam covered the road, the grass verges and every duka rooftop as far as the eye could see. Bar a similar deluge of remarkably ravenous crows, the mess would surely be around for days.

On the ninth morning, and with visas finally procured for all, we set off very early. Al wanted to clear the tar section of the road – some 300 km – in a day, as camping along that stretch was notoriously susceptible to nocturnal rip-off. In every duka we passed, plastic washing-up bowls of ants supplemented the usual monopoly of goods on offer. For a poverty-stricken nation, this was literally manna from heaven in the form of cheap and nutritious protein.

As we drove, Bangui's urban spread thinned out and the roadblocks went up; three in a row, all manned by surly army officers looking as if they had no doubt we should be conducted to the nearest wall for a bout of automatic AK47. The police and army in CAR are almost a law unto themselves, paying their own wages through extortion of innocent motorists. At each of these three barriers we were summarily fined: once for not having a warning triangle; once for a crack in the corner of the windscreen; finally, and most creatively, for not having flyspray in the cab.

The good road made up for the pecuniary delays. We made it to the Berberati turn-off as planned, driving into the forest again and finding a good gravel-pit before dark. Mick had told us about a new overland discovery: Ndoki, a game park on CAR's border with southeast Cameroon and northern Congo. This was our destination.

Mick had left the previous morning, driving off slowly with two people in the perspex roofbox painstakingly lifting the low branches of the campsite trees over it. I felt sorry for him – it was enough hassle keeping an eye on where the truck's wheels were going without having to think about the roof as well. Seeing his old friend had rejuvenated Al, even if he had been much berated about his courtship of both malaria and Helen. Mick himself had a girlfriend on board his truck. Sarah, as capable as she was good-looking, had effectively become his co-driver. Helping with anything from visa applications to the Bangui bank run, she tried hard to downplay her role but had become victim to the group's endless questions: Where were they going next? When? What would it be like? On one occasion I had heard the not unreasonable reply from an exasperated woman: "For fuck's sake, I don't know. I'm only shagging the driver!"

Mick's parting words to Al had been in line with much of the advice of the previous few days: "Sort your cock out, mate, give it some focus."

I took the wheel the following morning – the first time since spraining my wrist. It felt good to be back on a dirt track again heading south in ever-thickening forest, and it was much less dangerous driving than on tar. On the highway, the roadside had been littered with evidence of Africa's carnage at the wheel. Person for person, Africa has significantly more road deaths than anywhere else in the world, a league table proudly fronted by Kenya. We had passed the black and rusted wrecks of several double petrol tankers; the twisted remains of buses, minibuses and trucks; the upturned chassis of now wheel-less cars and a bicycle folded completely double in some unimaginably horrific accident.

Green now filled the screen again – I'd almost begun to miss it. With it came the more pleasant sight of villages, their menfolk walking hand in hand down the road, the children squatting to watch us pass or trying to race our truck by jumping over earth torn into rivulets by previous heavy rains. Each one called out the West African child's anthem for tourists, "Donnez-moi un cadeau." Extended families sat outside their huts under great trees. Surrounded by goats, chickens and scrappy dogs, the women and elderly prepared food on woven mats spread out over packed earth. In the near-empty dukas, bottles of diesel were now a feature of the roadside goods on offer, the vertical marketing possibilities of which were being exploited by one hopeful entrepreneur. Above his display of fuel-filled wine bottles he had hundreds of plastic funnels hanging up in the tree like multicoloured exotic fruits. Coincidentally we needed one, but despite our purchase it would clearly take some time before he needed to restock.

Another new business we periodically encountered was the 'monkey-man'.

Holding a dead primate up in one hand, the tail tied to the back legs so it resembled a novelty handbag, the monkeyman would enthusiastically try to flag us down
with the other. Even though our meat rations had not improved post-Zaire, we
weren't yet desperate enough to try fresh monkey-brain starters.

After a day's drive and another rough camp, we arrived at Berberati.

"Any guesses which way to Nola?" Al asked, looking at four unsigned roads
meeting at the roundabout.

"There's a bloke there with a book. He's our man," I suggested.

Asking directions is a hazardous business in Africa. To ask "Is Nola that way?"
would guarantee a 'yes'; to ask "What town is that way?" would bring an
unintelligble reply in the form of the name of the next village. It is a form of
politeness – you hear what people think you want to hear. I had developed a
system of seeking out hints of elevated education. The man, still walking as I
consulted him, barely looked up from his reading and pointed with his chin.
Continuing in the indicated direction, there really was no way of telling if he was
right. It wasn't until we reached Bania some 50km later that we were sure.

That night we had camp companions – friendly pygmies who appeared silently from the bush, naked apart from a flap covering their genitals. Had they
wished to finish us off with poison-arrows, they could have done so without us
ever having seen them. Some 10,000 pygmies make up the Ba'aka tribe who
inhabit this corner of CAR, living in groups of around twenty to fifty people.
The different pygmy tribes are estimated to number around 250,000, inhabiting
the forests of several countries: Zaire, Cameroon, Rwanda, Uganda, Congo, Gabon
and CAR – though it is hard to count them. Their knowledge of the forests is
unsurpassed. They can track animals and kill them with arrows or spears; they can
locate any amount of fruit and plants for food and medicine and are said to be
able to raid honey from a bee's nest by watching the flight of a passing bee.
Pygmies have always been part settled, part nomadic, but nowadays the period of
time they spend providing cheap labour to farming villages is increasing. Like
many forest peoples, they are close to losing their independence and culture, as
they face threats in common with the Indians of the Amazon: political violence,
logging and the migration of dislocated farmers to their land.

Despite their forest existence, our companions were not unaffected by the
spreading tentacles of the west. They wanted Marlboros and T-shirts as trade for
fruit and smoked game. Deals done, they smoked with haste, but evidently chose
to save the textile booty for Sunday best.

The Ndoki Gorilla research basecamp, part of the Dzanga-Ndoki National
Park, lies in deep, dark rainforest on the banks of the Sangha River. I hadn't felt so
remote from civilisation since Djanet. An oasis paradise, the beauty of the place
entranced the group. Clean and bilharzia-free water lapped the edge of a palm-
thatched hut that doubled as seating area and dormitory for those not bothered

to erect tents. The uniformed pygmy park rangers were knowledgeable, friendly and wildly enthusiastic for their task. These jobs are one of the ways in which several organisations try to accommodate local people and promote their skills. Classified a 'special reserve', pygmies are allowed to forage and hunt in most of the Park. An American woman led the research and protection programme for the two hundred gorillas recorded in the cross-border reserve, but we never met her. Not surprising – as she was usually tracking her beloved creatures deep in the forest. And the Ndoki, even just the CAR part, is a big old wood.

The first afternoon we took pirogues out onto the river to go hippo-spotting – a particularly dodgy endeavour, in my opinion – four to each dugout plus a boatman paddling at each end. About 500m wide with impenetrable bush on each bank, the Sangha drains the highlands of eastern CAR and delivers its volume to the great Congo after crossing hundreds of miles of Zairian swampland. For part of its course it marks the border between three countries. We were paddled upstream. Initial excitement gave way to silence as we all became overwhelmed by the serenity of the gently flowing water and the hypnotic sound of the paddles breaking its surface in unison. Within minutes I was asleep.

I awoke to find us being paddled directly into the lowering sun, its rays spreading towards me in a heavenly welcome. Wallowing hippos, only visible by their nostrils and eyes, had just been spotted near the riverbank. Seeing hippos in their natural habitat is an incredibly moving experience; they are so cumbersome on land, yet so graceful underwater. They dunked, strolled along the riverbed and reappeared nearer to our dugouts. I knew a tipped boat would certainly mean one of us bitten clean in half and I quickly planned my escape route in such an event – well, I might be needed to get the two chunks flown back to Europe. Hippos are, in fact, shy beasts and don't attack unless provoked, which we obviously weren't about to do. Safe, and with the sun an orange ball in the sky behind us, we eventually raced downstream back to camp. At the hut Robert snapped the necks of his two beloved chickens and plucked away their personality. Judge and Pickles, old friends of each of us by now, were rendered indistinguishable. Their white bodies, roasted in their old home, were delicious. Quite the fattest fowl in Africa.

In darkness the following morning, I drove the truck several kilometres towards a watering hole where we hoped to find elephants. Deafened by a cacophony of toxic insects, screeching monkeys and crashing branches, we had to trek the last three kilometres through the forest to where a WWF-built viewing platform overlooks a small lake in a wide clearing. As dawn broke, we watched flocks of African Grey parrots swoop in and land. Washing themselves and each other carefully, they chattered like happy day-trippers at the beach. Eagles glided above them, rising on the first thermals of the day.

Presently a troop of about fifty forest elephants emerged out of the bush, nonchalantly swaggering towards the water. The young, initially between the legs of their elders, grew boisterous and broke off to reach the water first. Mesmerised by the scene before me, I watched as the troop washed, drank, squirted themselves down and rolled in the mud. The parrots sensibly moved to one side but continued their own ablutions without obvious fear.

By nine o'clock, they and several other small troops who arrived later had gone. We began our march home. As we waded through a shallow river two pygmy guides suddenly sprinted downstream, shouting and slashing at the water with their machetes. They chased for about 200m before holding up a metre-long fish. Dinner.

Pottering along back to camp, a bit tired and hungry but feeling rather awe-inspired, I was ill prepared for the cab fire.

"Fuck me!" Al and I shouted in unison as smoke started rolling out of the dashboard, filling the cab with cloying, noxious fumes.

I killed the engine and fell coughing out of the cab. Quickly disconnecting the battery, I flicked open the front grill to find all the electric wiring aflame. Al pushed me out of the way and played an extinguisher over the fire – an item we had only just found when a CAR policeman had tried to fine us for not having one. When it all stopped smouldering we heard a sudden 'pshshshshsh'. An airline had melted through, clamping the brakes firmly on – a Bedford's singular safety feature. We looked at each other again, amazed at the sudden descent from the sublime to more overlanding chaos.

"Fuck me!" we chimed.

Given the dramatic performance, electrical damage was mercifully light, but we had to replace the airline to get moving again. I couldn't help thinking of the dire consequences of an engine blow or full electrical fire out there in the middle of nowhere. I was still effectively a trainee – at least in mechanical matters – but the next trip I would be on my own. Though worrying, I smiled at the thought. It was a long time coming and a challenge I was really looking forward to.

In a truck review following the electric fire, I discovered the brakes were losing fluid onto a rear pad. The seals needed replacing. The next morning I volunteered for the job while Al went gorilla-tracking with the group, led by three spear-wielding pygmies. He hadn't seen a gorilla yet and thought he might be on his last trip across Africa and at the time, I assumed I would be coming straight back. After dropping the group off in the forest, I started work on the truck where I had parked in the middle of the track.

With the back wheel off and the brake system dismantled I was working slowly and carefully, pleased to be mechanicing alone. I was determined to get it right first time and to avoid my habit of ending up with a bowl of nuts and bolts left over at the end of each job.

My quiet concentration was interrupted by a bee. I flicked it off my spanner and remembered a succession of painful run-ins as a child, the worst up my nostril. A few minutes later my nemesis returned, having presumably gone to fetch a few mates to look at the strange goings-on near their nest. About five buzzed round my toiling hands but I ignored them and they eventually flew off.

Apparently the spectacle of me on the tools was a sight too rare to keep to themselves. The next tour of my bravery was conducted by about a hundred. As I hurried to replace seals and pistons into the brake housing, they landed on my fingers and nosed around the spanner I was gripping. I felt a bead of sweat drop from my forehead and realised I had been holding my breath. I was tense, but knew I shouldn't make them angry. The ploy worked and they left, but then returned once more, quadrupled in number.

They buzzed around my head, which I had wrapped in a T-shirt, some settling on my eyelids, lips and on my now fumbling hands. I might have finished the job safely had one not crawled through a hole under the arm of my floursack boilersuit. As I tried to release it, it stung my armpit. Losing my forced calm, I punched the painful area with my spanner hand, crushing the offending bee under the blow. Bad move. Whether drawn by inaudible sounds or undetectable secretions I don't know, but a small squadron sped straight to the area. Some found their way through the hole into my T-shirt underneath. I was stuck. I couldn't drive away on three wheels and I could hardly work to replace the fourth with a shirtful of bees.

I stood up slowly, my blood pumping with the effort of quelling my innate desire for flight, and walked about a hundred feet. None had followed me, so I punched myself under the arm once more and slapped myself where I felt buzzing, killing all but harvesting a few more painful stings. For a moment I thought I had got away with it, so stuffed a rag into the armpit hole and walked back towards the truck. The swarm met me halfway. I ran through them to the wheel, threw it on and, screaming obscenities, tightened four of the twelve nuts. The angry swarm was all over me, stinging me around my eyes and the fingers of my right hand, the only parts of my body they could reach.

The wheel tentatively fastened, I leapt into the cab, shut the doors and turned the key. Hundreds of bees had made it in with me, so while the compressor built enough air to release the brakes, I fought my battle – I would have given anything to watch the cartoon-like scene from the other side of the screen. With my accounts book in hand, I batted, smashed and crushed but the more I killed, the more I whooped the troops outside into a frenzy. Thousands of bees buzzed at the windows and screen, incensed like a crowd watching the execution of comrades-in-arms. I was clearly winning, but as I dealt the deathblow to the last few in the cab, reinforcements broke through. Guided by bare instinct, they were somehow finding their way down between the windows and the doorframe, through the winding mechanism and up the other side, appearing through the black nylon bristles. Each new entrant flew straight at my face. Putting the truck in gear, I drove no-handed, whacking the last few suicide-fighters that made it through the assault course.

After less than half a kilometre the swarm abruptly stopped following me. Presumably I had crossed an invisible line and left their territory. I surveyed the scene of carnage around me. Little black bodies, some still waving legs and antennae in the air, covered the seats and dashboard. My fingers were a mess of angry red lumps and I had big welts around both eyes and lips. Taking off my sweat-drenched top, I saw my armpit and torso were in a similar state. Trembling, I drank a litre of water without pause, and then shut my sore eyes.

Mechanics and bees. The meeting of my two fears had nearly been the death of me. I started chuckling at a thought – *I see why those policemen fined me for not having spray in the cab* – and my mind wandered further. *What a story…!* In overlanding folklore it would make a change from dull old malaria. Soon I was laughing deliriously at the thought of the group returning to find no truck, a scattered toolbox, then up the track a lumpy body in a shroud of flour-sacking. It would be like one of those lateral-thinking riddles; *a man with an unopened parachute lying in a field…* My mind clouded over and I fell asleep.

I awoke feeling terrible. I could barely lift my limbs and my head throbbed. Along the line of veins down the insides of my arm, red marks traced them like bloodshot eyes. I was wheezing and my face and lips were grotesquely swollen. Evidently this was not yet over. I fought to unlock the fiddly padlock on the first-aid kit and pulled out the medical guide. *Bees, bees, BEES.* I found it in the index. According to the cheery authors, my body was in the process of self-destruction. In an effort to fight off the poison of a hundred stings, 'mast cells' were apparently over-compensating and poisoning me further. Cure? Anti-histamine. Popping a double dose for good measure and downing more water, I fell back to sleep.

"Forgotten something?" The next thing I knew, Al was outside the window holding up the toolkit. "Feeling a bit snoozy, were we? You missed half the wheelnuts." He held them out in the palm of his hand. I unlocked the door, revealing the furry mess around me.

"Shit, are you OK?" Al dropped the box and climbed up, bending over me with a look of concern on his face.

"I feel like shit," I croaked.

"What happened to your face? You're bloated, man. You look like you've had a bike-pump stuffed up yer arse."

"Can you get me some more piriton?" It seemed to have worked and I wanted more, despite the instructions I had read. Al fed me two more tablets

106

with more water, and then brushed up some of the dead bees.

"Christ, mate, we'd better get you home."

I was drifting in and out of sleep until much later in the evening. Still feeling weak, I got up to eat. The group, while I had been battling it out with nature, had been looking for it. They hadn't found gorillas, only their spoor, but had returned with fresh dikdik – stolen by their pygmy guides from a leopard's pantry up a tree – more fish and, ironically, delicious wild honey. Bushmeat dinner was wonderful, the little I could eat of it. After dinner Al produced a disgusting foot, shoving it under my net into my face.

"Those little fellas are the business!" he exclaimed. "Best tucker I've noshed in months, and see that?" He waved the foul thing ever closer to my nose. "Those pygmies got a bleedin' bush out of the wood, crushed the leaves, mixed it with oil from another tree and slapped it on. 'Sombolo,' they kept shouting. Dunno what it means, but every one of those little sodding jiggers did a runner at the smell of it." Tentatively, I examined the sole. He was right. Leathery and dirt-encrusted, but entirely free of fleas. "Incredible. I've ordered a truckload for when I come through again. Hope I do – it'll make me a packet."

I joined the group for another elephant viewing the next morning but declined a further gorilla-tracking expedition. They returned unsuccessful but laden with more game killed with bows-and-arrow by the pygmies. Bar the $90 pizza, we hadn't eaten so well in weeks and it was exciting to be living off the produce of the forest, even if we didn't possess the skills to kill, or even see it, ourselves. Pygmies, and presumably other forest tribes, have a healthy, plentiful diet and those few days in the Ndoki forest gave me some insight into how Zairies and others in permanent economic straits keep themselves alive – as well as the dangers they face in doing so. In gaining this first-hand understanding, we were doing what overlanding is all about. We had reached where no public transport reaches and had shared a brief part of our lives with an extremely impressive people; a people that tread the same earth as ourselves but treat it with such respect. It was a total privilege, and worth every second of the weeks of driving it had taken to get there.

Yaoundé, the capital of Cameroon, which we reached five days later, was a haven. It had the same European atmosphere I had last encountered in Dakar. We found ice cream, ready-roast chickens and crates of Johnny Walker at $3 a litre – cheaper than CAR diesel. At the campsite in the grounds of a mission on a hill overlooking the city, I spied sit-down toilets. It had been nearly two months, at Kampala's Sheraton Hotel in fact, since I had had the pleasurable sensation of porcelain touching buttock: a rim to circle my rim.

As I sat I pondered, taking no heed of the queue I knew would be outside. A whole subsection of overlanding culture revolves around crapping. People approach the problem in different ways. Some walk far from the truck – most in the mornings, some in the evenings – and others hold everyone up while they empty out en route. Some people, especially couples, I had noticed, would head off in pairs, sometimes groups, separating only at the last minute. The two shovels would be passed from hand to hand like a relay baton, some averting their eyes at the awkward shared intimacy; some stopping to chat like neighbours over a fence until one set of clenching muscles called an end to the conversation.

Then there was the crapping technique itself to consider. Balancing with the classic squat could only be achieved by Asians or athletes. The rest of us had several choices. Squatting 'One Foot Forward' presented the danger of spillage onto the heel of the back foot but had the advantage of holding the anus wide for efficient wipage. 'Twixt The Rocks', a hand holding the body weight on each rock, was fine until you needed to wipe. This either meant standing up, which then closed the crack to good papering, leaving a soggy feeling for the day, or dropping forward like a baby, arse in the air – very undignified.

Where possible I favoured 'The Fallen Branch'. With a natural railing to grab, I could guarantee no smelly boots and could perform with such accuracy that I could fill a pre-dug hole with a deadly aim. There were further advantages. My pants, stretched between my knees, provided me with an ideal bog-roll platform, keeping it free from dirt, wet or, worse still, a badly-aimed turd. I could wipe with a well-splayed arse whilst holding on tight to the branch with a free hand. With all methods it was easy to keep the area litter free. Paper, I found, stuck well to fresh turd which stopped it blowing away and this could easily be achieved without the dipping of figures, if folded correctly. A neat pile topped with paper, a skim of earth or sand quickly shovelled on, and I could leave little trace of my regular morning activities.

In the mission bathrooms there were also full-length mirrors. I had felt the beard sprouting on my face but had no idea how disgusting I looked all over – oil and dirt encrusted on my skin, my clothes in rags, and in my boots, my socks were stuck fast to my feet. We all looked like that, but I was still shocked at my own appearance. I would have to do some serious scrubbing before we went to the Yaoundé Hilton for happy-hour cocktails in the penthouse bar, the plan for the night.

The Olympics were on satellite TV. As much as by the athletes themselves, I was amazed by the organisation behind the event. Everything was perfectly planned: people moved between events with split-second timing, whisked efficiently by clean buses to vast stadiums. After two months of seeing mud-huts and little else, I felt a sudden urge to be embraced by the sophistication of Europe.

It didn't last long. The coverage finished and I looked around me at the group I had shared the journey with so far. I felt a wave of appreciation for my good fortune. And outside continued the road and all the adventures that were to come. Resplendent in jeans, trainers, a clean white shirt and a smooth face, I raised a glass to the group. While a jazz-band played, we all talked, laughed and got thoroughly drunk, feeling the close bond of shared excitement, drudgery, hard work and danger. I realised I had no specific answer to my question as to why they had come on such an apparently purposeless endeavour – all my theories had been right. Some had run; some wanted to know more about the world to add meaning to their own; some had wanted a partner and had found one; some hadn't and had still found one. They had all learnt, all experienced a way of life they would remember forever; and most importantly, they'd all had fun.

Claiming that I looked like I was having too much fun, Al kept the news from me until we reached Douala. London had decided to pull me off the trip. I was to leave in Kano and fly to London, as they wanted me to help sort a new Trans-Sahara route. Al was excited to be in line for the attempt at being first through, but my upcoming role of untrained diplomat didn't have the same effect on me. My attention was now firmly focused on driving, and I still hadn't run my own trip.

We had reached Douala in a day and got out again quickly. Towned out after Yaounde, we were keen for more rough camping, particularly as our menu had improved considerably with the availability of good food in Cameroon. The bar was and up and running again, and so was the oildrum oven. The only downer on the truck, apart from Al's unwelcome news, was that Hector had come down with the dreaded malaria, this time tested and verified at a clinic. I had given him our last Wonderdrugs and had also restocked with another ten boxes.

Possibly the only other bit of bad news was that Charlotte had politely refused my Yaoundé advances, deciding on my behalf that I was still in love with Kathy – I must have overplayed my hand in the mutual heart-opening sessions. In truth, she had shown great perception. If I did ever think about Kathy it was with complete reverence, but to avoid obsession creeping in – after all, I was never going to see her again – I did my very best to avoid such pondering. To balance that out, though, Lesley and Al were speaking again, though like Charlotte and me, not sleeping together. Helen had given him the bullet. Oddly, Al seemed happier with his situation that I was with mine. Focusing his cock, no doubt. All other couples were as I had found them, with the half addition of Becky and Robert, who were dilly-dallying between sharing a tent and not.

Finding a palm-fringed beach after dark near Limbe we camped, looking forward to a swim in the morning. We woke to find a layer of litter, shit and seaweed covering the beach. Then it started raining. This was overlanding – easy times could last for only so long. Plan B? Climb Mount Cameroon. But the incessant rain put the mockers on that idea too, so the group voted to crack on for the Mamfé-Ekok border with Nigeria and invest the time elsewhere. I am sure that we all now live with the same regret that we glided past such unrepeatable opportunities with barely a backward thought.

Hector wasn't responding to the drugs. Worse, rather than conking out like everyone else had, he started behaving erratically. First he tipped a lunch table over, and then he punched Dan, fortunately the only one of the group big enough to take a wallop from Hector without suffering damage. Isabel was mortified and begged me to do something for him. We were nearer Calabar in Nigeria than Douala, so decided to press on to find him hospital treatment there if necessary.

From time to time, Hector would launch himself at someone – it was like having a timebomb ticking in the back of the truck – so we brought him to the cab with us, Al and I alternately squashed against the passenger door by his wide girth and wider shoulders. Music and laughter seemed to calm him, but he wouldn't sleep. I visualised a sharp crack from behind with a mallet – he'd never know.

We crossed into Nigeria without any hassle from border control. A friendly bunch with a pet monkey who had been trained to apply the entry stamp, they gave us no clue as to the behaviour of the army officers we would soon meet.

Zaire and CAR like a good roadblock, but in Nigeria they are a national institution. The army love them, the police live for them, and even customs officers were in on the action, each however working separately from the other. Roadblocks were also a favourite method of highway robbery. Not the 'official' kind we were used to, but the kind where you get stopped by bandits at night at a hastily erected pole, then get your brains blown out for your car, your watch or your box of matches if that's all you've got on you. No one in their right mind drives at night in Nigeria, at least not outside of major city centres.

We reached our fifth block within three hours of the border. This, the army variety, had two staggered strips of metal spikes and was manned by two gun-toting officers. As mean-looking as their CAR counterparts, at least they had smart uniforms and someone had evidently banned sunglasses. We were fed up; Hector had just puked on the cab floor and we were in a hurry to get him treated. One officer raised his hand but the other, behind him, looked as if he had waved us through. I looked at Al with quizzical brow. He nodded 'Go for it.' I agreed and swung round the spikes, nipping through the narrow gap between them. Bad mistake.

Our gung-ho "Fuck you, muthafuckaaaaaahs", delivered with below-the-windowline V-flicking and macho merriment, were shortlived. Twenty metres from the block, we heard a sharp report of rifle fire: three bullets. I slammed on the brakes. Looking in the back, I saw the whole group were bent double, arms

110

uselessly covering their heads. Fortunately I couldn't see any obvious writhing in agony.

"The bastards!" Al howled. The smell of vomit had evidently really pissed him off. "They cannot do that."

In these scenarios there was, I was soon to learn, a choice. You either bend to their bullying or you climb on your high horse. Al chose the latter and was brilliant. But you've got to be confident that it's going to work.

Meeting him at the trailer, me having shimmied along my side of the truck to get there, we checked on the group – shocked, angry even, but all OK. Al then turned. He marched towards the officer who still had his gun pointing at us, me deftly walking in his shadow.

"What the hell do you think you're doing?" Al yelled. Nigerians speak perfect English. "You could have killed someone. We're tourists!" He was still ten metres from them and continued at the same volume. "I want your names, numbers and the name of your commanding officer. This man," – he pointed to the second soldier whose gun was now pointing at the tarmac – "waved us through, and you" – pointing at the first again – "try to kill us!"

The barrel of the gun, which I had a very close eye on, wavered with the second officer's resolve, and then dropped. Al had already won, but in a risky manoeuvre. The officer did try though: "You drove through a roadblock when I signalled you to halt." He had said the words, but without conviction.

Al was upon him now, face to face, and I had bravely stepped up to his side, happy now that both barrels were aimed at the road. "Well, you and your colleague should co-ordinate your signals. My driver and I didn't see you." He had gone haughty, which sounded odd on him. "We saw a clear wave through. Now, paper, pen and numbers. I'm going to Lagos where I will see first the British Ambassador and second, your commander."

OK Al, that's enough now. I was holding back a smirk.

There was a brief standoff. No one was going anywhere in search of a pen.

"Will you pay for the bullets?" the officer suddenly asked to break the silence. "Then I can let you go."

Chancers to the end. But given the need for a speedy resolution, it seemed reasonable. When I got back with a $5 note, Al had struck the final deal. Thinking ahead to our possibly poor reception from the group, who had taken the brunt of the incident, he had found a way to heap blame on someone else's shoulders, thus side-stepping our mistake. In return for the bullet-cash, the officer approached the back of the truck and apologised to the group.

Hector, possibly overcome by his own fumes, had finally fallen asleep between us, lying heavily on Al's crotch and dribbling slightly. Al made heavenward rolls with his eyes, grimaced, shook his head, but let him be – he was better out cold regardless of the uncomfortably close proximity of mouth to member.

Later however, at our rough camp in bush well off the main road, Hector flew into an uncontrollable rage. Like a wild bull, he began smashing into everything in his random path: tents, tables, stools, even parts of the fire went flying. I could see sweat pouring out of his forehead and the tendons in his thick neck standing proud like Roman columns. The group had scattered and I was dancing nimbly like a boxer in front of him, trying to calm him down. Perhaps some recognition of me or what he was doing flashed through his mind; or maybe, like an elephant afraid of a mouse, my diminutive size had him puzzled. He slowed and eventually dropped to the ground, holding his head and howling in pain.

"You've read the book cover to bloody cover. What the hell do we do now?" In this situation Al was finally stumped.

"We have to treat him with a different drug. We've got quinine."

"Get the shit and give it to him then."

In the cab I found the quinine, then quickly thumbed through the pages of the medical manual again. ***Quinine. Apply per rectum or inject intramuscularly.*** I felt I couldn't shove a glass phial up a man's arse, so I rummaged for a needle and syringe. I could hear Hector was up again; stools were crashing against the truck.

"Hurry the fuck up!" Al shouted. "Ow, ya Argy bastard...! Tim, where's those sodding drugs?"

"It's got to go into the muscle – and the arse is the quickest," I added as I rushed past Al to get to the brighter light in the cook tent. A further flick through the book had revealed this unsavoury prospect. As I was filling the syringe from the phial, five of our biggest guys and Becky were wrestling Hector to the ground.

"Bring him over here, hold him over the table and drop his shorts," I said, feeling suddenly calm. Someone needed to be in control and the job seemed to have fallen to me. Well, my brother *is* a doctor.

Jamming the needle deep into a hairy right buttock, I injected the quinine. Hector was struggling and shouting abuse in Spanish, but was held tight. We stayed that way until he went limp.

"Are you sure that's enough?" Al said. "We could bang another lot up there now he's gone floppy."

"That's the dose in the book. Just get him to a tent." One or two were still standing amidst the wreckage of our camp.

At Calabar Hospital, Hector had been put on a drip. On regaining compos mentis, he had revealed that he'd thrown away the Wonderdrugs, as he 'didn't like tablets'. This news hit me hard. How could I have been forced to inject someone who had brought such a situation upon himself? I wasn't a doctor, and though calm at the time, I had afterwards felt deeply shocked at the violence and my involvement. It was too much responsibility. With hindsight, the incident had scared me more than anything I'd come across on the road, even my own battle of the bees.

Ruminating over the two days it took Hector to recover, I got deeper and deeper into my fear, building it up into an unbreakable wall of negativity – negativity directed towards my job. Accidents were one thing; even illness was to be expected, but I had had enough of malaria. Pete looking like death; Al half-dead in the cab for days on end; the graves at Bumba, then the bog-hole in Zaire where the group had dropped like flies, tended like war-wounded in our ridiculously named cooktent. 'MASH' wasn't a joke any more. In my mind our canvas kitchen had turned into a dangerous place; a place of serious, possibly deadly disease. Without speaking to anyone during those forty-eight hours, I had made up my mind and penned my resignation letter, faxing it from the hotel we were staying at in Calabar. It was decided – *life just couldn't get worse than this.*

We left the next day before any reply that might have arrived. In the cab I finally broke my silence and informed Al.

"Oh – he speaketh. Christ, Graham'll rip you out a whole new arsehole – he's got you penned in for a trans-Africa but told me not to tell you."

"You what? Why don't they tell *me* anything? It's been like that since I started and I'm supposed to be a driver now. Anyway, I'm not doing it," I sulked. "I've resigned." Inside however, I was already wavering, suddenly regretting my typically impulsive behaviour. My desire to run a trip fought with my genuine fear. I fell back to rumination; arms folded, chin on chest.

"Let's forget it for now," Al muttered. "Hey – wanna hear some good news?"

"Go on."

"Me and her are back on, mate. While you were sulking, we were shagging. Full-on, mate. My sack, Sir, is empty." He hit the steering wheel emphatically, a proud smile on his face, then turned to me. "Smile then. You should be happy. That's what you wanted me to do, isn't it? Me and Pauline, eh? Happy together, forever?"

I find it difficult to smile when I'm sulking, but I managed. I was happy, and Al's expressive face showed me he was over the moon. They had always got on brilliantly; having great fun together even throughout Al's wanderings. It was almost as if Pauline had been waiting for him to get it all out of his system.

Apart from the continued good cheer of Al and the majority of the group, the first half of the crossing of Nigeria had nothing going for it. Good tar roads were rendered useless by constant checkpoints, something the European in me just couldn't get used to. *What the hell do you think's changed since your colleagues stopped us ten kilometres back there* was the subtext behind my false smiles and contrived patience. What was the point of all these aid-built roads traversing the continent only for a rash of poles and spikes to spring up and ruin their efforts?

But Nigeria eventually redeemed itself. It is, after all, a big country in Africa, and Africa is big on beauty. Apart from being a major West African depository of forest elephants along with fine game in number, the Yankari game reserve sports possibly the most beautiful natural spring in the world. The delightfully named Wikki Warm Springs lived up to Al's promise of paradise – and some. In a steep tree-covered valley, clear, cool water bubbles up in huge quantities from below a fifteen-metre sandstone cliff at the valley's head. A riverbed of shimmering, perfectly white sand lies below a uniform metre of water, the surface dappled by the sunlight slipping through the overhanging foliage. Vines hang down for safe Tarzan swinging sessions and the permanent replenishment of spring water keeps paradise sparkling clean.

On a well-kept lawn above the valley, vast mango trees threw shade over our campsite. The reserve was such a favourite with Al, and such a total hit with the group, that he put a ban on truck maintenance. Yankari is a place for pure unadulterated enjoyment and we all took to that task with fortitude. Even the resident baboons – the sole blemish on our mini-break as they stole anything and everything – had caught the fun bug. Between robberies they spent their time on the branches above the spring – and once at the end of one of the wooden picnic tables we used for lunch – sat on their red bottoms, furiously tossing themselves off.

On the lunch occasion, Isabel spotted the show first. She had long been struggling to come to terms with overlanding and had endured more than her fair share of shocks. Spying the wildly wanking primate, her eyes went out on stalks and she dropped her fork.

"Madre mia!" she exclaimed shaking her head, before pelting the unspent beast with oranges until it found a new perch high up in the branches above us. With fresh abandon it immediately started its five-knuckling once more, quickly building up to an astonishing pace. Isabel led the move to alternative seating, not directly below the obvious ending.

We spent two mornings out on the reserve, mainly viewing at remarkably close quarters the abundant elephants. With no other tourists around we felt like we had a Garden of Eden to ourselves. Al and I befriended the Park Warden. James was a Brit who lived in a large house hidden behind tall trees, the lawn of which was our camping area. He was out most of the time, but one free afternoon took just the two of us on a fishing expedition.

Further downstream from the springs, the river widened and spread into marshland. James' favourite spot was at the end of a five-hundred-metre walk though tall grass, following plainly visible hippo tracks. Armed only with rods, I was feeling nervous, but James explained that they rarely ventured out of the water during the day, as it was too hot for them. Nonetheless, as we walked I managed to ease my way between the tall and, I hoped, tasty-looking figures of

Al and James. Fish were plentiful and, sipping cold beers from our coolbox, we chatted lazily between frequent catches, often lapsing into comfortable silence. When I would get to thinking again...

How can I leave this job? Malaria fears aside, every day was incredibly varied and interesting. Some days we were wallowing in shit and living in misery, but others we were floating in a state of bliss, every sense awake to the intense happenings around us. Apart from checkpoints, no part of the day was ever boring. *And I've just thrown it all in.* As I watched the taut nylon line quiver in the light current, malaria troubles crept back into my mind, but they were dimming now. Everyone was fine.

I thought of emerging from Bethnal Green tube station, the dust and litter blowing in my face; grim weather in grimy towns, packaged food and miserable newspaper stories. *What have I done? Here I have a role, and more responsibility than I could ever achieve in England.* My friendships were by no means as close as at home, but I had fun meeting new people and some would surely develop into lifelong friends over time. I loved the comradeship between drivers. They talked like a bunch of Vietnam vets, swapping tales of disaster or elation. How had I got on with my clients in London? Did I laugh like I did now? *Ah well, it's done now.* There was a good reason at the time, surely, or I wouldn't have done it. I should just get on and enjoy the moment... *What happens, happens for a reason...* The line tugged sharply and I hoisted out another whopper.

With popular consensus we decided to stay an extra day at Yankari – it was as if we were afraid to leave in case paradise disappeared. That evening, down by the springs together with Charlotte, our feet gently splashing the moonlit water, I spilled out my recent decision and subsequent doubts to her. She of course listened patiently, and then gave me a hug. Pulling myself away, I slipped my clothes off and dived into the water. It felt fabulous at night, somehow even more refreshing than during the day. Glimpsing Charlotte's fine-shaped silhouette as she too undressed, I found it hard not to surreptitiously stare.

"You can look if you like," she offered, standing with one arm on her hip and the other in her hair, her body bent provocatively.

She dived in. As we floated downstream together, months of build-up blossomed despite the cold of the water. She approached me and we pressed our lips together. A momentary touch, no more than a nudge, sent shivers through my body and I pulled her closer.

"You can put that away for starters," Charlotte objected as she pushed away backwards, laughing as glistening water tumbled over her shoulders to caress her breasts. "You're still not over her."

For God's sake, you're right! But how the hell do you know?

In an old colonial bathroom, I found myself combing my hair using an ornamental glazed fish as a mirror. I could see Charlotte showering behind me, the image broken up by the varnished scales. Reluctant to break the Yankari spell by entering the menacing streets of a city, Al had booked the whole group into a rundown hotel – a colonial country club in its early life – not far outside Kano. The wild game we had recently viewed had appeared plentiful and delicious on our dinner plates the night before: crocodile, something beefy – buffalo perhaps – and wild boar. I looked again at the fish as Charlotte wrapped her hair in a towel. We were even sharing a room now, but it occurred to me that even in our easy intimacy, I had got nowhere near the depths of passionate feeling that I had experienced with Kathy. But then this was different – much more natural; so comfortable. What was a strong relationship supposed to feel like, I wondered? We had just had our last night though, so I would never know if it was that.

On the hill dropping into Kano, we had an accident. Pottering down as usual, using third gear for a brake, we felt a sudden bump that jolted the truck forward.

"He bloody did hit us," Al confirmed, applying the previously redundant brake. "I saw him haring down in the wing mirror but I thought he'd overtake."

Outside, a small Toyota, already in a fearful state, was stuck fast to the back of the trailer, two men surveying the impressive damage to their bonnet. Seeing us, one started shouting.

"What were you doing going so slowly? I don't have any brakes and you got in the way. This is your fault." I laughed at his outrageous logic, but he was serious. "You will pay me money for repair. I will get the police."

"Get the sodding police then," I chuckled. "You just said you didn't have any brakes." He disappeared.

We got to work separating the bent metal from our rear. When the car was free I put two stones under the wheels, intending to drive off. The second man grabbed my arm. "The policeman is coming. You will stay." He was strong but I wasn't worried. I was almost looking forward to the cops jeering with me at their complaint. Al was more cautious. "Don't bank on them being straight," he warned.

Experience, of course, knew more than common sense. The policeman listened to the story, surveyed the damage, almost entirely to the car, and quickly pronounced us guilty. Either we paid up $50 or we would be imprisoned. Al, normally a paragon of virtue when it came to corrupt officials, preferring almost anything to feeding the disease, coughed up without a murmur.

"I don't get it, we could have got away with that," I complained once the incident had passed.

"Not in Kano, my friend. It's almost an independent state up here. When the Muslims aren't scrapping with the Christians, the cops are fighting with the lot. We'd have been behind bars for sure. At fifty that was a steal."

Suddenly, fatigued by the consistent gross injustice of Central and West Africa against native and visitor alike, I felt pleased again I was leaving.

Urgent. Flight booked for Tim from Kano to London tomorrow. Come to office. To arrange Sahara traverse for Al in three weeks.
Also to prepare for running TransAfrica Ex-London October 14th.

There it was, in black and white – no mention of resignations. Either my fax hadn't got through or they were ignoring it completely. Perhaps they knew more about the emotional ups and downs of African overlanding than I did. I thought of asking, but Al cut us off.

OK, bibi, love and cuddles, Al.

"Well, there's a thing," I said uselessly.

"A thing indeed." Al was grinning broadly. "Surprised?"

"You're telling me."

"I'm not."

"Eh?"

"While you were dealing with that insurance this morning, I called Graham and told him you loved it here really. You do, don't you?"

I didn't know whether to hug him or belt him one.

My farewell party was brilliant. Knowing the décor we would find, Al had got everyone to dress for the occasion. Flares were fashioned, massively collared shirts were bought in the local market and wigs were constructed from wool, paper strips or palm-thatch. In a 70s-built hotel right next to the truck park, we started early, drinking the night away under a ceiling sprouting red plastic cylinders. At 4am I climbed, legless, into an airport-bound taxi, the group all there to wave me off. Except Al and Pauline. They had nipped upstairs earlier, 'just to see if the bedspreads are turd-brown velvetine' and hadn't reappeared. In the cab I found a note on my baggage.

Thanks, you interfering bastard – you're as bad as Mick.
But you're both right, Pauline's worth the focus.
So, forage in the undergrowth of many a foxy lady for me eh?
Keep yer sack empty 'Driver'. Love + cuddles, Al.

"Hawkins would like to see you," Graham said as I put my foot on the bottom stair of Operations. "When he gets back we'll all go to the pub for a chat. By the way, I think you should know. You're booked on a plane to Morocco tomorrow morning – and Hawkins is booked to go with you."

Graham smiled, relishing my disquiet. Conversation would surely be intense; if the boss travelled, it was to the epicentre of any trouble that was a strategic threat to his company. He had long since given up travelling for pleasure.

Hawkins met us in a pub on Palace Road, late and flustered. "Got bloody stuck on the motorway. Damn traffic. Don't normally use the car, but I had all that stuff of course."

No one had a clue what 'stuff' he was talking about.

"Drink?" he offered. A turned-out pocket revealed only loose change. "Ah…" Graham was already holding out a note, which Hawkins took. "Sort that out later, eh?" I couldn't help but smile as he passed the note on to me.

"English," Hawkins announced when I arrived back with the drinks. "Won't go on about it, because Graham here tells me he's spoken to you, but we were pleased with your work on the Touareg thing." He did go on about it anyway, before getting to the point.

"Thing is. That French of yours. Godsend. And I need you to help sort out another little problem. What we need is a new trans-Saharan route."

Hawkins outlined the options. I'd had plenty of time to pore over my Michelin map, and I knew there was precious little to choose from. In the east, Eritrea was trying to separate itself from Ethiopia. In the centre, Sudan too had a dangerous civil war that never seemed to end. A free crossing of Libya was out of the question and with trans-Algerian routes shut, that left only Mauritania in the west. Entry to the south from Senegal was fine, but Mauritania's northern border with Morocco caused the problem. Even though there was a tempting red line on the map that joined the two countries, the road itself traversed a heavily disputed area: the Western Sahara. Supposedly under threat from the separatist rebel movement, the Polisario, the border had been closed for fifteen years.

"So in fact, we've only got one option," Hawkins concluded. "What we've got to do is get the Moroccans and Mauritanians talking. Then we can get that route open." Hawkins stopped talking, sipped from his pint, and managed to look not in the slightest bit daunted by the prospect.

Only two days later I found myself in Rabat, at the office of Morocco's Minister of Tourism. Remarkably open to such requests, he had agreed a meeting over the telephone. The Minister listened carefully as I translated Hawkins' explanation of the benefits to Morocco of opening the Western Sahara to overland traffic. He asked us to prepare a further presentation, which he would attend on the Friday.

The meeting over, Hawkins was ecstatic. "Bloody good start, eh?" He bubbled. "Right to the top on day one, *and* a reply by next week if we're lucky. Right. Where can we find a computer? This has got to be good."

In our hotel business centre, Hawkins sat at a workstation. I leant over to start the machine and a blank page appeared on the screen. Hawkins' eyebrows furrowed as he picked up the mouse and waved it at the page, clicking furiously. "Can't work these damn things. Pen and ink man myself, and I'll be buggered if I'll change. Let's write it out, eh? And you can translate and type it later."

We retired to a table on the terrace by the pool. Hawkins opened his briefcase and from an assortment of tools, string, business cards and empty food wrappers, pulled out paper and a pen. I produced a map and he glanced up. "Ah good, good. Glad you're along. Black coffee and orange juice please." I caught the waiter's attention and ordered.

Muttering his thoughts out loud, Hawkins worked tirelessly. Lunch came and went, coffee appeared at regular intervals with a nod to the waiter, and on our wobbly plastic table under a gaudy parasol, with children splashing and screaming in the water behind us, the document grew.

We described the history of the company, the opportunities for Morocco and our tourists alike, a proposed itinerary and exaggerated some statistics involving the potential spend of groups in transit. Hawkins swore me to secrecy. If it came off, he told me, he wanted the kudos of 'breaking the Sahara barrier' for his company.

After reading it through for the third time, Hawkins handed the hefty sheaf to me. "All yours," he pronounced. "Best French please. And I want it ready for typing tomorrow."

Hawkins' attention to every word had been impressive, and I thought back dolefully over my hurried offerings to college tutors – the last time I'd had to translate anything into business French. This volume was to be presented to the minister in charge of one of the most important portfolios in government, an aide to the King of Morocco himself. I was somewhat daunted.

I immediately set about my task, having stopped off briefly on the way back to the hotel to purchase a large dictionary. I was still working when Hawkins got back to our shared suite. To the background of snuffles and snores, I worked on through the night, finishing the translation in time for breakfast.

Croissant crumbs and jam mingling to make a mini continental breakfast on his moustache, Hawkins chatted about lawnmowers. I mustered the energy to explain my theory on the virtues of maintaining an old Atco, like my father did, rather than purchasing a Flymo.

"Just what I've got at home!" he shouted excitedly. "Give your lawn a proper trim every time, don't they?"

Whereupon, he suddenly switched to business. "You get that presentation finished, and I'll see you here tonight." Leaping up, Hawkins relieved his face of his breakfast with a flourish of a paper napkin. He examined the smear, opened his briefcase, and popped the napkin in. "Don't forget to sort the bill!" he shouted over the heads of other diners as he pushed his way out of the restaurant. As usual, I had no idea where he was going.

I typed all day. I added brochures, copies of relevant sections of the map and had three copies bound.

In a bigger office, panelled in leather and filled with an acreage of polished hardwood furniture, I flipped the transparencies and frenched. The Minister, flanked at the far end of the oval boardroom table by two women and two men – the senior team from the Department of Tourism – held the tips of his fingers together and listened. Hawkins sat next to me, fiddling with his pen and incessantly topping my glass up with water.

The meeting over, Hawkins took charge of the telex machine;

```
Hello Graham, Hello London.
Minister definitely interested in proposal.  Will contact
me in office next week with decision.
Al Casey then through Mauritania to Morocco - Insha'allah.
See you Monday.
BIBI
```

Insha'allah – Arabic for 'if God wills' – denotes both a sense of powerlessness and optimism in an environment controlled by the gods. That about summed up where we stood.

I could imagine Hawkins wiping his eyes with genuine emotion as he delivered the crushing blow from back at his desk in London.

```
Attn:   English
Hotel Hassan, Rabat.

On Tuesday, the Moroccan Minister of Tourism granted us
permission for Casey and group to cross the border from
Mauritania and travel north via the Western Sahara.
However, the commander of forces in the southern town of
Dakhla has overridden the decision, citing danger from
Polisario.
Overlanding costs spiralling.  Decamp to Rabat campsite.
```

Find truck parked there.
We are trying to arrange you a meeting with the Minister of
the Interior.
Await further orders.
BIBI. Hawkins.

Western Sahara has been a land under conflict for decades. The territory stretches from Mauritania north to a horizontal line between Tindouf in Algeria and the Atlantic – its 'border' with Morocco proper. The desolate territory is rich in natural resources – mainly phosphates and fish – but fighting has stifled development.

The indigenous population – the Saharawis – were governed by Spain after colonisation in the 19th century. The Spanish finally withdrew in 1976, but despite a UN resolution declaring the right of Saharawian self-determination, Spain secretly granted control of the province to Morocco and Mauritania.

Resistance came in the form of the Polisario – The Popular Front for the Liberation of Saguia el Hamra and Rio de Oro. Formed in 1973 while still under Spanish rule, this group quickly became a mass movement that spoke for the entire Saharawi people. On the day the Spanish withdrew, the Polisario declared an independent Saharawi Arab Democratic Republic (SADR), but Moroccan fighter-planes chased half of their population out of their territory. Algeria, in an unheard-of gesture of support, ceded the fleeing Saharawis a swathe of land near Tindouf, where many still live today. Run almost entirely by women, these refugee camps have proper housing, schools and health centres, and are mostly self-sufficient in food. The women also have another role. In a bid to increase the Saharawian population in readiness for the return to the Western Sahara, their homeland, they deliberately strive to achieve a high birth rate.

Meanwhile, the Polisario continued to fight, making daring raids deep into Mauritania, the weaker of the two countries. Eventually Ould Daddah, Mauritania's president at the time, reluctantly agreed to allow a force of Moroccan troops to be stationed on Mauritanian soil. Even with this help and that of French bombers, the Polisario could not be routed, and in 1978 the Mauritanian army backed a coup to remove Daddah. The new government signed a peace agreement with the Polisario, relinquishing all claim to their land. Furthermore, they described the war as 'unjust'. In response, Morocco declared the whole of the Western Sahara part of their country.

To repel Polisario raids now targeted at their own economic installations, the Moroccans used arms supplied by France, Britain and the US. They also set about building a huge, fortified wall. By 1989, with the SADR now recognised by 76 countries as an independent state yet held by the Moroccans, the wall stretched 1500 kilometres along the southern border with Mauritania and up past Tindouf into Morocco proper. On the international diplomatic stage however, the pressure was on, and in 1990 a UN deal finally ended the fighting. The people of the Western Sahara were promised a referendum; they could choose between independence and integration.

Over a decade later, the region's inhabitants are still waiting while the Moroccans obfuscate. Despite the UN's original agreement to base voting rights on the last Spanish census of 1974, Morocco wants their 200,000 settlers to be allowed a vote too. Currently, UN peacekeepers verify each case on an individual basis.

It has cost the world some $50 million a year to keep a quasi-governing UN peacekeeping force in the SADR, more perhaps than it would have cost to resettle the entire Saharawian community from their prolonged exile in Algeria and set the whole territory on the road to a bright economic future. I can only begin to imagine the sense of injustice I would feel were I a Saharawi. A whole world of nations has on several occasions agreed their eligibility to their own country, yet decades on they still live in tented camps on its occupied borders.

Being high season, Rabat campsite was full of characters on their travels. 'Characters' seems a weak word. In fact, my latest arena for a renewed life in limbo was more like an asylum for the unhinged and rootless.

The first I met were a young British couple. They had spent two blissful years in Huddersfield planning their African trip, while converting their Mercedes van into an overland vehicle. After only a week on the road, however, they had breached a relationship milestone. I spent my first few afternoons sitting between their sniping, until finally the woman eloped and the man cried. Subsequently, he became a constant companion on my town walkabouts, when he would plod along beside me wearing a mindless expression between verbally reliving his previous two years of harmony.

Returning from one of these strolls one evening, we arrived in time to see a fight. Two retired French couples, celebrating their release from working life with a joint campervan trip through Europe and Morocco, had long since colonised the centre of the site. I had noticed that the smooth running of their compound and luxury RVs was a job in itself; much effort had been expended by the men in the erection of a roped perimeter and the laying of a stone patio. A chance meeting in the communal wash block could easily lead to a full hour of description, down to the last detail, of the capabilities of their matching Citroens. Now, they were having it out with the German Bikers

The bikers – motorcycle couriers from Bremen – had conspicuously lavished Deutschemarks on two young English girls they'd met on site. Stuck without transport or much cash, the girls had apparently gladly swapped their chastity for tours of Rabat on the Germans' throbbing two-wheelers and free beer in the evenings. That left the rest of us listening to greasy-biker roars of achievement interspersed with encouragingly loud moans from the girls as two couples reached successive pinnacles of ecstasy for half of each night. The fight concerned both this constant disturbance and that of their equally noisy machines.

The two pensioners' wives were screaming abuse as loudly as the well-ridden English girls. Robin and I joined all four to watch the dust-up, in which the elderly messieurs were doing rather well. Ex-factory workers, and of the generation that 'know a thing or two about hard work – I can tell you', they hid strong muscles under flabby bodies. One had a German in a full nelson, his own leather jacket trapping his arms. The German's legs flailed weakly while he tried to wriggle free of his heavily studded garment. The other pensioner was running rings around the second German, dancing with the skill of an ex-boxer and throwing air punches in his general direction. The second biker stood, hands on his hips like a fat matador, swivelling on one heel to keep facing his aged tormentor. When the first finally broke free of his leather, he ran to his friend. Lifting their fists they stood back to back, whereupon the pensioners joined their wives in the hurling of fine French profanities.

Like all fights I have ever seen, it dwindled to a mutual slanging match, conducted as the Germans walked pushme-pullyou to their own territory, the scene of the original crime. The girls joined them, standing by their men in bodily support of their right to shag at top decibel. This they continued to do, that very night, with perhaps extra gusto.

Further notable arrivals were another couple on a motorbike. The French pensioners greeted their entrance by standing side by side on one of their patios, arms folded over bare browned chests and stomachs drooping over belted shorts. Oddly, that day both wore ships' captains' caps. One pointed towards a distant corner to which the copulating couriers had finally moved after finding flat tyres and disconnected batteries on a succession of mornings. The rider ignored them completely and parked unnaturally close to the Citroens.

There is normally a natural order of things on a campsite. Some prefer a central position; others like myself seek the security of the perimeter. No-one, however, crosses the undrawn boundary into someone else's space – apart from Italians, who get used to sharing small patches of grass as they all holiday for the same two weeks of every year. The couple got tented almost on the pensioners' patio.

At an opportune moment, I strolled over. The girl on the back was Danish; the driver a New Zealander. Within minutes I was bored by the detailed description of his bike. Not so the pensioners. Finally meeting a man after their own hearts, they extended the rope to welcome them permanently into their compound. With the evening sun and bottles of vin rouge going down at a similar pace, I listened in agony as they swapped mechanical minutiae with barely a pause for breath.

It was lucky that I was so well occupied as I drifted through the days until my meeting, because when it came, the Interior Minister informed me that the decision still depended on the military down south. With that, London finally decided I was to visit them in person.

With a classic double-take, I saw the name of my company in large letters on a small placard. With only twenty passengers disembarking from the twin prop at Dakhla's scruffy airport, and me the only foreigner, the board was possibly surplus to requirements, but it was nice to be met and driven to a hotel. To this day, I have no idea how the besuited man knew I was coming. The three-minute journey to the sole hotel was conducted in silence and I never saw him again.

Dakhla, the administrative capital deep in the south of the Western Sahara, lies at the end of a narrow, forty-kilometre peninsular, often only two kilometres wide. The residents therefore have eighty kilometres of their own beach, all of it too hot to sit on. They live on fishing, both the trawled variety and a little touristic game fishing. Other than that, nothing appears to happen. Satellite TV keeps most people – when not at the mosque – inside, either in their homes or in teashops, depending presumably on their position on the fish-production employment ladder.

In the morning I left the confines of my imaginatively named "Hotel Sahara" in my office-boy gear bound for the province's military headquarters. My briefcase and I stuck out badly. While walking, I looked at the peaceful scene around me and wondered if I wanted to open the floodgates to thousands of overlanders a year. How would it look in ten years? With tourism comes jealousy and hassle. Ultimately, however, I decided, the decision wasn't mine to make. I was just the current cog keeping the bigger cogs turning. It would happen with or without my personal involvement.

As it turned out, the name I had – Commandant Jamal – wasn't a military man at all. In a confusing system unique to that province, he was in fact a *Monsieur* Jamal, Adjoint de Chef des Affaires Generales, Province Oued Eddahab: the top man. Like his title, his courtesy knew no bounds, and he was completely up for the project from the start. Jamal obviously knew a great deal already, but politely questioned me until he had elicited my version of every scrap of information I had. He then offered to prepare a submission to Rabat. That worried me, as it was they who had sent me to him, but he assured me that with his endorsement permission to travel would simply be a formality. Telling me to return at 5pm, he stood and saw me out of the office.

At 5pm sharp I knocked at his office door. Jamal had prepared a long telex citing details of Al's group and truck, concluding: **the authorities in Dahkla**

**see no reason for the esteemed group not to enter the
Western Sahara from Mauritania.**

Apparently, with a stamp from Rabat, I would have it in the bag.

The following day Jamal presented me with a signed copy of Rabat's telexed
authorisation. He then pointed out an addition he had made to his original telex;
**this will go ahead only on condition that we receive a
letter of approval from the Mauritanian embassy in Rabat.**

That night I sat down to write a report for Hawkins:

The Meeting

*M. Jamal was positive from the start. He was impressed that the company were taking
the matter seriously enough to send me to Dakhla.*

Results:

*1. We have authorisation (enclosed copy) for Al's group to enter the Western Sahara
from Mauritania.*

*2. The Future: Jamal assures me that once the precedent is set, future applications
would not need to go to Rabat. We should simply send Jamal details of each trip three
weeks in advance.*

*3. The spanner in the works: Jamal holds no faith in the "unruly" Mauritanians. He
will not allow entrance until he sees a letter stating agreement from the Mauritanian
Embassy in Rabat.*

Of course everything had gone too well. A visit to the Mauritanian embassy the
minute I got back to Rabat brought the following result: a Mauritanian visa –
which Al's group had all acquired on their recent arrival in Dakar – constituted the
right of entry and exit at any Mauritanian border. As the border with Morocco
wasn't officially closed, only unused by foreigners for fifteen years, the Mauritanian
Ambassador to Morocco refused to issue a letter to Jamal.

When I told London they advised me that they could allow Al only one week
in Dakar. If I couldn't organise authorisation in that time, I was to fly down to
organise shipment of his truck to Casablanca; they would find someone else to
run my proposed trip. I couldn't face the prospect of ending up back as a trainee
and realised I simply *had* to get the problem sorted out.

My plan formulated itself overnight. I woke up thinking that the Moroccan
Minister of the Interior was probably more powerful than he let on. After all,
Commandant Jamal had known everything before I arrived and had definitely

been primed to act – he had signed the authorisation in hours and Rabat had ratified it equally swiftly. If I wrote direct to the Minister to explain the impasse, perhaps he would help. I could request that he then wrote an official letter to the Mauritanians explaining Jamal's requirements. With such a document I could fly to Nouakchott, the capital of Mauritania, see the government there and use it to get a return letter for the Mauritanian Ambassador in Rabat. Simple – all could be achieved with the flourish of a quill. Of course Part Three depended on Part Two, but Part Two couldn't happen without me writing Part One. I extracted a pen from my case.

The Minister, I was told by his aide, would deal with it immediately. I waited only a couple of hours to see Part Two achieved and flew to Nouakchott that afternoon.

The largest town in the Sahara, Nouakchott is no pretty place. Substituting crushed shells for tarmac and with dunes crawling across town as they feel fit, it sounds almost romantic. But in reality it is a 60s-built town of stark utilitarian concrete. Lacking any entertainment, you are left to wander the streets, blistering hot with a constant wind whipping fine dust into any unprotected orifice about your person. Food is unimaginative, hotel rooms look like prison cells and both are outrageously expensive. The Mauritanians didn't even manage to build their capital by the beach – it's a six-kilometre walk to the fine stretches of white sand that might just have provided a pleasant backdrop to the place.

Stifling even during the night, by 8 o'clock the next morning it must already have reached 40 ˚ C. In my familiar guise as office-boy, I was to be seen staggering with my case up a dusty road in the direction of the government complex. The buildings, as ugly as all the others in the city, were at least air-conditioned. Before talking to anyone, I tried to dry myself off, pulling my sweat-soaked shirt from my body in a bid to get cooler air between it and my skin. I had only walked two hundred metres.

Everyone was very friendly and it was even more accessible than the Moroccan government. I couldn't help considering what the British would make of a sweat-soaked Moroccan or Mauritanian turning up at the Houses of Parliament sporting a nylon tie and asking for a quick meet with the Minister if-you-please. No one there batted an eyelid at this damp foreigner's request.

Within an hour I was in consultation with the honourable Monsieur le Sécretaire-Génerale du Ministre du Commerce, l'Artisanat et Tourisme (beat that, Jamal!), an affable man in a full western suit, including waistcoat. He listened, he looked puzzled; he looked at the brochure, he saw dollars. He took the letter and said he would speak to his Minister of the Interior.

"When?"

"Oh, today, tomorrow."

"Please, it's important. I will come back tomorrow."

"Fine."

Title length evidently has an inverse relationship to importance in Mauritania. The next morning I elicited from him a shrug, the morning after that he simply refused to see me, sending a message to the door of his office that there was nothing more to say; that I was to wait for the Minister proper to find time.

How long could I stay in Nouakchott alone? A quiet town anyway, in the fierce heat of late summer activity had almost ceased. Only me and a few dogs were to be seen plodding the streets. Our tongues lolled, our heads hung at the same angle and even they sweated. The only difference between us was that they didn't carry briefcases. I was bored, lonely and frustrated. *Dogs with cases?* The heat was boiling my brain.

Thursday proved to be a repeat of the previous five days. A week in Nouakchott alone is not something I would recommend – it was time for a further flourish. It was long, it was patronising, and when I read it now I cringe at its words, the rambling French and its lack of any protocol. The letter was addressed to the Mauritanian Minister of the Interior.

> *I would like to bring to your attention the situation in which I find myself. I am the director* [lying already] *of a company dealing with thousands of tourists and millions of francs. On arrival here I delivered a letter from the Moroccan Minister of the Interior to one M. le Sécretaire-Génerale du Ministre du Commerce, l'Artisanat et Tourisme requesting urgent assistance from your government with regard to tourism.*
> *M. le Sécrétaire-Génerale du Ministre du Commerce, l'Artisanat et Tourism granted me one meeting and refused me many more. I must say I am astonished. Have I in fact been refused?*

The worst bit – this hurts to read:

> *The fact that there actually exists a ministry which deals with tourism suggests to me that the country has an interest in welcoming tourists. He might have a lot of work, but those in authority cannot forget the opportunities of tomorrow because of what they are doing today. I hope someone can administer to my simple request or explain to me why not.*

Then, in some kind of weird, belated attempt at sycophancy:

> *I must say that I have been welcomed very openly by the inhabitants of your fine capital* [especially the dogs] *and I have a great desire to introduce this very favourable experience to my clients.*

The ultimatum…

You can contact me at the address or phone number above. I shall be in Nouakchott until Tuesday 6th October, after which time alternative arrangements will have to be made.
Tim English [do you realise who I am?!]

If I was *astonished* by the behaviour of the Minister of Everything and Tourism, I was even more so at what happened next. I might have needed a few lessons in international diplomacy, but I appeared to have hit on Rule Number One: Do It By Letter. On the Monday morning I was called down to reception at my hotel, whereupon a young runner handed me a sealed envelope. In it was one letter for me *thanking* me for bringing the matter to the Minister's attention, and one for his ambassador requesting his complete co-operation. The boy earned probably his most substantial ever tip. I was out of there in minutes, Part Three in the case.

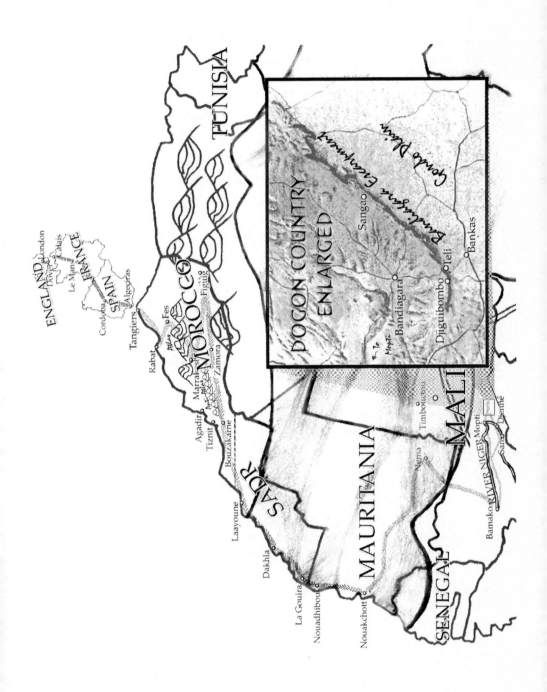

Even while I was talking him through my suggestions for Mauritania procedure, Graham's attention lurched to a new crisis delivered by Hotline. A driver, responsible for a motorcyclist's death under his truck, was now locked up in Asia. Hawkins was in Kathmandu again but had sent congratulations on hearing the news that Al had crossed the border into the SADR. He had also expressed his agreement with Graham that I was only to take my trip as far as Bamako. As a special dispensation in acknowledgement of my malaria fears, they would send a driver to replace me when I reached there. I was destined to fail to complete my first trans-Africa overland before I even started, but it was a satisfactory compromise as far as I was concerned.

I allowed myself a weekend to see as many people as possible, belting in a hire car from London to Brighton, Brighton to Bath and Bath to London. Sunday lunch with Charlotte in the sunshine by Richmond Bridge – she had a job in London and was going to stay a year or so – turned into dinner on the High Street. All that resulted in my waking up late on Monday morning and leaving hurriedly for Northamptonshire with a hangover.

Being the man actually destined for the driving-seat of a truck undergoing intensive preparation at the hands of eager trainees had a marked effect on my enjoyment of the workshop. It was a more confident man who told stories at tea breaks and bought rounds at the Three Queens – I had just been paid a year's wages. It was a man who now knew himself that allowed the trainees' ribbing of his preference for organising stores and equipment to interfering in mechanical issues. Why bother? These trainees, like those in my day, were mostly highly skilled mechanics who I assumed would make a better job of such things than me.

I did have one dabble. Adrian, an experienced South America driver, was also between trips. In my clean overalls, I passed small pieces upon his request as he stripped a gearbox and rebuilt it with reconditioned parts in an unbelievable two hours. All those bits; a three-dimensional jigsaw, but without the picture. He was a patient, skilled and chatty teacher. I felt like a surgeon's assistant, and hoped I would never have to deal with such mighty endeavours on the road.

At my pre-departure meeting in the office, I scanned my first full group for signs of their willingness to get involved. Faces and body language give no clues to such things, however, so I would have to wait. The typical group profile puts most people between 25 and 35, but can vary from 18-year-old schoolkids to 65-year-old Aussie ex-teachers – the latter guaranteed to be the most positive and useful by miles. What I saw before me was youth. Bar three, they looked like a bunch of students. They sat in silence while I tried – eliciting worried glances from Graham and Dean flanking me – to put The Fear into them.

Africa was dirty, I told them, often dangerous, sometimes dull and the home of delay on an unimaginable scale. I briefed them on the problems of the new

Mauritania route and covered the long list of jobs and responsibilities they would be expected to take on. 'Expect the worst and you will enjoy it the most' was the crux of my doom-laden message. My final words – "This is not a holiday" – certainly weren't designed to give anyone the impression they were going to enjoy themselves. Dean opened a question-and-answer session, which met with silence. I went to the pub – a flea in my ear courtesy of Graham – feeling in total control.

In compliance with UK law, the group were to be separately bussed to Dover, where I was to meet them in the truck after a solo mission down from Victoria. The following morning's departure, like a side-show in south London life, featured drivers, trainees, office staff, parents and friends of the expedition members – and Japanese tourists wondering what on earth was going on. The crowd, occupying a wide pavement outside a fruit and veg shop, watched while the trailer was packed then waved the coach off. Lacking only a fanfare of bugles I then left, feeling great as I U2'd down the road without a soul on board.

I bought the beers on the ferry, and finally I had an opportunity to meet the group. At first and very brief acquaintance, they seemed excellent. They demanded stories and I obliged with one that seemed appropriate; Mick had related it to me in Bangui, when we had discussed our respective dealings with disaster as novice overlanders. On his first solo ex London, he had got his truck stuck in a campsite in Perpignan. All was well when he pulled up, but after a night of incessant rain, when he tried to leave, the truck sunk axle-deep in mud. A tow truck couldn't pull it out, nor could a six-wheel-drive electricity-pylon erecting machine that happened to be at hand. To his intense irritation, he eventually had to pay for two JCBs to pull him clear. He was three days into a trans-Africa.

I didn't even make three days before my own bogging début. At lunchtime on my second day, not far from Le Mans, I pulled up on a wide patch of well-kept grass for lunch. With my penchant for aesthetics, I had left the main road to find a pretty Touraine village in which to enjoy our Camembert sandwiches and crispy salads. It wasn't even raining but I just couldn't get the truck to leave that lovely spot. The more I tried to move, the deeper we sank. Four-wheel-drive wouldn't grip.

By the time we had finished digging and sandmatting our way out, the village green resembled the trenches of The Somme. The police, who caught me up on the main road and dipped fingers in muddy sandmats to present evidence in refutation of my denial, fined me a thousand Francs, saying it would go towards the funding of the Flora and Fauna police. Needless to say, the group asked the inevitable question: "How are we going to get through Zaire?"

I answered truthfully – as far as I could tell, given the extraordinary truck capabilities I had witnessed in bog-holes – "The mud's different there."

We had our first party at a massive opencast rubbish tip in central Spain. The group had previously commented positively on my rough camp-finding skills, galvanising what I already considered to be something of a talent – we had swum in cool fresh water on the previous two nights: once in a Pyrenean lake and then in a pretty Spanish river lined with poplars. In response to such praise I had put in still more effort and had turned off the main road again that night, having spotted a large flat-topped hill on my right. On discovering the reason for its neatly planed summit, it was too late to find anywhere else. Cervezas and rough vino flowed while screeching seagulls and revolving ravens dived at the neighbouring house-sized piles of Iberian refuse.

Charlie, already cast as the camp fool, got it all going by 'demanding to have some booze'. A Withnail and I party ensued, complete with bowls of decorative vegetables, loud Jimi Hendrix and what was to be the following day's chicken stuffed in the kettle – the latter, much to the vociferous disgust of our resident German doctor, Miriam. Her prim image plummeted later though, when I spotted her leaning against the truck drunkenly talking to someone. Looking down to check out her long attractive legs, I was puzzled to see her feet steaming. I then clocked a dark patch spreading across her tight skirt. It slowly dawned that Miriam was quietly pissing herself mid-sentence.

Later, I got caught in conversation for an hour by Denise. An Irish lady, and like Miriam obsessed by her ablutions – I had already given some desert warnings but water was currently plentiful – she usually had her nose in idealistic books. *Ireland before the Famine* and *Fat is a Feminist Issue* were both hers. When talking, she came out with increasingly dramatic stories – from helicopter crashes to divorce – and never asked questions. I gave up trying to talk and later heard her tell her boyfriend she thought I was shy.

All in all we had an excellent night. I was beginning to get to know everyone better and my team training was going well; making and breaking camp had already reached an art form. Other jobs had been amicably shared out and were approaching similar levels of sharp execution. The food was very nearly acceptable and the group had for the most part responded to my six-till-six routine. They were no doubt bored by the sound of my voice; my inexorable exhortations to disciplined overlanding included plate-disinfection, 100% successful peg-retrieval, minimal water consumption, considerate trailer-packing – in fact endless rules on health, safety and security. But it was all part of my plan – to get them into shape for Africa by the end of a week in Europe. All I had needed to do was get them dirtier. The river and lake had been mistakes; the tip, a total success.

The early rising, the most unpopular aspect of my drill so far, was rewarded in a stage-managed appeal to the group's psychology. By my reckoning, the distance across Africa wouldn't change, but the time spent at the all too infrequent stopovers and attractions could expand. I wanted to prove early on that they would see and do more by getting up early. So when we drove into the beautiful town of Cordoba, I announced a non-brochure extra: an afternoon to be spent at their leisure using the hours we had earned ourselves. After five days on the truck they all scurried ecstatically into the centre.

It wasn't until we reached the campsite in Algeciras that I realised I had a ferry trip, a border crossing and a Mauritanian visa application to deal with the next day. So far I hadn't planned anything at all apart from the training. As Pete had predicted, I had been too busy on the personal issues, and had spent more time chatting than plotting. That night I mapped out an itinerary and gathered up my documents for the following day, then did my French Franc and Spanish Peseta accounts. It was well gone midnight by the time I had finished. I had given myself a timely reminder that it was *me* who was entirely responsible for whatever happened on the trip, a feeling I was excited by, but far from used to.

The old faces had all left Rabat campsite by the time we pulled in the following evening. Leaving the group to implement their finely tuned drill, I sat in my cab and sipped beer. Running my eyes down the pax list I had ready for the morning, I wondered how much I knew about everyone after eight days on the road as leader.

Hege, Heidi and Else, two blondes and a brunette, were Norwegian. Each as gorgeous as the next, they caused quite a stir wherever they went – initially of course in the Victoria pub full of drivers and trainees, and subsequently in French villages, Spanish supermarkets and, I imagine, Cordoba's main plaza. But they seemed to have acquired a certain street wisdom despite their youth, and had impressed me by building a reed bivouac at the river rough camp in which they slept comfortably in overnight rain. Sleep came rather too easily though; they were the chief lier-inners and often missed breakfast.

Miriam, the 'German' surgeon with those great legs and a bust so large I felt my personal space invaded, was actually, I noted on my list, Swiss – more German than a German. The complaints had already begun and I could sense more trouble ahead. We did, however, have one thing in common. She liked a bit of punk music – I would concentrate on that.

Katrina was as slow moving as a snail, but the only trail she left was one of artistic grace. Evidence of her presence when she moved on included beautifully folded bits of paper, little carved objects or simply bottle-tops and shells arranged with elegance. Australian – outback Australian – she had the inbuilt set of capabilities being nurtured in that environment provides. She had already made her own toothpaste from fine sea shells as well as her own soap and, considering her mollusc-like pace, was very sporty – she went running most evenings. She had peroxided her hair blonde for the trip, and when showing me the beautiful rings on each of her slender fingers, including her thumbs, she explained that she had made those herself too.

Belinda, an American law-school fundraiser, was clearly going to be the Charlotte of the trip. She displayed an early passion for clearing up and a clear passion for early rising. Belinda had none of my guilt about physically hustling people from their beds and took on that role happily. Only the Norwegians appeared to escape her attentions. Perhaps one of them had barked or bitten – Heidi was particularly ferocious in the mornings. Irish Denise had teamed up with Klaus, a rather loud German, on a Caribbean cruise ship; staff, not wealthy punters. He was the keenest of fire-builders, which in fact annoyed me as my post-driving therapy had traditionally been the ritual of axe-wielding and lid-flapping. Now I just drank more whisky – *must find him another job*. They made a glamorous couple. Already tanned, he had several sets of extremely clean safari gear with matching socks, while she just looked ready for the ball at all times, if of course you favoured inch-thick makeup as she did. Of all people, Denise and Klaus needed to encounter mud the most.

Our only other couple were on the short 'old' list along with Cool Elaine. Canadian Bob and Nicola were in their 50s, had been married in that decade (at 15!) and were still so completely in love they were almost as one. Bob was like a Swiss army knife on legs and Nicola held his gadgets for him, producing them from a bumbag whenever a crisis arose – his pocket-lamp collection could easily light a small town.

Cool Elaine, another Aussie, had herself nicely sorted out. She had accumulated 'units' of property in Cairns and lived off the rent, mainly travelling or volunteering for environmental projects around the world. She was practical and capable of any task, always done without attracting any attention to herself. Socially, she had that talent of making everyone feel special by subtly dragging out their very best. Perfect overlanding material. She had already formed a special relationship with Phil, a rather nervous young New Zealander. He had been in trouble for dealing soft drugs and his concerned parents had assigned him to us for rehabilitation – his father had done an Africa overland twenty years previously. Certainly I ran a very tight ship in terms of drugs; they could do what they liked in town, but *nothing* was to be carried or smoked around the truck. Elaine had already slotted herself in as counsellor, motivator and mother. I was looking forward to seeing the change in him – I had a few character-building plans for Phil myself.

Charlie, also Canadian and a hippy, guitarist and stand-up comedian, was actually a rancher by trade. Only twenty, he was confident of his position in the group and had a cheerful manner that could easily infect his audience. Every group needs one, and Charlie was entertainer par excellence. When he wasn't propositioning Katrina or the Norwegians, he was plying me for tales of squalor from further down the road. "I'm sure looking forward to getting ma hat and ma boots all messed up in Za-ear." The Cowboy from Quebec.

Charlie had teamed up with Brett. Recently made redundant from Melbourne county council, Brett had pocketed a hefty sum in severance and was out to enjoy it. Charlie's straight man, he was as dry as Katrina's toothpaste and had TV stardom in his bones; he talked like Paul Hogan and, with his noticeably hooked nose, looked like Muppet Gonzo. He was also on the 'very involved' list – Aussies generally were.

Fat Tom, Tall Tom and Welsh Tom. Sporting a popular overlanding name, they were typically British: generally reserved but periodically incredibly witty. Fat Tom had a great 'stand-up' routine which everyone took the piss out of: at times of truck endeavour he was always to be found … well, standing up – just staring, hoping that by looking at things they would put themselves away. Tall Tom always went for a run after lunch and Welsh Tom I knew very little about, only that I was suspicious of anyone who wore Penguin paperback T-shirts. I had never seen anyone with a library of clothes before. *Must spend more time with him.*

Bergs and Ronnie too. Bergs was a fisherman from Iceland, wore black oblong glasses before anyone else realised they were cool, and had so far kept himself to himself, apart from talking to Ronnie, an American hippy who lived in Kyoto, Japan. Both seemed very pleasant, but were quiet. According to the list, Ronnie was a musician and although he often drummed on washing-up bowls, stools and saucepans, he had yet to bring out any instruments, which I was assured by grumpy trailer packers he had with him in abundance. *All in good time.*

And what did the group see? I tried the same analysis on myself. The group saw someone who was distant all day, especially when driving, but usually friendly at night. He spoke to everyone but gravitated towards Charlie, Brett and the girls. He showed near reverence to Elaine but constant cheek to Canadian Bob. Phil was sometimes under his wing and Miriam got his back up.

He was 'strict', almost like a teacher, but everything ran efficiently. He had high expectations, but also of himself. He blundered constantly, but would fix it up and eventually laugh at it. There was plenty of money and time for buying good food but he kept banging on about it being the real job of the group; 'eating well is the core of high morale'. He allowed plenty of breaks but driving days were long. Camp was as clean as it could be and parties were encouraged, particularly if they had a theme. He had a morning routine. Rise in the dark, chop wood and start the fire. Loud music – often the James Bond theme – for an alarm, three coffees and three Marlboro Reds while the cook team cooked *hot* food for breakfast – or there was a complaint. Checked the truck, ate last, ready to go first, engine deliberately sputtering exhaust onto any laggards brushing teeth by the water tank.

Putting the list to one side, I pulled out some photos. They were of the streets of Bethnal Green. I had taken them to remind myself of how revolting it looked there and now they did the trick for the first of many times. I was glad to be where I was, with this group of people, randomly thrown together to share a few months of our lives.

Katrina was talking to Charlie when I eventually took my place by the fire. Everyone else had gone to bed. I poured a big slug of Johnny Walker.

"You should go for a Capricorn," she was saying.

"No way, babe, I'm not cutting myself down to a one-in-twelve chance when it's already tough enough with a full dozen-in-a-dozen."

"Rubbish – handsome, blond hair, great sense of humour. You can get who you want, Charlie."

"Yeah, but I'm a drinker. I should stay off it though … it makes me feel too good. I start to think I can achieve things."

"Charlie, you've achieved a lot."

He took my whisky bottle and poured liberally into his beaker. "What, rounding up a bunch of cattle for a living?"

"That, yes, and you're here."

"Well, how about you and me then? Now we're both here."

I laughed. He was as bold as Al. Katrina leaned back and sighed, realising he'd missed the point of her pep talk.

Looking her straight in the eye, he drawled, "It's long, Katrina. Long like those beautiful fingers of yours. Perfectly round like those rings."

"Charlie…" She shook her head. "I'm going to bed. See you in the morning."

"Don't remind me you said no when you do," he called after her.

"That's the trouble with this stuff," he said, raising his glass to me. "I always forget that other people remember."

"Anything wrong, Charlie?"

"No way, man, I'm gonna have the trip of my life. Now tell me more about those bog-holes in Zaaaaa-ear."

We didn't head to our tents until dawn broke. We got through Zaire and onto women. We went round the world, some of it on horseback; we lived in an Ottawa flat doing office jobs. We finished the whisky and opened a second. Sitting around a fire telling lies – that's how blokes get to be mates, I guess.

A trickle of traffic was already taking the new route. Two other overland companies had followed Al through, and independents had quickly gravitated to the scene fearing that the only Africa overland route might close at any time. I had already forwarded our details to Jamal, so we had two weeks to explore Morocco and get down to Dakhla. I did the basics: Fes, Marrakech, the High Atlas and on to the oases in the south.

136

From there I chose a back route that crossed the foot of the Anti-Atlas between Zagora and a town just south of Tiznit called Bouzakarne. There were some sandy wadis, which the group had to get the truck through using sandmats, but generally it was so rocky that I couldn't leave the track; lunch was usually served in the middle of the road.

One wadi was particularly wide and became the scene of my first whole group sulk. Having got me going, I ploughed on through deep soft sand, managing to keep the momentum going until I reached rocky land. In the mirror I could see the group more than a kilometre behind me. Miriam, deliberately dawdling, reached us last – over half an hour later.

"I suppose you're not going to let me wash now."

"I can't, Miriam. It's the desert. There's nothing for miles."

"There's loads of water. I saw you fill up."

"Yes, but we might break down."

"We'll all get crabs, you know!"

That stumped me. I was up for a bit of dirt, but was hot on health and hygiene. Yet thinking back, I couldn't remember anyone complaining about lively genitals before. *I know where this is coming from.* The day before I had found both Miriam and Denise brushing their teeth at the water tank, leaving the tap on as if we were permanently attached to the mains. I had let them know my displeasure. It was a cultural clash. Normal European life, where the environment is tamed and all but impotent, compared with the real hazards of Africa where nature still has ultimate power. We would be going down the beach route of Mauritania in just a few days; salt water on one side, desert on the other. Miriam and everyone else who thought like her would have to learn.

"I have medicine for crabs. You can wash again when we hit the main road." Miriam swung away sharply in fury, her chest slicing through the cold atmosphere like an icebreaker.

Crabs became almost the sole topic of conversation that night. It continued all day and the night after, Miriam fuelling people's natural fears. She was the subversive. Due to her profession she wielded considerable power and used it to gather people around her. I had a year of group experience behind me but I couldn't have foreseen this – even I developed a scratch.

I had my supporters too, the ones who were really into my ethos of the trip: Brett, Charlie, Becky, Katrina and all the Toms had made their allegiance clear. The Norwegians were split; two for me, Hege behind Miriam and her second-in-command, Denise, for whom it had also become an issue of sexism. Elaine occupied higher ground, an observer, along with her protégé Phil. It was getting ugly, overwhelming the enjoyment of our beautiful surroundings. In my usual position in the cab that night I wrote it out in a letter home:

The Water Wars:
It's The Mutiny Of The Dirty starring Miriam, an offensive German on a
germ offensive. She's rallied her rebels with well-worded warnings of what
might appear in their pants – pincered crustaceans with a penchant for
pubes.
Her sergeant, sidekick and sister-in-soapiness is Denise, an idealistic Irish-
woman with ideas on odours. The battle lines are drawn, but I have a few
fierce friends myself; supporters of smelliness who watch the water tank.
With a canine commitment to refraining their followers from flagrant flan-
nelling, we wear our T-shirts with pride:

THE RESERVOIR guardDOGS
Dryer Than Beau Geste's Bollocks.

Driving the next morning, the desert now mainly sand again, I came across a fork in the track. I stood on the cab, I consulted my map and I peered at my compass. *No bloody idea at all.* I was aiming south as well as west, so I plumped for left. After lunch, the track petered out to nothing. We weren't exactly lost but we had to go back; a whole driving day wasted.

Camping only a few kilometres from the previous night's spot, I took stock of my situation. I was on one side of a group rift and was uselessly trying to bring the others into my way of thinking. Were I in hospital I would have listened to Miriam's superior knowledge, but here it was me who was supposed to be in charge; here I knew best and I didn't need to argue. I had to do what Pete would have done – lead, and to hell with trying to 'teach'. Popularity and appeasement – neither were issues. I finally worked out for myself that sometimes a leader has to pull away, regardless of how he feels on a personal level.

With that detachment the problem largely burned out by the time we reached Dakhla, and it was the commonest of activities that would finally bring us back to a homogenous unit. A campsite had already sprung up, indicated by a freshly painted sign. After booking in I went to see Jamal, who told me the army would provide an escort in three days' time.

Arriving back at the site, I saw Denise washing her clothes under the truck tap. I asked her to stop. As she did so our eyes met and joined our body-stances in fighting a short battle of wills. A tap on my shoulder broke my stare, and I turned to see the camp proprietor showing me a sponge and soap and pointing a thick hose at the dirty truck. As he pressed a trigger, a powerful plume of water blasted the dusty metal, splashing both Denise and me. "You want washing? " he cried. Her eyes and mine met again, this time creased with barely contained laughter.

Inspired by limitless water, I suggested a whole truck clean. For creating team spirit a truck clean is as good as a bog-hole. Every item of goods and equipment is brought out, washed, dried and replaced in similarly cleaned lockers. Seats are thrashed until not a speck of dust emerges; cooking equipment is cleaned in hot water and pots, blackened by fire despite coating them in washing up liquid before cooking, are wire-wooled until they shine like new.

The group divided themselves up and worked in small teams, laughing and joking in harmonious travail. Even Fat Tom scrubbed, bashed and swept with the rest of them. I spent the same three hours as everyone else clearing the clutter from my cab. The music played loud and the Blues Brothers inspired the inevitable post-cleanup party. Though suits were hard to come by, trilbies were fashioned, sunglasses worn and dusters used in number for the 'shaking of tail feathers'.

Maintenance was up to schedule – to my mind anyway – so, capitalising on improved group relations and free of any tasks while we waited for our convoy, I decided to follow up the Blues Brothers night with hosting a dinner party.

The venue presented itself: a row of three fig trees that cast their low branches wide. We placed tables and twenty borrowed chairs under them. Else took charge of stringing up the Christmas lights I had brought, having been well impressed with Al's set. We all did out best to smarten up and took our seats for a supper that might have been eaten by stockbrokers in a Notting Hill restaurant courtyard. I had received plenty of help, but was still very proud of my pumpkin soup and roast chicken with the varied legumes of Dakhla. Apple crumble came two hours later after I had restarted the fire for the oven.

The dinner seating choices made visible the trip couples that were beginning to form. Charlie and Katrina flirted constantly, leaving me slightly jealous; Beccy and Brett seemed to be getting closer – she rallying to his every need, he soundly rounding on her with his rapid wit; and there were suspicious mutterings about Else and me, even though, true to form, I was in the throes of making a good female friend. Chewing on a shared bowl of crumble, a few wines to the good, Else was discussing life with a little too much melancholy.

"Do you find that every decision you ever make is the wrong one?"

"Cheers."

"No, not on this trip."

"Where then? It sounds like you've got something to tell me."

"No, I wasn't really talking about you, Tim. I was talking to myself, I suppose. I was just thinking. This trip. It's the best decision I've ever made. It feels fantastic. I feel fantastic. It's like I've started life again. If I went back now, I'd already have changed."

"Last chance 'til Nouakchott. There's a plane to Casablanca every afternoon from here."

"Ohhh, you're not listening ... I guess I just wanted to say we're all enjoying it, Tim, and we're glad we've got you as a driver. It'll be fun in Zaire, won't it?"

"Hmm, yes, Else, of course,"

Else had struck a well-hidden nerve. I was really enjoying the trip too, particularly now we'd become a team again. But I hadn't told them I was going to be replaced in Bamako. The idea suddenly seemed a waste of all my efforts. Should I risk the malaria-ridden forests? I could still remember how I had felt at the time, but it seemed distant; different, now I was in charge of an excellent group. It was my turn for melancholy now. I let the silence grow.

Grey, indeterminate meat in a watery soup; fat globules floating on top, rising where they touched the side of the bowl. The only edible part of the meal, a salad, had been wasted – thrown in by the waiter as he put the soup in front of me. I watched as it slid through the ooze to get gently warmed at the bottom of the bowl. I ate bread.

We were in a small hotel in Nouadhibou, which I had booked into in celebration of our successful entry into Mauritania. Although the country boasted some of the finest fishing grounds in the world, our hosts could provide us with none. Jamal's men had been superlative. They'd gone at our pace for a long day's drive, sorted our exit past the army post at La Gouira, and then guided us through the minefields and sandwall before the border. Now all we had to do was cross the country.

Our robed Mauritanian guided us along desert pistes for two days. Occasioning only one glimpse of water in that time, we reached the point where the track becomes the beach. The beach was an obvious route to follow, but the guide came into his own by finding us a safe haven between the dunes when the tide rose to cover it entirely. With the sound of crashing breakers behind us, we camped for our third night and reached Nouakchott in the morning.

When planned, the Route de L'Espoir that stretches 1000km to Nema in the east was supposed to bring trading opportunities to the hardy folk peopling its route. In reality, it has simply led to a mass exodus to the 'bright lights' of the capital. As we left the capital behind us and turned inland, we could see the living conditions of those who had chosen to stay put. Tented settlements dotted land that looked incapable of nourishing the smallest crop, and with no discernible water supply, survival seemed improbable. Even though conditions in Nouakchott's extensive slums were renowned to be atrocious, the desire to try their luck in the city seemed forgivable. I wondered what choice I would have made in their shoes, but soon found the concept too alien even to contemplate.

With the more densely populated landscape of sub-Saharan Africa next on our route, I decided upon a security review. At a dinner meeting the following night, I reiterated the need for constant vigilance of both equipment and personal belongings and reminded the group that everything moveable and valuable was to go in the trailer overnight. Admittedly it seemed petty, given our isolation, and I myself had lapsed into leaving stools out, but we were only a few days from Mali. To reinforce my message I made a grand display of packing up and locking everything away. With my alarm set for 3am, I joined the others in sleep.

We were an absolute pushover. On the back of the truck I picked up boots, clothes, souvenirs, a wallet and two cameras. From the ends of the beds I scored the bags of Bob, Beccy, Charlie and all three Norwegians. I put everything in a large heap the other side of the truck and went back to bed. Niggled into getting up again, I checked my cab to find that I'd left the passenger door unlocked.

In the morning there was a brief panic as I kept my nocturnal nicking quiet, but the pile was quickly found. It turned out that the group felt the need to have toiletries at hand for the night, which was fair enough, but when I asked them to show me what else was in the bags, Heidi and Nicola also produced passports. I had seen the results of losing those once before and certainly didn't want to again.

The group loved Bamako, and I remembered my fondness for its joyful energy despite many inhabitants' spartan existence. Everyone was enjoying their first taste of 'real' Africa, particularly after the long desert journey. Charlie waxed lyrical about the music, the colour, the vibrancy – and the women. On returning from a nightclub after our restaurant dinner, we found him with a woman he had been dancing with much of the night. The pair were leaning on the front of the truck in the mission where, grinding her hips against him, she was submitting enthusiastically to the desires he had voiced at length to me earlier in the evening. Not only bold, I thought, but blatant. Had I known, I would have suggested a comfy bed in the Majestic.

Promising a longer Bamako stopover on our return, we set off the next morning towards Mopti, Djenné and the Bandiagara escarpment – the Dogon trip. On the busy tar road that services all but one of Mali's major towns, we were following the course of the river Niger. Packed buses, rocking wildly on raised suspension, strained to overtake us, running parallel until I dropped back to let them in. Time and again we avoided oncoming vehicles by mere inches. Sometimes, Peugeot 504s – the West African version of Ugandan matatus – managed to slip their way into this already intricate arrangement. In a public exhibition of precision timing as good as any Red Arrows display, they squeezed through non-existent gaps in virtuoso displays of recklessness.

Indifferent to these skirmishes, Charlie and Katrina were in the cab, creating a pocket of atmosphere of their own.

"She wasn't a prostitute," Charlie protested.

"How do you know?" Katrina seemed more offended than jealous.

"Cos I didn't pay her."

"OK then, what was her name?"

"Fanta."

"Fanta? If that's not a stage name, then I don't know what is!"

"Perfectly reasonable actually, Katrina. I can introduce you to a Coca Cola in Nigeria if you like." Immediately regretting crossing over into their airspace, I found myself drawn into their argument.

"So, do you think Fanta was a prostitute?" Katrina turned her fiery eyes on me.

"If she was a professional then Charlie would have paid. They don't go in for voluntary services for clients from overseas… Oh-oh, hang on to your hats boys and girls!"

I swung off the tar to let an overtaking 504 through in front of a truck, spitting up a plume of gravel and saving the lives of its ten occupants in one quick flex of a bicep. Katrina didn't notice a thing.

"But they were screwing within hours of meeting!"

"And you've never done that?"

Katrina dropped eye contact and turned to gaze through the windscreen.

Why didn't you just concentrate on driving, Tim? Then another thought crept into my consciousness with a life of its own: *Well if this stops Katrina and Charlie from getting it together, I've still got ten days.* I pushed it away guiltily.

"There is middle ground here," I continued. "She might have been a good-time girl."

"She was that, all right," Charlie grinned. "Anyway, why are you so interested, Kat? We weren't going anywhere, were we?"

Katrina sighed. "In answer to both your questions, I don't drop my pants as quickly as you two would like to think. Sex is important to me, not just an instinct like a rampant dog's. I was brought up to... No. Tim, could you stop? I want to go in the back."

I stopped straight away. I felt tacky. Charlie looked even worse. No one else wanted to come up front so we were left sharing the sullied air.

"I loathe myself," said Charlie at length. "Kat's the best I ever met and I've screwed it up."

"Literally," I replied.

"What'll I do?"

"I dunno. For now, keep quiet, Charlie. Keep *clean*."

The thought crept back, but I didn't fancy my chances much now either. Charlie and I were tarred with the same brush, and I hadn't even had the 'good time'.

My vision of a memorable riverside rough camp met with mixed success. The view of the great Niger, post rainy-season brown, swirling and swollen, was wondrous. But the millions of mosquitoes – spawned on marshland where flooding had begun to recede – blighted us. Dinner was cooked by a reluctant, neck-slapping team, and then eaten individually under nets, our camp beds circling the fire in a perfect kaleidoscope pattern.

When I found my net coated in a thick layer of mossie the next morning, I realised it was time to dip our nets in Permetherine, a further anti-malaria feature our trucks were now equipped with. There is a peculiar satisfaction in killing mosquitoes, particularly if they squirt evidence of gorging on your own blood. Incredibly free of any discernible bites, I spent half an hour on my bed exacting a more generalised revenge. Creating creases in my net to trap dozens at a time, I squidged them between eager palms, each time muttering, "You bastards have ruined my trip."

In San's enormous market, memories of innocence and ignorance made me smile as I sat in the same café as I had with Pete a year previously. I felt so much better now; on my own, in control, running a good trip with an excellent group – the only problem being Katrina's permanently averted eyes. To my dismay, she had teamed up with Denise and Miriam, forming a coven of previously and presently wronged women. The detachment of the first two I had resigned myself to, but I missed Katrina's positive spirit.

Bergs came into the cab for our final run up to Mopti, sitting between Else and myself. He was feeling ill and correctly assumed the cab would be kinder on his stomach as the truck swung violently to avoid death. He was distinctly green and sat quietly while Else and I talked.

"I heard what you said to Katrina," she said. "She's really upset."

"It was a joke. I wasn't even really involved."

"Well, she seems more annoyed with you than Charlie."

I had got that impression myself. I'd noticed they were talking again, albeit with cursory politeness.

"Well I wasn't shagging on the bumper."

"But you're the driver."

"So what?"

"Tim, what you say counts. It's the same with Denise and Miriam."

"Listen, I don't have time to keep arguing with them. I've got a trip to run." Bergs gurgled, then burped.

"They only do it because they feel you don't respect them."

"And don't I?"

"No, it doesn't look like it. I think you don't know the influence you've got. It must be horrible to feel disliked by the driver, and you've made it so obvious. They're going to keep fighting you 'til you seem more fair."

It was that word again; the 'Rachel' accusation. But this time, with Else's calm portrayal of my poor leadership, I could see more clearly what she was getting at. Whether I liked someone or not I had to show respect. Perhaps after all it *was* important to spread my time around more evenly, if only because I was in charge.

"OK. Look, I'll try again with Miriam and Denise. But what can I say to Katrina?"

"Just apologise."

Just then Bergs lunged at me. His mouth yawned, and a sound like a horny walrus burst from his lungs. For a moment all I could see was a sheet of vomit spread like a map before me. Half of it reached its intended destination, being whipped by the wind out of the window, while the rest cascaded into my lap, laying mountains and rivers of half-digested lunch across my legs and shorts.

"For fuck's sake!" I shouted, braking sharply. "If I count so much, why didn't he go for your side?"

The lengthy cleaning process, with Miriam mocking my use of quantities of water, delayed our arrival into Mopti. We eventually reached a hotel bar by the harbour and set up camp in half-light amidst a troop of hustlers and souvenir sellers.

Built on three islands between channels of the dissipating river, Mopti already looked a fascinating town. Filled with wooden pirogues and their larger cargo-bearing cousins, pinasses, we had glimpsed the busy and colourful scene of the harbour on the way into town. It was dark now, but we could see hundreds of lights bobbing up and down in the foreground, the air humming with the calling of unseen cargo handlers and passenger hawkers.

Everyone wanted to go out after dinner so I volunteered to stay back as truck guard – I needed to look through notes on organising the Dogon trip. With three days up there, I worked out, we could afford an extra day in Mopti. I saw a chance to bring my adversaries back on board.

We were having a breakfast meeting. "So that's the Dogons and Djenné," I concluded. "Where would you like to spend the extra day you've earned?"

Way back in Morocco, Miriam had shown me a list of highlights a friend who had travelled West Africa had given her. Amongst them was Mopti. My question was loaded, and aimed at her.

"Well I'd like to stay here, but I don't suppose you want my opinion." I ignored the barbed half of her suggestion.

"Well, that's possible. You might be right. There's a fish market to see, the salt-traders, the Bozo fishermen camps if they're still here – you can get a pirogue to take you there – and the old town sounds good. Any other ideas?" My rather strong advert silenced further suggestion. I hoped I hadn't been too obvious.

"Could we have dinner out tonight?" Klaus asked.

"Good idea. I can give you all a sub and you make up the rest. That OK with everyone?" Nods and murmurs of agreement.

"We went to the Bozo Bar last night," Denise ventured, my other fish hooked. "The food looked great and it's right on the harbour."

"Sounds excellent. I'll hire a truck guard – unless Charlie wants to man the bumper again."

Closing the meeting, I stood to take my notes back to the cab. Else brushed past, elbowed me in the ribs and winked.

"Thanks," I mouthed.

The Bozo was a terrific venue. When I popped over to thank Denise and Klaus after dinner, they offered me a beer. Miriam, Canadian Bob and Nicola gathered around and we formed a neat circle. They all enthusiastically told me about their day: the riverboat trips, the mud-brick mosque and the welcome of the buoyant inhabitants. We drank and laughed, the circle widening as more people gravitated to our end of the table. I paused momentarily to count up and found that for the first time since Fes, the whole group were sitting and talking together.

The Dogon area is steeped in history and culture, and I had been encouraging the group to read up on it in guidebooks. Living in their isolated territory, the Dogon people have protected their ancient traditions from all but the most recent invasion: tourists. Their unique villages occupy the plateau at the top of a huge sandstone escarpment, the plains below and, perhaps most dramatically, the cliffsides themselves.

We set off via Bankass to Teli. As the road thinned out to little more than a footpath after Bankass, Gérard – our guide – took us between walled compounds surrounding square mud-built houses. The houses' grass roofs sat like wigs at different jaunty angles, coming to individually shaped points at the top like bunched hair. Small, enclosed fields sprouting bright green onions contrasted sharply with the parched earth and brown rock surrounding them; the children with distended stomachs who worked them stopped their play to wave us on our way. Behind Teli the 300m cliffs were slashed with angry horizontal scars that created precipitous overhangs. Fallen boulders lay strewn below the village, which was tucked protectively under the base of the cliff like a joey in a kangaroo's pouch. They provided a ready source of building materials. I could see pockmarks like bad acne on the lower reaches of the high brown wall of rock. On closer inspection they turned out to be the windows and doorways of homes carved directly into the cliffside itself.

In Teli, Gérard took us straight to the chief's house, ushering us into a palm-thatch shaded courtyard to await his arrival. I was, I hope, not the only one expecting someone in feathers or animal skins, face slit with tribal scarring. Disappointingly, a short man in jeans and T-shirt appeared and welcomed us as 'esteemed visitors'. We sat on uncomfortably low stools while he went through a collection of masks, clothes and jewellery that he urged us to buy. He was, he said, saving for a new moped.

The few purchases we made were supplemented by a charge for our visit 'for the preservation of our culture and community'. I bought a woollen top for a musician friend at home who specialises in wearing strangely adorned shirts. This one had pairs of woollen bobbles hanging off it like multiple sets of testicles. Initially suspicious of the authenticity of its origins, I was delighted to see some locals who did indeed wear such finery, along with matching bollock-bobble hats.

After a late lunch, we filled water bottles and followed Gerard to the base of the cliff. Out of any breeze, and with the sun's intense heat radiating from the stones, it was still more sweltering there. He guided us up a narrow stony path until we reached what he described as a graveyard. Above us, carved into bare rock, were numerous tombs where the bodies of Dogon ancestors were said to have been laid. A very long ladder reached up to them. It was the job of the 'guardian', who sat placidly on a clay pedestal while we wandered around with cameras, to refresh their shrines with offerings each morning and evening. The paraphernalia of his calling surrounded him: clay pots, some on their own pedestals; poles with straw dolls on the end and some animal skulls. Around him wooden facemasks stared out from clay-smothered walls where they hung next to similarly featureless mud faces moulded directly onto the clay.

When we had finished trifling with his ancient culture, we split up and followed tracks to whatever appealed most. I just went to a suitably lofty rooftop and sat alone, staring out across the immense vista ahead of me, thinking about our presence there on the borders of the Sahara, paying guests of a people with a history and society so different from our own it was barely fathomable. We would have our fun, take our photos, and then move on. *Perhaps it does make some sense*, I thought. We would each take away specific memories of parts of the world we wanted to visit again; we would skim now but maybe come back selectively to study in detail later on – overlanding as a taster session.

Tired and thirsty, we made our way back down. Gérard negotiated a large room for us to sleep in, and then Charlie, Elaine and I, quickly caught up by Phil, went with him to buy meat. Cooler now, the shops were open for business, which simply meant that in some huts, wooden hatches had been propped open. In the 'window' of the butcher's, hunks of fly-covered meat hung from string. We declined fleshy purchases, filling our bags with onions instead, the sole vegetable available from the 'greengrocer's' next door.

Back at our lodgings, Gérard launched into further dinner negotiations and I was asked to select a kid from a pen of bleating goats. The first one I pointed at was grabbed, but it wrestled free of captive hands. I reflected on the random nature of our fate as I pointed out three more before one was finally tied at the ankles.

Firmly of the opinion that if one is going to eat meat then one should be able to see it killed, I invited the group to the ceremony. Only Elaine, a vegetarian, and Bergs, a fishetarian – though not entirely so during our trip – declined. The goat was placed in a shallow circular pit, some sort of prayer was incanted, and then I was presented with a knife to slit its throat.

I said 'see', not actually *do* the killing. I held its quivering chest with one hand and pulled back its head. The kid's eyes peered at me while it bleated mournfully. I started rubbing the blunt knife against its bulging windpipe, sawing away like a useless carpenter. Fortunately the goat was quickly rescued from my incompetence and met a swift end at the hands of the expert owner as he poked the knife behind the windpipe and forced the blade towards him. In that one swift movement the suffering ended; a gush of blood spilling into the pit. More words were muttered while the kid was suspended on a rope and stripped of its skin, amazingly all in one piece, even its legs; it was like seeing someone take off a boiler suit. The skin would go to make a water carrier, or more likely one of the suspiciously shaped brightly painted shoulder bags on sale in the chief's house.

My enthusiasm for witnessing the slaughter of my own sustenance had diminished, along with everyone else's. While we sipped diffidently at onion soup, most of the delicious spit-roast meat went to the children who had eagerly watched the ceremony with us.

We climbed the escarpment early the next morning, the sweeping vista getting better at each turn of the twisting path. As we reached the narrow gullies of the plateau edge, we stopped for breakfast under an overhanging rock. After a couple more kilometres walking on the plateau itself, we reached the village of Djiguibombo. There, stone houses were surrounded by a stone wall in a totally stony landscape. Its existence seemed inconceivable, but its charming inhabitants were real enough. They offered us small doughballs and coffee while we rested in their shaded 'town centre' – two stone benches on a stone plinth.

From there we linked up to a circular route around the savannah and walked past terraced fields of the ubiquitous onion and a few forlorn and ancient baobabs, following the cliff edge back to Djiguibombo late in the afternoon. Exhausted, we were shown to our quarters, a small compound with a toilet hut and two benches outside it. Seating was ignored as everyone dropped daypacks and empty water bottles where they stood, sprawling on the gravel desperate for rest.

Gérard had warned us that it would be cold overnight but we had ignored him. Only 300m above Teli, however, it was an entirely different climate. Over a doughball breakfast we all huddled around the fire, having slept fitfully on thin mattresses, freezing in sweaty T-shirts. Too cold to hang around, we descended back to Teli where I gave the group a choice: hiking through the string of villages along the foot of the escarpment, or driving back to Mopti. They quickly chose the latter. Despite ceaseless expressions of wonder, and promises to return for weeks of hiking and climbing with friends from home, to a wo/man they voiced a preference for a night together drinking cold beer in the Bozo bar.

Hmm, maybe overlanders do just want to taste the goods and nothing more. But it served to emphasise one thing: the real pleasure of overlanding is often simply to be found in the groups themselves.

Charlie and Katrina cuddled on the terrace overlooking the harbour. I saw their silhouettes bend towards one another. Like crude shadow puppets, I made out lips touching an upturned forehead. *If they've made up,* I thought, *how come I'm still being cold-shouldered by Katrina?* I was a few days from having to leave the group, and my favourite – if I was allowed one – was the only person I now didn't have good relations with.

In Teli I had told everyone I was being replaced, but not the reason why. It was Miriam of all people who had come up with the idea of writing a petition to the company to protest at my removal. I'd had to work hard to put the mockers on that one.

Lunching by the Niger the following day, we had our first view of our next destination. Djenné, dominated by its famous mosque, stood before us in the middle of the river. Heavy traffic wasn't allowed on the causeway, so we arrived by ferry – the proper way to reach this ancient island town, the most beautiful and famous in all the Sahel.

The group dispersed into a crowd of hustlers under instruction to meet at Chez Baba's at 4pm. My first job was to help 'Clubfoot' find a doctor. Heidi's recently acquired nickname was a result of a hiking injury, the enormous swelling, actually on her ankle rather than her foot, indicating a vicious bite of some sort rather than a twist.

Already used to excessive attention, Heidi smiled at the onlookers as she hobbled along. Taller than me, she was able to use my shoulder as a serviceable crutch. Injury, real or otherwise, would appear to be a good deterrent to in-your-face hustling; the myriad guides kept their distance – odd, as I actually wanted one for once. Selecting a boy who was holding a Maths textbook, we slowly followed him in search of healing.

We eschewed the temptation of the traditional medicine men the boy first introduced us to, in favour of a pharmacy. The shopkeeper became a doctor simply by stepping from behind her counter into a curtained cubicle in one corner of the small room. She ran both hands over the bulbous appendage before twisting it this way and that until Heidi winced. Then she pronounced her diagnosis: possibly a bite or it could be a sprain.

Fair enough, but which? Looking closer, she discovered what looked like a pair of pinpricks.

"Spider," she blurted confidently. I had heard of wounds where spiders had supposedly bitten which turned out later to be where they had laid eggs. I didn't fancy witnessing the sudden explosion of Clubfoot's ankle into thousands of eight-legged furry babies. Neither, I suspected, did Heidi.

"Has it laid eggs?"

"That never happens. It's a bite – poison."

She certainly knew more than I, but I wondered if it could have been a scorpion or something else. It didn't matter much, as she prescribed nothing more than skin cream for the irritation and a hot bath. I bought the former but couldn't promise more than a bucket for the latter. Clubfoot would have to hobble for a few more days yet.

Heidi bravely decided to join me for a tour of the town. The boy was still with us, and each time limb reorganisation halted our three-legged progress, he studied his Maths until we signalled our departure. We visited the empty marketplace, the top of which provided a good vantage point for a clear view of the Grand Mosque – entrance was banned for non-believers. Looking up from his book, the boy casually announced that it was market day the following day. I had heard of it and it came highly recommended. *If we could make up time…*

At Baba's I enquired about staying overnight and was offered the roof terrace for a song. Meals were also cheap so I could pay the whole cost. When the group had gathered I asked if they would swap a very long day's drive for a morning at the market. It would have to be one night on the road rather than two.

"It's always bloody early anyway," Katrina pointed out. Her first words to me in a week, but she was smiling. "So it would be great." The group echoed that opinion.

If just visiting Djenné already felt like a trip back in time, pushing through the crowds on market day makes you feel particularly medieval. The marketplace fills with all the peoples of the Sahel, each bearing their rich offerings. The hundreds of stallholders compete for decibels, offering anything from fruit, vegetables and live animals to pottery, colourful fabrics and gold jewellery. Separated into small groups as we were, I briefly glimpsed Katrina trying on a ring and holding her hand out to Charlie for approval. Then the crowds closed in around them once more.

That night was my last with the group on the road and the theme of the party had been decided in Djenné – a medieval feast. Shortly before San, I turned off down a rough track, shying away from the river in favour of sparse bush.

Only two small boys found us as we created the scene. We draped fabrics in the trees for tapestries, mounted candles on the end of tent poles for torches and spread the Christmas lights between bushes – just because we liked them. The group made ruffs, crowns and capes. We could have done with the twanging of a few lutes but settled for Ronnie and his Japanese stringy-thingy. Charlie juggled under an improvised jester's hat and the rest of us roared, as loud as we could, while quaffing beakers of 'mead'. No one knew what mead was but we named our bucket of red-wine punch thus. When Ronnie tired of serenading us at our long table, Canadian Bob produced some Gregorian chant music. Possibly not the same era, but it felt about right.

Interrupting a throat-punishing guttural guffaw I was having with the three Toms, Katrina pulled me to one side. She was wearing a beautifully made gold tiara balanced gracefully on the spikes of her blond hair. It matched the new ring I could see glistening on a spare finger. Throwing her arms around me she gave me a big hug. I found my arms resting on a large false behind she'd created. From it, a long train flowed, gathering thorns from the ground.

"I'm sorry about last week," she implored. My shoulder muffled her voice. As I kept her pressed tight to me I ignored the thought that I might be overplaying my hand.

"No, Katrina, it was my fault. I was rude and thoughtless. I'm sorry."

She snuggled a little closer, wiggling her hips to gain extra contact. I was aware of the Three Toms' eyes boring into us, but was too full to wine to care.

Looking up she whispered, "Well, let's just both be sorry." She lowered her head back to my shoulder and we started swaying to the music.

"Mind if I have this dance?" Charlie appeared from behind the truck, doing up his flies as he spoke. He gently pulled Katrina away from me. As my hands trailed off her hips we looked intently into one another's eyes. There seemed to be much left unsaid. I returned to the Toms.

"What are you up to?" enquired Welsh Tom. He had a Singing Detective T-shirt on below a cardboard crown.

"Just saying goodbye," I reassured him, before latching on to Tall Tom's next witticism with a mediaeval laugh that made my throat burn. Presently, Else came over for a dance. The music had changed to something more rhythmic, much to Bob's annoyance.

"All made up then?"

"Looks like it, doesn't it?"

I flew into Heathrow on Boxing Day. I had spent the whole flight honing my one ambition, and had even written it down: *I want to finish a trip that I start.*

It was Adrian who had arrived in Bamako to take over. Working together on the truck for a couple of days in the Lebanese Mission, I had got to know him even better than I had in the workshop. I decided the trip would be more than safe in his capable hands, and it was probably a blessing that I'd got out of a potentially dodgy personal situation. Besides, I had noticed Adrian and Heidi striking up a swift friendship – *perhaps some things are meant to be.*

After two days with my parents I repaired to London to stay at a friend's who was on holiday. I had been told to report to the office on January 3rd, so I still had New Year's Eve to look forward to. I didn't feel like travelling, and most of my friends already had arrangements, so I caught up with everyone over the wire.

Charlotte asked me to meet her in town that night. We ate in Chinatown then walked the cold streets arm in arm in the direction of the Thames. Crossing at Waterloo Bridge, we wandered along the embankment past the National Theatre. At the end of a small pier, we embraced. Small talk had given way to our normal easy flow of conversation and now to mutual attraction. We kissed. A photographer must have thought us an interesting picture as a flash went off before a figure scuttled away down the embankment. Feeling intruded upon, we descended to the riverside. With the tide low, we could walk along hand in hand in the clear moonlight. Presently we found ourselves under London Bridge. We wrapped each other up in our coats for warmth, closing the winter out of our intimate little world. I felt as if we were the only two people in London; as if we had it to ourselves.

In The Anchor adjacent to the bridge, we warmed ourselves up with mulled wine and discussed future meetings. It looked bleak, particularly as she was going back to Sydney and I to destinations as yet unknown, but we resolved to spend New Year's Eve in a London hotel together – in two days' time.

The next night my mother rang. She told me I had received a phone call at home. "It was a bit strange. It was a German voice, I think. A girl. She just said to say she was looking for 'Monsieur L'Etranger'. I didn't pry, you know me, but I gave her your number."

That brought a quick halt to the conversation. As soon as I put down the receiver, the phone rang again. I grabbed it. Another friend. I had a distracted conversation and aborted that call too. I turned on the television and opened a bottle of wine. Still distracted, I went for a walk, checking the answerphone was left on.

'Monsieur L'Etranger'. The nickname I had acquired in Dakar; the person who'd given it to me – Kathy.

I was still awake when the phone rang at three in the morning. Nervously, with achingly long gaps in our conversation, Kathy and I started to fill in our respective six months. She was still in Basle, she said, and felt happy but lost. She missed Africa and said she missed me. Having had no contact at all in that time, we found we were still talking when it got light. By then we had arranged to meet in Paris for New Year's Eve. We rang off and I suddenly panicked; Charlotte would be getting ready for work. I had to call her straight away.

No chat or small talk; I just blurted, "Charlotte, listen, I'm really sorry, but Kathy called out of the blue. She's invited me to Paris and I'm going tomorrow." Swallow. "You know I had to say yes. You told me yourself nothing had changed deep down. Charlotte, I'm sorry."

Silence – just my breath echoing into the receiver. "Charlotte, I'm really so–" The phone went dead.

In a small hotel not far from the Pigalle, Kathy and I found our souls, minds and bodies entwined once again. We talked, laughed and walked the streets. Paris was beautiful. Bitterly cold from a sharp frost, the trees stayed covered all day in their white icy shrouds like so many jewelled wedding dresses.

We ate in good restaurants and back street bars; we drank champagne and rough wine; we spilled croissant crumbs and coffee on rumpled bedclothes. I felt abandoned to something called love, even stronger than the last time. Oddly, the other person who entered my mind in those three days was Katrina. I told Kathy about her.

"Do you love her?" she asked, after listening to my story.

"Don't be stupid. She was a friend, that's all. I just wanted to tell you how strange relationships can be in overland groups. It's you I love."

"Don't say that. I told you not to say that word to me." Kathy suddenly looked cold. I knew she didn't like me saying it, but she had just used the word herself, albeit not to me. It was our last night and we were somewhere in the middle of it – I had lost track of time. We started arguing.

"What are we arguing about?" I cried, suddenly coming to what I thought were my senses.

"We are arguing because we must." Kathy looked at me with her quirky smile, her eyes beaming once more with intense passion. I didn't even try to understand her strange comment.

"There is something I must tell you," Kathy later whispered in my ear. I was waiting for the magic word. It had come up, we had argued about it, albeit circuitously, and now we were once again joined in its name; it was time.

"I'm getting married... next week. Helmut knows I'm here with you. He told me to come." I lifted my chest to look at her fully, to check her face. The expression told me she wasn't joking. I went blank for a moment; closing my eyes and forcing the truth from my mind. A thought finally made its way through my barriers, bursting into my conscious.

Helmut – what a crap name.

SOUTH AMERICAN CIRCLE

VENEZUELA

COLUMBIA

ECUADOR

GUIANA

TRINAD

GUIAN

FR

Manaus

Belem

Rio Amazonas

PERU

Lima

Cuzco

La Paz

BOLIVIA

BRAZIL

CHILE

PARAGUAY

Asuncion

Rio
de Janeiro

Santiago

URUGUAY

ARGENTINA

Fortune favours the lucky. My escape was already planned: London had booked me a flight for January 5th. To Rio. Still wrapped in my cocoon of self-loathing, I had caught only snippets of Graham's explanation of running trips in South America: usually two drivers ... dodgy trucks ... hotels ... Peruvian bandits. What I did register was that the driver meeting me at the airport was Al. And what better tonic to a broken man?

I heard the shout first, then glimpsed a pair of gleaming fluorescent shorts coming my way at speed. Dropping my pack, I lifted my hands to create a set of horns of my own, then we clasped each other backhanded around the neck.

"Wankaaaaaaaaah," he cried through my throttling, "you wankaaaaaaah!"

I know, Al, I know.

A taxi took us through the deserted centre of downtown Rio. It was hot but not Mali hot. Al told me about the local policemen's tendency to earn extra cash by killing street children who hung around the shops; the traders paid them well. Groups traipsed the streets, already quiet even though it was only eight in the evening. They scavenged for booty in the refuse of that day's commerce, working separately from packs of dogs that rooted around for their own pickings.

Adjacent to the centre is the district known as Lapa. Part of Rio's Old Town, its tall terraced streets at least had signs of normal life. Neon did the job blank streetlights should have been doing, casting intermittent dim shadows behind wandering groups of poorly dressed people. They were heading to Lapa's dilapidated main street, Calle Amor as it was known according to Al's enthusiastic commentary. There we would find our hotel, the Marajo.

The neon became more insistent as we turned into the narrow street. Downtown Rio nightlife is distilled into this thin strip of gaudy bars and brothels. One side of the street was unwalkable as cars were sprawled up over the pavement, hastily parked with no thought for neatness. On the other side, a row of low trees flashed like Christmas trees under the houses' balconies, from which the neon hung. Lovehearts, beds, reclining women and beer bottles floated in mid air, flashing lazy, stroboscopic pulses of red and yellow, catching one another up, overtaking, sometimes momentarily in unison.

At the bottom of the street, a blue heart – how I could relate to that! – flickered rather than flashed. Below it, a sign spelt out 'Ma jo'. Behind two huge windows, blazing fluorescent strips put the occupants on display to new arrivals. I looked in. It was like watching two televisions in the window of an electrical store. On the right, a bar with an animated clientele permanently on the move between red plastic-covered booths; on the left, two concrete steps went up to the glass doors of reception. A man stood behind a tall marble desk stretched along the left wall. He stared at the scene in the bar opposite him, hands on top of the counter as if holding himself back from joining their frivolous lives.

The receptionist looked right as I struggled to push open the heavy glass doors. At the desk, too high to rest my elbows on, Al introduced me.

"Senor Michel. Senor Tim. A new driver. Your best room, sir, and make sure it's a 'special'." Al winked, and under his breath continued, "Miserable git, but Michel's a diamond. He'll sort anything for you. I'll give you an hour, then we're off to The Office." Al strolled towards the bar. As the doors opened, a roar of welcome filled reception, echoing from the high ceilings. As they swung shut behind him, the sound was cut off like a man being gagged.

Having followed Al's entrance to the Marajo bar, Michel's eyes returned to meet mine. In a red bow tie, black trousers and white jacket that revealed stains of leftover wine and food, he looked out of place, like a relic of a past age.

Using my basic Spanish I asked Michel how long he had worked there. He proudly told me that he had first stood behind that very counter forty years previously, having moved from Argentina. Lapa, he said, had been a desirable area of town then. "They've all gone to Ipanema now. They live in concrete tower blocks and never come to Rio." His uniform looked as if it was the same one he had worn that day.

"Do you drink here as well?" I asked.

"Never! I just watch."

My room was indeed special. In the centre was a round bed covered by a purple bedspread; one pillow had fallen to the floor. Above the bed was a ceiling of mirrors. Flicking on the TV set which was suspended from the ceiling, I heard a loud grunting and moaning coming from under the bed; loud speakers were set into the base. In a fine reconnaissance of her posterior, a Brazilian on the screen was pumping his prodigious length into the well-rounded ass of a Negress. I watched for a while, mesmerised. Was it like an American aerobic show? Were the Marajo's less singular customers supposed to follow what they saw on the screen? While I showered, the couple under the bed became more rhythmic, alternating one grunt to one moan. A scream – then the grunts took over and turned into a roar.

Al was shouting over the music in the Marajo bar.

"…too right, mate. More fun and games. Graham reckons we're best off together as neither of us knows a thing about South America. How's your Portuguese?" Al said it with an exaggerated lilt at the end, talking as if he had cotton wool in his mouth. It was his version of a Portuguese accent.

"Nowhere, but I can do some Spanish."

"Same as me, I'm just going to shout 'til we get to Paraguayo."

Realising I didn't know anything about the route, I felt a sudden rush of panic. I didn't want to feel like the trainee again. Co-driving would be great, particularly with Al, but I would have to bone up on trip notes. Al seemed to perceive my disquiet.

"I think we're only going half way together. Then you're up to Quito for an Andean Adventure back to Rio on your own." We were both still shouting and I wanted to get the detail I had missed in blanking Graham.

"Yeah, that's right. I remember now. Graham told me we'd meet on my way back too. Where's this 'office' you were on about?"

"I'll show you." The regulars clapped Al on the back as we left. "Prostitutes and pimps, the lot of them," he said when we got outside. "But what a laugh!"

At the end of 'Love Street', on the corner where we had turned in, stood a small shop, its two windows facing two streets. Inside, a dozen men sat in fours around three rickety tables. Behind a glass counter displaying dubious meats, the barman sat on his freezer, guarding it like Zongo on the Mali train.

"This the Office?" I asked. "Quiet isn't it?"

"It goes off sometimes." Al nodded hellos back to those he received. He was obviously recognised there too.

We ordered beers and sat outside on the root of a tree that had broken through the tarmac pavement. Al told me how much fun he'd had in Rio doing a truck turnaround with Craig Hutchinson. They'd been flown out together three weeks previously. Craig and a trainee had left Rio on New Year's Day to do the 'Across The Amazon' trip, the ten-week northbound loop to Quito. "Great spot for Christmas and New Year, Rio," he concluded. "How about you?"

I told Al about Charlotte and Kathy, and then moved on to my Africa trip. Knowing Al would appreciate the story, I described Charlie's bumper antics, therefore mentioning Katrina as well.

"Phew, how did *you* end up in that sort of shit?" Al enquired after my lengthy résumé. "It's not exactly your scene is it – three at once? That's not a love triangle hombre – that's a bloody rectangle!"

"It wasn't three. It was two – Charlotte and Kathy."

"Ay ay, if you say so. What are you going to do now?"

"Nothing, just drive."

"And mend your ways like me?"

"Yeah – what about you and Pauline?" Al was used to my reticence.

"Bloody brilliant, mate. She's gone back to Australia; I'm here. No really, we had a few days at my sister's in Dorset, and I said she should come out here to see what's what; y'know – with us. Just before I left Northampton, some scrag-end turned up at the drivers' house. I could have portioned her into oblivion, but no, I'm going to try that focusing."

I laughed at his latest vocabulary. It would be great to work with Al again. Right now, I needed his outlook on life, as well as his friendship.

Al woke me up next morning. Banging on my door he shouted, "Put your cock away hombre – Paulo's here. See you in five."

Paulo was the company taxi-driver. He knew when drivers would be in town and made himself available for us at all times. A handsome young man, he had a small flat near Copacabana beach, paid for with the hard-earned rewards of two years gold-digging in the Amazon. He told great stories of gun-toting brigands plucking nuggets from the anal passages of fellow miners. He himself had set off with a specific target, and once he had dug up enough to buy the flat for him and his wife, had left. He also owned his taxi outright.

Paulo drove us through Rio's sprawling suburbs; sometimes through tree-lined avenues where tall walls hid whitewashed houses; sometimes along busy highways where cardboard huts could be seen under the overpasses. Dodging trucks, motorbikes and fellow cab drivers, even at Paulo's excessive pace it took forty-five minutes to reach the bus depot where the truck was parked.

The depot lay below one of Rio's favelas, the shantytowns built on hills where no mains water or electricity reaches. Lawless areas run by mafia barons, drugs and crime fuel their micro-economies, and the inhabitants are beset by the ensuing violence. Some of the bus company workers lived there, their ambition always 'to get out'. The depot itself was enormous. Behind high metal gates with watch-towers on either side were the workshops, huge like aircraft hangars. Dozens of black and white buses poked like piano keys out of the hangar mouths. Divided up into various trades – mechanical, upholstery, spray painting amongst others – hundreds of men in smart overalls worked round the clock to keep Rio moving. Beyond the workshops was the bus park itself, where hundreds more buses lay in long neat lines. Our Bedford nestled amongst them.

"What a place! There's nothing you can't get done here." I was excited by the prospect of expert hands working on any vehicle under my jurisdiction.

"Yeah, but you've got to book ahead. Half the time it's quicker doing stuff yourself."

"Do they have parts?"

"Millions – but not for Bedfords. They still come from Northampton with the groups. But if you need a seat repairing or a new paintjob, you're sorted here. Don't forget, these trucks never go to England. This one's been here for don-keys'."

It looked like it. A more modern Bedford than I was used to, it was still shabby. To protect passengers from the bitter cold of the Andes, it had a hard body with sliding windows, which looked disproportionate to the size of cab. I mentioned it to Al.

"Fuck your aesthetics, hombre – it's the engine that worries me. I've got it booked in with the boys today. They're going to check it over, but we've got no spares anyway."

Rio de Janeiro was everything it was supposed to be: fast, frenetic, flash and fun. Everywhere I looked there were signs of gross opulence, but the more Paulo drove us to and from the depot, the more I saw of the city's slum dwellers.

Favelas were on every spare patch of land, with those who couldn't find space there spilling out onto the streets and pavements themselves.

I loved the nights out in the city. Every night on our way back from the workshop we had a beer at The Office. With our oily shorts, dirty hands and sweaty brows, we blended in well with the local clientele – street cleaners, market traders, pavement mechanics or pimps. After a shower we would meet in the Marajo's reception area. Al was always there first, lying in a booth reading a *What's on in Rio* monthly guide, from which we would select a restaurant. With our shared passion for good food, we fervently discussed our choice from – we counted them – sixty-two countries.

The restaurants were usually in the modern beachfront suburbs of Ipanema and Copacabana to which we would taxi – in Rio, you don't walk. After our Japanese, or Ukrainian, or Swiss, or French, or Brazilian Churrasceria, we would head to the beachside cafes for coffee and more beer. Beautiful prostitutes sat on knees stroking significantly less attractive European faces; security guards' truncheons bashed street children's wandering fingers; cars, from familiar broken Toyotas to Jags, Mercs and Porsches – with the ubiquitous locally made Beetle in between – cruised the 'strip', the dual-carriageway that separated us from the white beaches themselves. Rio is an amazing city. If we ran out of things to chat about there was always more talk-fodder: 'Do you think that one's a bloke or a proper bird?' 'Would you ever buy a Harley like that?' 'What do you reckon those poor kids live on?' Or…'That's never Ronnie Biggs, is it?'

I even loved working at the depot. The boys were really friendly and incredibly professional. If the job was small – a bit of welding, a stitch in the driver's seat – they would do it straight away, waving off proffered notes in preference of a beer at lunchtime at the Office 2 just outside the depot gates, where an Italian made fine salami sandwiches. With a reasonable amount of time to complete the turnaround, Al and I could work at a steady pace, ticking off jobs from an improvised job-sheet. We did a strict eight till five, knocking off like *real* people.

Paulo kept us up to date with the mind-boggling spiralling of Brazilian inflation, charging us a few thousand more Reals every day. Since he was always on the level, we could then gauge what to pay everyone else. In some ways it was worse than in Zaire, but disguised as some of the noughts had recently been lopped off in another central bank devaluing exercise. Taxis, restaurants, even small bars like the Offices had taken to using codes to price their services. That way they could show that they had changed nothing, only slotting in a new price based on the daily percentage inflation rate. We changed dollars only as we needed them.

A trickle of expedition members started arriving at the airport. To avoid them losing everything before even reaching the Marajo, Al and I took it in turns to meet them. We both enjoyed watching their reactions as Paulo's car turned into Calle Amor and they saw the Marajo for the first time – long imagined from months of office-job musings. For those we guessed might find it funny, we ordered a 'special' from Michel. He thoroughly enjoyed blank-facing them if they complained – one or two did. To all we passed on his one simple rule: don't walk in Rio!

On the eve of departure we held our meeting. We sat on a table in the hotel breakfast room while the group trooped in to take seats facing us. Al had bought new shorts in an Ipanema surf shop especially. They came with a matching aquamarine hat in the shape of a surfboard, which he wore sideways on.

"You'd look more sensible with a bouncing hammer," I commented.

"Mate. If you're going to look a wanker, you might as well look a proper one," he countered.

The group looked on in bemusement as I held up a map and Al traced the route as best he could from his sketchy knowledge. A full three months to Quito, the first month – crossing Southern Brazil, Paraguay, Argentina and Northern Chile – would be short on stopovers and long on driving. The real action, Al said, would start once we hit the Andes on the Chile/Bolivia border. From there we would work our way up more slowly through Bolivia, Peru and Ecuador, stopping off at an amazing variety of attractions. If the group weren't excited by what was on offer, I certainly was. Finishing, Al bowed with a flourish of his hat and the straight man took over for his 'gloom-show'.

"You're a mean bastard, aren't you," Al said as we organised taxis to get everyone to a restaurant for a group meal. "Even I was scared by the time you'd finished."

"Get them off to the right start and you're sorted."

"After that speech, mate, I reckon half of them'll have slipped off home by tomorrow morning."

Like a sexy dress drawing your attention away from the personality of the woman inside it, the truck sat outside the Marajo with a shining bright blue paintjob – company colours from a previous decade, but these trucks never got the update. It looked fantastic. "Is it a new one?" someone asked. In fact, the chief mechanic had warned us we were very low on compression; the engine had no power and could blow up at any minute.

Just getting out of Rio took two hours. While I pottered, keeping firmly in my chosen second lane, cars darted in and out in front of us, careering across all four lanes to gain inches. Al pointed out the driver of one we overtook. He was writing on a clipboard with a bandaged hand, his head completely wrapped in bandages too. His windscreen bulged outwards in a shape that clearly matched it. "Reckon that's how he got like that in the first place?"

Soon bored of looking for more driving mummies, he pulled out the pax list. We started putting the ages and jobs to the faces in the back of the truck as Al covered up the names. With our guesses resulting in miserable failure, that game finished too. Al leant back, rummaged around in his shorts, and then announced a 'first-to-get-a-stiffy' competition. "No hands!" he ordered.

"No way – you gave yourself a head start!"

"Aw mate, I was just lining it up. It kills if it gets stuck on your thigh."

Entertained thus, we were soon off the highway and onto a hilly stretch of road that curved through the tree-covered coastal mountains. The truck had to be in second gear to get up them, and to make matters worse there were endless speed bumps. Progress was pitiful.

"Not far to Parati now, but this is going to be a long old trip," Al lamented. "Still, we'll hire a boat and go swimming. Then we can see what's under those T-shirts. Saves the bother of guessing."

On the side road down to Parati we stopped at a supermarket to shop – already overlanding in South America seemed strange. Our tripnotes told us we would 'lunch at Parati campsite'. It was nearly four o'clock.

"You do the camp set-up with the group," said Al. "I'd better go and find out about the boat." He walked away, and then ran back. "And mate, don't let them see those notes, eh?"

I set to with my training. It took over an hour to get the cooktent set up and the same again to help everyone with their two-man tents. Al came back with word that we should be at the harbour at 9am. Leaving four rather peeved cooks to start supper, the rest of us walked to the small town.

A national monument, Parati is a Portuguese colonial-built gem. No cars are allowed into the centre and the only buildings taller than a single stone-built storey are four churches. The bars were already packed with Rio weekenders. Getting back for dinner, we found the cookteam sitting on stools around a table of chopped vegetables. They looked annoyed – the gas had run out and I hadn't shown them where to find the lights. Realising I'd been a little hasty with my desire to get to a bar, I set them up, then helped cook. Al went back to the supermarket with two volunteers to stock the bar, which we had also forgotten earlier. Regardless of Al's attempts at entertaining antics, the evening was rather desultory. We both later decided that it was completely our fault – we would have to split responsibilities.

The beautiful town of Parati faces an even more beautiful seascape – a huge lagoon dotted with tree-covered islands, some with enticing white beaches. The boat looked like a pirate ship, and apart from a small group of flashy Brazilian men in white shorts, T-shirts and sailor's caps, we had it to ourselves. While our group sunned themselves at the bow, they sat under a canopy at the stern.

"Caipirinha!" shouted one of the two young boatmen. Tanned and muscular, they looked like Club 18-30 reps and had all the same tricks up their sleeves. "Brazil's sexy drink. It's why there are so many of us!"

Made from Cachaca – a sugar-cane spirit – mixed with fresh limes and crushed ice, caipirinha is extremely powerful, especially when you start at 10am. Very soon the boys had us diving for champagne bottles in the deep clear water, jumping dangerously from the rigging and flashing body parts. Viewing was going even better than Al had expected. We lunched on an island, anchored off a couple more for a stroll through the forests, then lazed on the beach of a final one while the sun went down. Back at camp, everyone was completely pissed and badly sunburnt. Cooking was once more a random affair, but we had had our start-of-trip party, and even earlier than usual. Parati had quickly broken the ice.

A morning truck check revealed a list of complaints developed in only one day's driving. Al and I spent the morning securing the clutch housing, replacing a wheel bearing and fixing a brake-fluid leak. While we were doing that the radiator sprung a leak – the whole thing would have to come out to be welded. For good measure Al had a go at fixing the handbrake, a perennial problem that had been mentioned in the handover notes. His attempt fared no better than previous drivers', however, and the bricks stayed under each wheel. Between trips to and from the town and beach, members of the group passed various polite comments: "Don't you have time for fixing it between trips?" " Is it going to be all right?" and from the same optimist, "There's always teething trouble with new vehicles."

Camping once at a beach and three times at service stations, it took four days of non-stop driving to get to Foz do Iquazu. Service station camping is a Brazilian overlanding norm. They have large grassy areas set by for overnighting or picnicking and often have a Churrasceria on site with a few rooms above it. Brazilian truckers are the main clientele of these roadside establishments, filling up on slabs of char-grilled beef, then climbing upstairs for a night's entertainment from resident ladies. Al formulated a plan for opening such an oasis of indulgence in England. To be called 'Al's Cow and Sex', it would be a winner no doubt.

For us two drivers, the highlight had been more mundane – there was always a well-lit grease pit where we could spend the evening working under the truck in relative luxury. We had now moved on to renewing brake lines, replacing the diff' gasket and sealing holes in the exhaust. Routine maintenance, we told the group.

Straddling the border between Argentina and Brazil, the UNESCO World Heritage designated Iquazu Falls are beautiful and astonishingly powerful. We spent most of the day walking between the viewpoints, and then took a boat-trip

163

to the base of the falls. The enchanting day held further benefit. With evenings spent under the truck, it had been our first proper opportunity to get to know the group.

Annie and Lena had come together. Two vivacious and attractive young Dutch girls, they had just arrived from working at a Radio Station in Curacao. They were both entertaining, but while Annie was a bit dizzy, Lena was quite sensible, almost serious at times. Matthew, an understated but very witty Englishman, had recently left a live-in relationship and a long-term marketing job. He was tall, round to the point of being cuddly and sported a vicious crew cut, a statement of rebellion against his recently curtailed career.

The Stars and Stripes were represented in the shape of David. A law student – what else? – he was sharp and perceptive, to a point anyway. It was he who had twice declared the truck a new one. If he had humour, he hadn't yet shared it with Al and me. Hidden behind his beard, David seemed to me distant, an almost suspicious character. He had found a fast friendship with Phil, another Englishman who preferred his wit cutting and very dry. Phil was fairly quiet, but most of his utterances were well worth waiting for. He too had dropped out, this time from a career in the City, but he hadn't left his prep-school looks at home.

Isabel was instantly noticeable for her beautiful wide smile. It quite simply lit up her face and radiated warmth to those around her. An Aussie doctor, she was as down to earth as her small-town Queensland upbringing would imply and apart from showing a fierce temper at times, promised to be an excellent group member. She had got into the overlanding way quickly, I had noticed – her superb starburst T-shirt, which Al had tried to negotiate a purchase of, had not been changed since the day we left Rio. Her fellow countryman was Kevin, the only one who could possibly be described as 'old', but was probably just forty. He had recently completed the company's longest trip, a year from London to Kathmandu via Africa, and was now on a six-month South American Circle. He was already fed up when he started in Rio but, given his unfortunate reason for being there, he'd probably been fed up when he left London too: in the space of a month he had lost his job and his wife. A short conversation on the topic went like this:

"Oh, I'm sorry. Divorced or deceased?"

"Cancer."

He looked like it would take a lot to make his handlebar moustache turn upwards on a smile.

Our couple were Marco and Barbara. They were from Switzerland, where, as Barbara told me, "all our national products melt: snow, chocolate and cheese." Barbara was constantly amusing and had already become the heart of the group. She was fully involved with everything and always found time to help some more, giving a funny commentary in her half-English as she went. Her boyfriend, Marco, was quieter and quite dry. He tended to let Barbara steal the limelight.

Another Dutch woman was Helga. A real looker too, with enormous piercing blue eyes, she flirted heavily with everyone but had contributed little in terms of group involvement. I thought she might be the first to complain. Unless that accolade went to Aileen. A blond Irishwoman, she looked as if even her house doorbell would emit a growl. So far she had done little but cast dirty glances to and fro.

Sally obviously lived in a world of her own, but it was a place it looked like it would be nice to visit. A stout, jolly, sunny secretary from Croydon, she was another constant worker, apart from when she forgot she was working. A table-wipe would often end in a still hand and wandering eyes, generally skyward. She tended to sit next to Richard, a tall handsome Scotsman – a butcher – with a ready smile and quiet manner. He was taking longer than the rest to open up to the group.

Sam was the group's baby. At 19, he was a pain in the arse from the word go. He babbled constantly, got excited by everything and drank too much. His recently completed public school education had left him ill equipped for such complex tasks as tent erection and plate washing. He always wore black T-shirts, generally Motorhead, Whitesnake and Black Sabbath – groups that seemed old even to me. Given all that, he was very likeable.

Foz forms the apex of a triangle of three borders. After a record-breakingly slow three-hour packup, we crossed into Paraguay over the Friendship Bridge. Compared with an African border, it was ease itself, our passports stamped in seconds by polite officials. What was more difficult was actually driving across the enormous structure. The people in our path, staggering along under loads from electrical goods to car tyres, filled the entire road. At the other end of the bridge, Ciudad del Este was like one big open-air airport terminal, every shop spilling the latest in electronics, perfumes or pallets of booze. Paraguay is duty-free and Ciudad del Este – along with Asuncion, the capital – bases its economy on this fact. We gave everyone an hour to shop. Barbara and Marco, our bartenders, excitedly sprinted into the first offy, while Al and I dived into an electrical store. We both bought altimeter watches of a size that might go well with a gold medallion on the chest. Reflecting our different priorities, I also bought a new truck stereo while Al bought a Gameboy.

From a truck, Paraguay just looks like one big ranch. The whole roadside is fenced with barbed wire behind which fat edible animals roam, faces to the grass. For reasons of communication we had to get to Asuncion in the north, but were also obliged to go south to the Missions, entailing a long drive down and then back up the entire country. On the flat prairies the truck would hold a steady 80kph, but the slightest hint of activity on the truck's hill-detector would cause a dramatic slowdown. We hit a long incline. Bored of the view, duller still at 30kph, I asked Al, "Do you fancy this Mission business?"

"What, being one or going there?"

"Crawling over ruined ruins. I've seen pictures. There's not a lot left, and a Welsh castle is ten times older."

"It's in the brochure, so we go there. Keep driving, you lazy bastard – there's only two roads in Paraguay anyway, and you're half way down one of them."

There were two enthusiasts for the ruins when we got there. David and Kevin had boned up on the history of the Missions, and in a post-dinner rundown had almost created a semblance of group interest. It waned after only an hour of early morning viewing, but we all had to wait another hour and a half, filling ourselves with tea and biscuits, until David and Kevin finally came back to camp. "Jesus Mission next," stated David.

Jesus Mission lies at the end of a long mud road along which there were a few pools of water. Our South American trucks didn't have four wheel drive – it's not generally needed – but somehow I managed to get us stuck in a pitifully small puddle when I pulled over for a piss-stop.

"Nearly as rough as Zaire, eh?" Al remarked.

"I did it on purpose," I lied.

"Nice one – let's stretch it out."

It really wasn't much of a bogging, but Al and I oversaw some considerable excavations. After two hours of digging, the roadside looked like the foundations for a new mission. Afternoon now, Al eased the truck back onto the road to cheers from the group. But it was me, I suppose, who had just created the first group division.

"Either we miss lunch or we miss Jesus," I called to the group. "Can we have a vote?"

"Let's lunch," Matthew urged, heralding a sea of arms up-thrust in agreement.

David came into the cab that afternoon so he could more comfortably read about what he had missed. He made a point of striking up absolutely no conversation.

Argentina is expensive. That was part of the reason for driving straight across it; the other was that in the central prairie, the Pampas, there is very little to see. After five more days driving, the moans inevitably started. Centred mainly on the horrifically low speeds our truck attained, they also concerned our frequent breakdowns. On this occasion, we had simply puttered to a stop on the extremely busy Cordoba ring road.

"We'd be safer on the hard shoulder of the M25!" I shouted above the sound of speeding traffic. The cab was tilted and Al, like me, was looking at the engine, puzzled.

"Yeah, but a lot colder. Where's that pipe supposed to attach?" It was on my side, where trucks were whizzing by inches from my arse.

"It looks like a diesel feed."

"Well, is there any diesel coming out?"

"No, but there is under the filter."

"Well put the fucker back on then."

I had already started fiddling, but the flanged end of the metal pipe had broken off and the nut was gone.

"It won't go on – it's knackered."

"Come here, let's have a look." Showing unusual caution, Al slid around to my side of the truck. "You're right. It's sheared," he agreed. "We'll have to get the group out again."

Whenever we needed spares we had to get into the lockers under the group's seats. Twenty people filed out onto the highway and squashed themselves up against the roadside fence. We found the nut, but it took two hours to put a new flange onto the tough metal pipe, trying every tool we could find until finally bodging it with a hammer and nail. At each failure a hacksaw had shortened the preshaped pipe.

"Al, that'll have to do or it won't reach." Diesel was still dripping, but we bled it through and the truck started. With air in the mixture however, the engine coughed rather than rattled.

"Into town then," Al sighed.

Cordoba centre was even busier than the ring road. Kangarooing and stalling our way through, we eventually found a diesel fitter. With some efficient customisation, he fitted a replacement pipe and we left town. We had woken up 20km before Cordoba and were now camped in a service station only 10km the other side. The group's patience, already thin, had run out. David led the deputation.

"We've written a complaint and I need a name to address it to. It's not about you, but about the truck. I totalled it up. We spent over $50,000 dollars between us, and this is *not* what we bought." Behind him, Kevin, Helga and Aileen stood impassively, adding weight to his proffered missive.

"Hmmm, that's a lot. We could get a new truck with that," I said, feebly trying the humour angle.

"The name please," David repeated, brandishing a biro. I could see the lawyer was in no mood for mediocre jokes, so I chose the Pete acquiescence method.

"Sure, Graham Chatwin. I'll fax it from Santiago for you if you like."

"No, I'll take a copy and post it myself."

As one, the posse turned and marched back to their stools.

167

It was as easy as that! But they had a point. The truck was a disaster and was adding hours onto each day's driving in what was not the most suitable part of the world for an overland trip. Even if we could do nothing about that, we did need to liven things up a bit.

On the map I found a likely looking yellow line heading for a small mountain range. It turned out to be a dirt road, which meandered up through delightful rock formations, giving fine views to all as it switched back and forth. Stopping at a viewpoint at the top, I noted we had scaled 2000m according to my altimeter, 2100 according to Al's – *a discrepancy that needs to be sorted.*

"That's better, eh?" I had sidled up to David. "Beautiful, isn't it?"

"I could have hiked it faster."

The descent down the steep escarpment on the other side was equally dramatic, and for old Sahara hands like myself, the desert after Chepes even more so. At camp under a pinnacle of sandstone, Al and I started on some African stories around the fire. Whenever possible we still insisted on the fire, even though gas was readily available anywhere. Ostensibly it was for the purposes of romantic rough camping, but it was possibly also due to a desire to make things just a little more difficult; to spice up a journey that could so far have been done in a bus; to make it an *overland* trip.

That fact wasn't lost on David. After another few Zaire stories interspersed with Hoggar and Djanet nostalgia, he had once again had enough. Halting our hearty laughter at the end of the Craig's-truck-in-the-Congo story, David interrupted.

"You two really should have stayed there. You didn't like the Missions, you obviously don't like South America and, what's worse, neither of you know anything about the place. And all this fire crap – there's gas sitting right there on the trailer."

I opened my mouth to argue but stopped myself. Again, he had a point. Several in fact. I wanted to say that half the fun of overlanding was the travelling and camping itself, and therefore the open fire. But maybe that *was* an African thing. I did like South America and was especially excited as we would soon reach the Andes. This section, I felt, was like the crossing of Europe during a Trans-Africa: an intro, a benign training ground. As for not knowing anything, he was right. But it was in the spirit of expeditioning to find out – overland leaders often led trips 'blind'. And he was no doubt correct to get annoyed with our rattling on about Africa – that definitely needed curtailing.

David's outburst had been met with silence, the casting down of eyes and the shuffling of feet. Al had got up and walked off, so I put on my best primadonna voice and replied, "Complaints, David, are best off made in private, then written down if you're not satisfied. The name, don't forget, is Graham Chatwin. Anyone for a beer?" Murmuring turned to audible muttering, then at last to full-scale chat again.

"Let's crack open a Gato Negro or two. Cheer us up, eh?" It was Matthew. "You'll join me in a plastic beaker of wine, David?" By the time I had got back with Al, dragged from the cab, the awkward moment had passed. We would have to get David up to the cab the next day to talk it all out.

The open talk didn't get us that far, but the next rough camp did the job for us – although for me it was slightly overshadowed by belligerent canine behaviour. Approaching the Andes the terrain became more fertile, and as in Paraguay was divided up into huge ranches fenced off with barbed wire. This made it difficult to camp. Eventually, however, we came across a gate peopled by a team of seven properly uniformed gauchos on horseback – the real thing, not churrasceria waiters. And they would be delighted to put us up – particularly, they told us upon looking into the truck, as they lived together for months on end and hadn't seen a woman in all that time. "Pobre bastardos!" Al whispered in an aside.

Following their graceful posse down a long track, we arrived at a tumbledown stone building. They pointed us to a circle of large logs placed around a charred patch of ground – camp. While the group set up, the gauchos unsaddled and went inside their house. I went in too, to introduce myself properly; first introducing myself to their dog sitting in the open doorway. It sniffed my hand, moved politely to one side, then bit me, a snarling set of gnashers hanging on to my ankle. The beast had drawn blood. In profusion, in fact. Interrupting their own messy ablutions already taking place, the gauchos washed and dressed my ankle in their filthy kitchen sink.

Later, around the fire, we were charmed by the handsome and grizzly bunch. Still resplendent in their authentic kit, they did indeed make some of the women in the group raise an attracted eyebrow; but with a detectable pong in the air the gauchos' washing facilities weren't working in their favour. Their natural charm even included the provision of dinner. Excellently cowboyish, they served us oats and beans, muddy coffee for afters. I found it an odd choice though; given their job of rounding up cattle from ranches the size of Wales, there wasn't a hint of steak on offer. Maybe they too had gone off the idea of killing their own meat.

The gauchos joined us for breakfast. Following our return gesture – fruit salad, yoghurt and fried eggs, most of which I later found in piles behind the logs – they offered us a burn around the ranch on their horses. David was suddenly ecstatic. Standing up expertly in his stirrups, he set off, whooping like a cowboy. For him, and indeed the rest of us, that ride perfectly sealed the first of many truly memorable South American experiences.

After a day's drive to clear Mendoza, we camped in a spectacular gorge in the Andean foothills. Rising early, we breakfasted through a magnificent sunrise, and then started a long haul up the 4000-meter pass. From the summit we beheld what looked like the whole of Chile, and immediately below us the forty-corner switchback road that snakes down dramatically to Santiago. In overlanding terms that road marks the entrance to an enchanting, fascinating and mind-blowingly beautiful continent. But a decent truck helps. Cautious of hot brakes as ever, particularly our unreliable ones, we descended in our usual second gear. And first for all the corners.

The Hotel Maury is situated right in the heart of Chile's capital. Al and I were just as excited as the group to be in a hotel – a feature of South American overlanding that would rub off on us very quickly. The group paired off for their rooms and organised to have their washing done.

We had arranged to meet at 7pm. Al had found a city guide and proposed a Mexican restaurant. After tacos and a few rounds of caipirinhas, we found a sleazy underground nightclub, which no one left until four. In a boozy haze, David and I shouted apologies at one another and declared the earlier incident forgotten.

While the group slept off hangovers, Al and I took ours to the Post Office by way of one of one of Santiago's many topless coffee bars. It is a strange experience to be served expresso by a pair of shapely breasts at 9am on a bleary-eyed morning, but a pleasant one. Telexing London, I commented on the poor state of affairs with regard to the truck, to which I got the reply:

```
List spares for Quito.   Send immediately.
Concern re faxed complaint from group.
Are you keeping up with maintenance?
```

Maintenance? Are you kidding?!!

We retired to the truck park. Slowly working up to another day's work with rehydrating Cokes, we started with the very lengthy spares list. Later, after organising a horse-riding and rafting trip for the following morning, we went out for another group meal. We all ended up at the same nightclub. In a crowded booth away from the music, Matthew was telling the assembled what he thought of the trip so far.

"….it's not right, it's just not right… and you're so keen not to make a mistake you go downhill slower than you go up it. It's not right."

Unable to control both his laughing and his clenching muscles at the same time, Dan farted loudly between his disjointed words. "And the things we end up talking about, the *detail* we go into – it's just not right. I know every cut of meat you can get from a sheep, a cow *and* a pig – I do – Richard told me; he's a butcher. We talked about it for two whole days." He farted again, the sound of which pushed him further into his hilarity.

Matthew pulled his T-shirt over his head to close us out. His body shook, racked with mirth. As the shirt alternately ballooned and then traced the shape of his wide-open mouth, I could hear him trying to find oxygen between sobs. Evidently taking the opportunity of a minute's personal space to make life-changing decisions, his head suddenly popped out and he planted a kiss on Isabel's lips. Startled – there was a moment's sloppiness while she too puckered up – the response was sincere. We had our first couple. Al came over to hear the reason for the cheer.

"Yaheyyyyyyy – get her T-shirt off, Matt! Then pass it over here – it matches these shorts."

Horse-riding, already a rather painful affair for the behind, was killing my head too. The rafting had been cancelled due to a general lack of stomach stability after a second night's clubbing, but Al was happy. He was showing the first signs of a passion I hadn't noticed in Africa – a love of animals. Galloping to and fro with instant expertise, he exhorted our plodding posse to do the same. By lunchtime he had easily covered four times the distance of the rest of us, and was eager for more. But to his intense disappointment, we voted a curtailment of the longer circuitous route home and turned our nags back in the direction they had come. That night was spent by one and all in an early bed, Matthew and Isabel still in separate rooms.

Like all South American countries, except perhaps Paraguay (Argentina, apparently, gets exciting south of the Pampas), Chile could be explored for months on its own account. Like everyone I knew its shape from the hot fruit that bears its name – one was held up in a singular moment of imaginative resourcing by an otherwise totally unmemorable geography teacher. What I didn't know was its tradition of isolation and its totally unique internal geography.

The fruit in fact provides an insufficient simile for the country's shape. At nearly 4500km long and never wider than 100km, it is more akin to my well-chewed pencil. Straddling numerous temperate zones, Chile boasts nearly every climate and landscape the world can offer. We would cover no more than a third of its length and, in true overlanding tradition, would only skim the surface of what even that small portion had to offer. But when you can stand on an ice-white salt lake in the middle of a huge desert and see the Pacific on one side and some of the highest glaciers in the world on the other, you know you've reached an extraordinary place.

As we drove north through the Cordillera de la Costa, the routine of climbing and descending in the same gear continued unabated for days. Finally reaching the edge of the Atacama Desert, we stared in wonder at the eastern horizon. Before us, a line of perfectly conical snow-capped volcanoes marched into eternity; the tallest, Licancabur, a staggering 6500m, clearly visible in the distance.

Too distant. In recompense, we stopped at a small hill shaped like a suet pudding and finally let David off his leash. He shot off up it. The rest of us, feeling the first effects of thin air, met him on his way back down. He called out that he was off to find another one. From the top I could see the Salar de Atacama, the salt lake shimmering like snow in the distance, but a distinct lack of climbable puddings. Had David had altitude hallucinations at the top? I looked a long way down to see him doing press-ups behind the truck. *A man like him is on the wrong type of trip, poor thing.*

David agreed.

"We've just driven past half of the finest peaks in the Andes, Tim," he puffed huffily when I got down, his words only just decipherable. Fit or not, oxygen is still a prerequisite to successful argument, but he tried. "And I'm pretty damn sure we're gonna do the same in Bolivia and Peru. All you lot want to do is sit around that damn fire drinking your Gato Negro. Why don't we climb one?"

It *was* a desperate shame to be skimming past such a wealth of opportunity. Along with the mountains and salars, the Atacama desert has a fascinating history: its pre-Incan Atacamanian civilisation, said to be over 10,000 years old; its colonial era British mining and railway interests; the torture camps set up in the Pinochet years. Overlanding, however, is more like the organised end of backpacking, and not designed for targeted special interests. We would skim here and we would skim elsewhere too, but we would do the highlights and experience the awesome beauty of travelling off the beaten track in between.

"We haven't got time for a mountain expedition, David, and it's not in the brochure. You've booked an overland trip. You've paid to be driven round seven South American countries in three months. I'd love to climb too, but that comes later, when we do the Inca Trail in Peru."

"Well, I'd be better off backpacking than sitting around on this old truck." David turned, leant against the side and lifted one leg behind him in a stretch.

Reaching a roadside salar at last, we studied the crystalline makeup of the dazzling salt at close range. We touched it and licked our fingers – it really was salt. Beneath the salt was deep mud. This particular flat had a narrow, rocky road built across it, which we followed. In the middle of the salar was a mine; the road's purpose was to facilitate the extraction of lithium, the very stuff that powered our fine wristwatch altimeters.

At San Pedro de Atacama, the group voted themselves an afternoon off to wander around the charming desert town. Of Spanish architecture, it looked as if a pueblo had just been lifted from the Picos de Europa and dropped in the Chilean desert. White shuttered houses lined streets of dust, and the plaza, complete with decorative fountain and little church, was a large sandpit shaded by trees. I went with some of the group to the town's Archaeological Museum, which displays an interesting collection of prehispanic artefacts. It is mainly centred on clay urns containing desiccated but wholly recognisable bodies of

Atacameno people, which had plainly been forcefully stuffed into pots and the lids popped on. They sat with their knees to their chins and their arms folded around them. But grinning! Evidently a hirsute race, they still had very long hair, in dire need of a comb.

Sipping Cokes back in the square, we saw Al running at us, pink shorts flapping, arms pumping and knees to his waist.

"I've found a condor!" he shouted excitedly, skidding to a stop in the dust. "You've got to come and see it!" His animal obsession was evidently growing in proportion to his abstention from women.

In a small lane down a residential street, a fine example of these awesome birds was perched on a wall. The owner, tending his vegetable patch behind the wall, gave Al a dead mouse to feed it. He lobbed it at its feet.

"Look, I think it's eating it."

The bird was clearly doing nothing of the sort, but I didn't want to quash Al's enthusiasm. Faced with such a huge crowd of onlookers, the condor got flustered and spread its wings, flapping them slightly as if warning us not to approach any further. A good nine or ten feet across, it looked like a model aircraft.

As the group drifted off I stayed to watch with Al. Renowned as the most beautiful bird on the wing, condors are members of the vulture family. Circling and hardly ever flapping their wings once they have taken off, they are hated by shepherds as they attack young sheep and goats. Once full of kid, however, they normally find a tree in which to roost, and noosing a snoozing condor is apparently an easy job. Al's friend had obviously been caught napping; the poor thing was chained to a pole, a metal collar around one leg.

The day's final offering was Valle de la Luna. Chile's Moon Valley is a nature reserve that boasts nothing more than a fantastic desert landscape. Where salt mountains have been eroded, pillars and cactus-like statues of rock populate the desert floor. Above this sculpture park the hardier limestone mountains still loom large; they too cut into fantastic shapes, tendrils of rock dripping down the steep sides like candlewax. Such heights are always worth a climb, both for sunset and sunrise – the view, the colours, totally different for each. That evening I climbed up for one of my customary moments alone; one that desert scenery of this order of beauty inspires.

But by the time I reached the same perch for sunrise, Matthew and Isabel were already there. In fact, they were in sleeping bags. I couldn't imagine a more romantic way to conduct a courtship – until they were surrounded by fourteen people, with Sam jabbering inane innuendo, such was his excitement at the thought of what may have taken place there. With a dark purple haze turning orange, then red, then yellow, before disappearing to leave the original purple painted on the mountains, we all sat watching in silent rapture. The sun up, Matthew told us to 'fuck off' while he replaced his underpants.

In an effort to entertain David, a day off was granted and the group went off on their separate little journeys of self-discovery. Even Isabel and Matt split up for, I fancied, some contemplation of their happy circumstances. Moon Valley is a far cry from the outback doctoring and city marketing they had left behind, but both appeared to have found what they didn't even know they'd come looking for – at that moment perhaps personifying one real purpose of overlanding. Certainly the best result.

Instead of such worthy contemplation, Al and I crawled under and over the truck. This time a speedo cable, a worn kingpin and an oil-change. Nursing another bump on my well-dinged head, I added to the spares list we were to telex from La Paz – 'mechanics hat'. I didn't know exactly what I was looking for, but I assumed real mechanics suffered similarly from the myriad robust protrusions on a truck chassis.

Calama, the local capital, is an industrial town, but still charming due to the surrounding desert. As we pulled in we noticed that every other shop was flashing a bright yellow neon chicken at passers-by. At the time, therefore, Calama was proclaimed Chicken and Chips Capital of the World. It would soon be usurped. We had all been off truck-food a bit due to altitude sickness, so were hungry. I pulled up outside a parade of three pulsating, plastic birds, aiming for the apparent efficiency inherent in splitting our large number between them. Irritatingly, the plan was to little avail – in each shop the fry-up was started from scratch with each person's order. The time wasn't completely wasted though. In one of the three queues I pondered with happiness that we had discovered the cure for altitude sickness, which has dogged the medical world for aeons: head downhill.

The supermarket was better prepared and we stocked up. Half a dozen baskets were filled with five days' worth of food, another half, Gato Negro. I also slipped in a few of our favourite sweets that had replaced Ugandan Cadbury's. Golpe Bars are like Lion Bars, only inexplicably nicer, while Dinovos are just what they say they are – bubble gum dinosaur eggs. Delicious.

Ready for them there mountains…

We left in the dark next morning to get to El Tatio for the early morning geyser show. The rocky track up to their elevated position at 4,600m was torturous, the truck gasping for oxygen to help fire its limp-dick pistons in and out of their slack-muscled cylinders. Al, myself and in fact the entire group bar David and Kevin, were in an even worse state, never having gone to real altitude before.

Acclimatisation at 3000m does nothing for passing the 4000m threshold – as our alti-alarms simultaneously informed us we just had. I didn't know which was going to collapse first – me, Al or the truck, the wheel of which Al was wrestling with to get it over large boulders reminiscent of Algeria's dreaded Fadnoun.

"I feel fucking terrible," Al whispered, his voice cracking in the dry air. "And they've all got their eyes shut in the back – except David, who's taking snaps of rocks again."

"Can I have some headache pills?" Lena, our passenger of the day, enquired through thin lips.

"We've used them all. There's more in the back," Al replied.

"Don't worry." She shut her eyes and leant against the closed window, bashing her head with each lurch of the truck. We drove on.

"I know what its like to be a fly," I mumbled, trying to find anything to take our minds off the misery.

"Righto," murmured Al, looking dead ahead.

"Really, we did it in biology at school. They look through a series of tunnels. It's called compound vision, I think. The only difference is, with tunnel vision you've only got one to look down."

"Sure … oh, fuck an arse … I think I'm going …," Al did a precision vomit out of the window, clearing even the doorframe "… to be sick." He spat out the last few chunks.

"Can you drive?" he asked, wiping the back of his hand across his mouth. With her eyes still shut, Lena chuckled, then grimaced as her head echoed a particularly good thud.

"What? While I'm looking down the wrong end of a telescope? You'll be lucky."

"Fuck it then, I'm turning back."

While he turned the truck and trailer around in the narrow track, using a succession of tiny shuffles, I informed the group through the hatch separating us from the back. Actually only two of them – everyone bar David and Kevin were asleep. With their cameras poking out of the window, confusion mounted on their faces at the prospect of missing yet another mountainous delight. I was feeling so dizzy I couldn't even manage any explanation.

"It just can't be done. Sorry, we'll explain later."

From Calama onwards our watches, still in perfect harmony, had turned from toys to tools. The difference between camping at 3,500m and 4,000m is cold but comfortable on the one hand, hypothermia and heaving on the other. After following the Loa Valley – the last glimpse of green where a deep arable gorge cuts a swathe through the dark mountains – the dirt road starts climbing in earnest. Up and up, cresting hills and dropping into valleys, crossing sandy windswept pampas and passing mini-salars like frozen village ponds. With the backdrop of perfect volcanoes framed against a blue sky marking the border with Bolivia in the distance, we jolted along in a mountainous wasteland. No public transport would have taken a backpacker along such a route, one of wholly dramatic beauty.

Rounding a corner in the expectation of another empty vista as far as the eye could see, we were stopped by a pole-in-the-road, the first I had seen since Nigeria. The officials, as Al found out when he leapt out for a dog-hug, were much friendlier than either their canine companions or their African pen friends. They offered us a camp for the night, indicating a large shed in which their Landcruisers were parked. They looked downcast when we said we wanted to keep moving. A god-forsaken spot, theirs truly must have been the bottom of the hardship-posting list.

Further on, at Buenaventura, just before the Bolivian border, we found the dip our alti-alarms were set to look for; they beeped furiously near a disused mine at the bottom of a depression. An old man on guard provided the only sign of activity. He let us set up camp in the defunct mine's Social Club.

The old man was still at his post when I approached him in the morning. He was dressed the same, but with the addition of a trilby hat. I asked directions for the border. In a long drawn-out ramble, a pipe bouncing with each word, he basically pointed out the only road there was. Feeling a little stupid for asking, I listened politely while he finished his explanation. He stopped for a puff on his pipe. I was just about to sidle off when he squinted into the sun and continued, "When you come back, just do the opposite."

"Thanks, I'll remember that." Wise words. After all, I would indeed be seeing it all from the other direction at some point. More usefully, I made a note of the fact that his job seemed to be centred round the beady-eyeing of a pile of telegraph poles. For a few pesos they would make fine firewood and chopping therapy.

Our notes had warned us, but we'd chosen not to take any notice. In fact, our trip notes were full of warnings between there and Uyuni, the first town we would reach in Bolivia:

Great caution ... Salar de Uyuni ... salt crust tends to break, deep mud underneath ... 4 day bogging ... deep floods in wet season ... electrical short-circuit ... corroded seals, rusting engine ... mudflats worse than salar itself ... extremely low temperatures ... test river crossing on foot ...altitude sickness.

On and on they went, leaving no room for forward motion of any sort. So it seemed best to ignore it all. Either that or turn back.

The specific warning in question was that no vegetable products would be allowed across the border. We knocked up the border officials who inhabited a railway station. An infrequent locomotive runs between Calama and Uyuni but no one I had heard of had ever seen it; with the local population as sparse as the landscape around us, it was hardly commuter belt.

Immigration were the epitome of politeness, but, with the efficiency of all Chilean officials I had so far met, insisted on removing our stock of fresh veg. On further inspection they found our wood under the roof-tarp, which they said fitted into the 'vegetable' bracket.

"Please offload your wood and place it there." The man pointed to a patch of sand, black with soot.

"But we need it, it's freezing up here," I replied, clapping my hands around my shoulders for emphasis. The campfire had by now become a very popular part of the evening, even David now turning his nose up at the gas cooker.

"It's not allowed across the border."

"But we're going *out* of the country. What's the problem?"

"We have an agreement with Bolivia. They don't want disease to cross into their country either."

"What diseases? It's *wood*."

"Please unload it. Many thanks." He turned away.

You can't argue with polite assertiveness, so off it came. I thought perhaps it might account for the pile of telegraph poles, but they did indeed burn it. Even if we were foodless and fuelless, it was an overwhelming delight to meet evidently incorruptible officials, South America's most striking contrast to Africa so far.

A useful hint in our trip notes was to bypass the Bolivian border post – a track circled behind it – in preference for completing formalities with less hassle in Uyuni. But what about this? Here were the directions in our notes for crossing 200km of almost uninhabited, high-altitude, muddy, salty wilderness:

Follow deep tracks and edges always. Follow railpoles. Military camp 20k – can camp in igloos. Drunkards. Village with duckpond another 20k ENE. At two o'clock ranges going E-W, keep on left. Clump of 3 bushes left 20k. Left at graveyard. Follow road 7k. Road moves away ESE to follow line of hills across bog. See caves. Looking west = mountain. 10k low hills to East 25k = Rio Grande. Turn right to SE, then E. Ridges either side. 15k, low ridge on right. Follow track. Sharp left to E. 7k. Cross river. Hug sand at edge 9k. See river on R. Tracks cross deep mud. 15k junction, right. 2K = causeway. 3k SE End range. Switch N of low hill. Main road. Mud. Hills disappear. To Uyuni.

We had stopped where the border-dodging track split into three. Al read the directions to the group, and then passed them to me. I lit them, and from the flame a Marlboro.

"Could be a day, could be two, or could be a week," Al drawled in his best Deep South G.I. "Think of this as your South American Zaire experience everyone. When you get back you'll be able to tell your folks at home long stories of your own. The only thing we do know is that the Salar itself is flooded and we can't get across. That also means deep mud. No questions? OK, let's go, Go, GO!" John Belushi in 'Animal House' style, he charged round to the passenger door, fist stretched before him.

"You didn't give much of a chance for questions," I grinned from the driver's seat.

"Less said the better in some circumstances, eh? Which way are you going?"

"Let's see what happens down this one." We looked at two deep truck-width ruts in the mud and started our bumpy journey, the Theme Tune tape pounding out Rugby Special.

In the event, it wasn't too bad. The mud was slimy in places, but rarely deep. Many of the tracks went across the said 'sandy edges' where a few blades of pampas grass struggled for survival. We saw the 'igloos' well in the distance, but no 'railpoles'. We did get bogged in a riverbed as warned, and it took two hours to get out, as the bank was so steep. Immediately after that, however, we joined the three kilometre-long causeway. Made of piled-up salt, it traversed an especially muddy section of the flats. As we reached the end another truck joined it, the only one we had seen in days. I flashed it to go back but it came on at us, and then tried to squeeze past. Wrong, as there was blatantly no room for two trucks. In fact the driver just drove calmly off the edge into a ditch.

"What the hell did he do that for?" I cried as the driver suddenly disappeared from sight. Only inches apart, we had been looking at each other through our respective cab windows.

"Dunno, but he was smiling," Al said in admiration. "Did you see him? All grins, then whoosh, he was gone! Silly fucker."

"We can't leave him there, he'll never get out."

"Well, the causeway's dryer than anywhere else. Why don't we camp?"

Leaving room for manoeuvre, we stretched our tents out along the narrow dyke. While the cooks worked out what to make without vegetables, the rest of us set to unloading a truckfull of floursacks. They were as heavy as cement bags, and at 3700m great effort was required to move each one. The cooks served tepid tea – water was now boiling at below 90° – and we finished the job in the dark.

After a very cold and windy night I roused everyone early with the Bolero. It sounded wonderful floating across the wide-open spaces when I went for my early morning spade session. Squatting, I watched as Al hitched the fallen truck up to ours and gently pulled it up onto the causeway. The smiling driver made it clear he fancied a spot of breakfast before heading off on his way. I knew why he was hungry, because we all were. Boiling spaghetti at altitude is a non-starter, and the previous night's dinner now formed a large spiral pile on the causeway. Our breakfast of boiled eggs fared no better; they were still runny after eight minutes. He seemed happy though. In fact, judging by his perma-grin, the entire incident had bothered the gentleman not a jot.

Falling into bad South American habits so soon after being posted there, I booked us into a hotel the minute we reached Uyuni. It was cheap, dirty and we shared a dorm. But it had hot showers and central heating.

Annie and Lena took me on a tour of the little 3600m town. Considering its position, literally in the middle of absolutely nothing, Uyuni is a surprisingly busy place, much of the trade being in moving contraband goods to and from Chile. Immediately noticeable were the amount of people of indigenous descent. More than in any other Latin American country, Bolivians have kept their indigenous cultural traditions alive. It was interesting to see the Indian women in traditional Andean dress: wide skirts, heavily pleated shirts and colourful shawls. They are short and tend towards roundness, so their bowler hats – a female fashion I hadn't beheld before – top off their body shape nicely. Their facial features aren't pretty in the traditional western sense, but their sturdy frame was flattered by a ruddy, red flush over taut brown skin. They looked permanently exerted. I found out later it was sunburn.

One such lady was running a stall in the black market that specialised in confectionery. To one side I spotted a pile of Golpes and Dinovos. Strangely, they were cheaper than in the Calama supermercado, so I bought a box of each as a present for Al. To cheer him up. Shouldering the major worries of keeping the truck alive – he would have to take it north, then round through the Amazon too – he had become significantly quieter of late.

The true Chicken and Chips Capital of the World is, in fact, Potosi. At first storey level the streets are an Oxford-St-at-Christmas of flashing 'pollos'. It is also the place where more pisco is drunk than anywhere else in the world, even though it is Peru's national drink. Between gorging themselves thus, Potosi residents play table football. Ranks of petite footballers skewered on poles fill halls like pool balls would in the States. Even after drinking numerous pisco sours to garner the skilled wrist-action their imbibing evidently gave the locals, Overland All-Comers were whooped every time.

Getting to Potosi had entailed another day's drive from Uyuni. The permanent incline was indicated as usual by the speed of the truck, but was more graphically validated by the mapping function I had found whilst fiddling with my altiwatch. Instantly jealous, Al had made me swap seats and drive so he could get his alti-graph working too.

The Highest City of its Size in the World, Potosi is nigh on impossible to walk around. Not because of crowded streets or over-peopled pavements, but simply because it is very hilly and we were very breathless. It was all we could do to climb to three neighbouring establishments on the main street – the pollo-shop, the pisco-soureria and the table-footy hall – and entertain ourselves in the local tradition. Even the hotel was hilly. Connecting the three storeys on one side, one on the other, ramps had been built instead of staircases. The views were tremendous, the rooms delightful, but with the ramps creating a central atrium off which doorways opened to all the rooms, it felt like Pentonville nick. We clanked mugs and hollered to one-another from opposing railings. Overlanders must surely

179

irritate all other travellers when they descend on a hotel. But for those involved, group travel is much more fun.

Potosi's more traditional claim to fame is its mines, an enduring enterprise that gave the city its fine colonial buildings and now its status as a UNESCO World Heritage Site. The mountains surrounding it were said to be made of silver when the Spaniards arrived. Finding the myth true, they put many thousands of local people to work, ensuring them an early death in horrific conditions. The silver has gone – it built much of 17th century Spain too – but some locals still work co-operatively to mine small quantities of tin, zinc and lead. It still often leads to an early death, of blacklung or general poverty.

Armed with armfuls of coca leaves and sticks of dynamite as gifts to the impoverished workers, we went on a tour below ground. The lack of oxygen is compounded by the intense heat underground, so the miners chew coca leaves for energy, rubbing wads held in their mouths against a stone placed behind the gum. We tried it. Revolting. It also apparently helps with the effects of dehydration, but we had cleverly brought water to counteract that phenomenon.

Positively medieval in their functioning, the Potosi mines are no place for the claustrophobic. The tunnels are often little higher than a metre, and descents between levels are undertaken by climbing down long ladders through pitch-dark body-width shafts. A keen crowd, we asked for, and were treated to, the fourth and most difficult level. Getting there entailed a gymnastic walk over a slippery beam above a three-metre drop before reaching a knotted rope that disappeared directly down into hell. Helga and David had declined Level 4, deciding to wait for us at Level 3. Sensibly, Barbara and Marco hadn't come at all.

Hell was where the dynamiting went on in a suitably furnace-like heat. Passing our remaining gifts forward along our line, our guide handed the dynamite to the Level 4 miners. The five of them had been working in a constant harmonic rhythm, knocking heavy hammers against long chisels. They sniffed at the dynamite before discarding it into a pile uncomfortably close to the candles that vaguely lit their work. The guide translated their gruff thanks:

"Bolivian shit. Argentinean is better."

I had been told this by the stallholder where we bought it but, lacking the nose for such distinctions, I had assumed he was simply trying to rip me off.

"They're blowing in a minute," the guide continued.

"Great, where's the safety area?" I asked.

"This is the fourth level." His eyes said the rest.

The eleven of us moved to the back of the small cave and crouched down not five metres from the action. That the miners just stood to one side gave me confidence; that the guide picked his way to the back of our group worried me...

Boom!

That was no Bolivian shit.

While earth fell down on our plastic helmets, a pitiful nod to safety if ever there was one, our ears accustomed themselves to not having to bother with their job any longer.

"Are you all right?" David mouthed when we had finally got everyone back up the rope ladder to Level 3. He said more, but my lip-reading couldn't follow the American shape of his words.

Back outside an hour later, ears recovered slightly, we yelled with survivors' happiness, hugging each other like successful sappers. The guide threw his arms around me, grinning like a wild man.

"You like fourth level? It's the first time I stay for blow there. Very good, yes? Third level no good. There is safety gallery. No good."

It's not far from Potosi to Sucre, a little over 160km, but it's a long way *down*, Sucre lying at only 2700m. The Andean buses that overtook us with on-the-dot regularity every hour did so at noticeably high speed, even had David not been in the cab comparing theirs to ours. The classic mountain road – high cliffs on one side, precipitous drops on the other – was covered in loose gravel. Piles of the stuff had gathered at the outer edges of the sharp corners, pushed there by the wheels of the lost back-ends of skidding buses. Local buses now use these heaps to stay on the road. I wondered which unfortunates had had to take the necessary risk in starting the virtuous circle.

The switchback bends beheld another strange phenomenon worth noting. Perhaps faithful to deceased owners long removed from numerous rusting bus carcasses, mournful-looking hounds manned each corner. Always black, always immobile, and always on their own. After Al stopped to go for his customary cuddle, they were quickly named Bolivian Ghostdogs – by the time he'd got around to their side of the truck, his chosen hug had disappeared.

"They certainly have the manner of ghosts" – Al was story building – "for starters, what the fuck do they eat?" We had seen nothing but rock and gravel for hours.

That question was answered on the discovery of the first Bolivian Ghostdog Café. The establishment, nestled behind concrete-filled oil drums, was sensibly built on the inside of a corner. Happy black dogs gambolled outside it, quickly joined by Al who rolled in the dust with them. Inside – out of pristine mugs – we drank coffee that could have usefully tarred the road, but there was no evidence of previous human custom, not even chairs. The subsequent two roadside cafes were similar. We checked.

"Perhaps they're training camps," Al mused, looking back and waving at the mutts. "I wouldn't mind running one, in fact."

While the buildings of Sucre gave us an attractive first impression of the city, the receptionist at the Hotel Bustillo did not. Although he was polite and quickly found rooms to cater for our now complex requirements of double singles, singles, double doubles, straight doubles and triples, he had a nauseating habit. Whilst talking he would pick at scabs on his scalp. I knew it was scabs and not just an itchy-head situation because he would produce them on the end of a fingernail, examine them for, I don't know, size? texture? Then pop them in his mouth. Talking normally throughout the preliminaries, his speech would then become incomprehensible as he ground the crispy ex-cut between centre teeth.

"Salt with that, Sir?" Al asked. "Or vinegar perhaps?"

"Eh?"

"Nada – don't worry. Can I have our key please, I'm feeling a bit ill." He went to our room.

Apart from the natural gravitations and groupings that dictated the moveable feast of room division policy, I was presented with a fresh request for a straight double by an unforeseen coupling. Perhaps it was the long nights of plotting over quill and parchment during the Disillusioned Days, or the feeling of mutual abandonment brought on when they thought we'd exploded in the mines, but David and Helga chose that moment to announce themselves 'together'. It was a rather shy announcement. While the receptionist continued picking his way through our complicated list with the same diligence he applied to his hair, mumbled voices, accompanied by much stroking of beard and batting of blue eyes, asked me to keep it quiet.

"Of course," I confided.

I couldn't *wait* to tell everyone. Especially Al.

With some of the afternoon still to spare, Al and I went back to the truckpark. We had earlier ferried the group from there by taxi. UNESCO has declared Sucre a Patrimonio Historico y Cultural de la Humanidad, and somewhere in that lot lies a ban on city-centre heavy traffic. The official capital of Bolivia – La Paz is the commercial capital – it is another jewel of South America. Low colonial-built buildings, all a uniform whitewash, are set out in a grid pattern dating from the 17th Century. I was hoping to explore it all, but Al was thinking otherwise. As we looked at our sorry mode of transport, he listed the current truck problems; by now, even the Rio paintjob had succumbed to the Andes' punishing roads.

"The whole air system's gone haywire – we need to check it right through and definitely replace the governor and pressure-release valves; that pipe's dripping diesel again; the injectors need servicing, and if you ask me the steering's up the spout." The endless mechanicing was tiring and I didn't want it to further subdue Al. For both our sakes I really didn't fancy it and made it known.

"Did you or did you not successfully drive around some corners back there?" I asked.

"Yeah, but ..."

"Are there or are there not garages with good mechanics in the capital of Bolivia?"

"Yes, but we …"

"Correct, Al. We're going to get a taxi and find one. You need a rest. Come on."

Acquiescence wasn't instant, but with reminders that restaurant research needed to be done and that we could peruse for new music in the pirate tape shop I had seen, I got my way. We found a Volvo workshop with a well broomed, red painted, football-pitch sized concrete floor and a team of enthusiastic mechanics in matching red overalls. The latter was particularly encouraging, but that the guard dog was happy to be cuddled sealed the decision. The truck moved in.

It needed three days intensive surgery due to "muchas problemas", but with new injectors and a totally serviced engine, a quick stamp on the accelerator heralded an unprecedented surge of power. The whole brake system had been refitted with our own spares and they had found chassis cracks that needed welding. A snip at $300. We had supervised much of the work, but from above rather than scalp-scrapingly below. Between times, along with the group, we had played.

Our favourite spot was the market just near the Bustillo. Downstairs, Bolivian men ran fruit, veg and meat stalls, while upstairs women held the reins of power. Each rather bulbous lady presided over a small kitchen in one corner of a concrete-walled square hosting three tables. They cooked what they would cook at home, and every man, woman and child in town ate there in shifts.

Breakfast was our favourite; empanadas, eggs and sweet coffee served with typical market-traders' patter, most of it unintelligible but judging by the smirks it created on the other customers' faces, mainly dirty. The atmosphere was fantastic and as regulars, we were soon welcomed like old friends. The tape shops stocked everything from the 80s – a fine musical era, in my opinion – and many Mexican and Chilean crooners, though the one's we picked weren't as good as we'd often heard.

Evenings were spent in a Mexican, an Argentinean – even more beefy than a Churrasceria – and, the best, a Swiss restaurant. The Cactus served 'rushdie' – which caused a great clamour from Barbara and Marco – and cheese fondues. Delicious. But as always with that complicated method of eating, I applied a hot piece of melted Gruyere to the roof of my mouth, leaving it blistered for days.

Thankfully we couldn't find a club, although we did find a cinema playing early Dracula movies. Black and white already, and with lamentable projection, the image supposedly on the screen was undetectable. We joined in the Mass Screaming from the crowded auditorium as well as their Howls of Laughter – an enlightened way of movie watching and much more entertaining than Leicester Square Odeon for all its techno-clobber.

Inspired by fine dining in Sucre and perhaps egged on by me at the market, Matthew decided to break new overlanding culinary barriers on our first rough camp out of town. The setting was superb: a confluence of two shallow rivers in a wide sandy valley provided an excellent beach. The surrounding tree-lined hills rose up in waves of ever increasing height, giving us an endless vista despite our low-lying position. The only blot on the horizon was an audible one – Sam's turn had come round for music. Europe's appalling 'Final Countdown' was playing hard; worse still, in the original German version.

"Rignons," Matthew announced, holding a bubbling pan of suspicious looking brown lumps. "Kidneys for the not-so-savvy. Queue up on my left. I'm serving so we'll all get a fair share. No squabbling now."

The rumour had already spread that we had innards for dinner, and Matthew's offer was met with almost universal refusal. Marco and Barbara, Al and I, and Sam, who would eat anything as long as he didn't have to cook it, queued as instructed.

"Come on now, roll up. This puts the 'haute' in French cuisine." Matthew was waggling the meal in what he hoped was an enticing manner. Isabel peered into the pan and screwed up her nose.

"It looks like it's made from disgusting parts of unidentifiable things. I've seen nicer looking meat in surgery."

His new love was clearly not impressed either.

Those who would ate lavish portions, while the others chewed on stale empanadas – never nice after 11 o'clock. Upon finishing, Al got up and climbed to the top of the truck. Curious eyes followed him. He bent double, and then took a deep breath as he stood up again.

"Heeeeeeere, doggy, doggy, doggy." The sound echoed around the valley walls for some time. As it did so, Al sucked in more air. "Come on churros, venga a Papa." Then, with fingers in his mouth, he whistled piercingly. Others joined him. Soon, it sounded like England had just beaten Germany in, well, anything. Unbelievably, a dog arrived. One mangy hound, loping up the river-bed.

"Who are _you_, Al?" Richard piped up unexpectedly in his Scottish burr, "Doctor bloody Dolittle?"

The dog ate the lot – every rignon – licked its lips, wagged its tail then honked it all back up again. With a double take like he couldn't believe his luck, the hungry dog set to once more.

"Aaaah. So good he ate it twice," cooed Matthew with satisfaction.

Behind the wheel was without doubt the best seat in the truck over the next three days. Almost non-stop driving, and slow progress, it was nonetheless another consistently dramatic and exciting route.

Sucre's engine improvements hadn't lasted long in terms of power, but we were breaking down less. The Volvo mechanics had advised a total engine re-build, but that was impossible on the road and would be difficult even in Quito with only a week's turnaround time. After camping at the confluence we had joined the road that ran down one of the two valleys. Cut directly into the mountainside several hundred metres above the river, it followed every contour of the rugged cordillera, offering a permanently glorious view of jagged Andean peaks. At best a truck width wide, there were no gravel humps edging the road to protect us from any steering errors. If you got it wrong, you flew first, and then died.

As every bend was blind I started cautiously, but after a while I realised I could see ahead and spot any oncoming traffic – the odd bus or truck – up to fifteen minutes in advance across wide valleys. Once I'd let a vehicle pass I could put my foot down, swinging into the bends with absolute confidence that nothing would be on the other side filling the road. Lena had her hands in front of her eyes. Al was dying for a go.

"Not till after lunch, and it's only eleven," – I was having a whale of a time – "come to think of it – get the Golpes out." I spat my tasteless wad of Dinovo out of the window.

"Mind those overhangs. They're getting lower," Al's mouth advised before being stuffed with a whole Golpe bar. I glanced up at the rock face and judged us still safe widthwise. Al poured the coffee – it had taken some time for us to realise that Thermos flasks were in ready circulation in South America's economy. Mug in my left hand, I turned a sharp right-hand corner with the other.

With a tremendous bang and a piercing metallic screech followed by lengthy clanking, I dropped my coffee and grabbed the wheel with both hands. I con-trolled the violent lurch caused by bouncing off the rock, then pulled to a stop. Lena was screaming. Al was too, but it was muffled by wafer.

"Don't scream with your mouth full Al. It's disgusting."

"Schhuck chhou!" Specks of wafer flew at me.

"We lost the tent poles," I confirmed. Out of the window, I could see the metal holder bent back, relieved of its duties.

"Chew losh the shucking poles eh?" – with a huge gulp Al swallowed the Golpe whole, his eyes nearly popping out of his head – "any hands or faces stuck on the rocks out there too?"

"Shit, I forgot about that." I leapt out.

The group were all fine, if a little shocked. We retrieved the poles and put them up on the roof with the wood. Setting off again, I asked Lena to refrain from mentioning that the incident may have been connected with a mobile coffee break.

At 2500m, Cochabamba, the 'breadbasket of Bolivia', has a very pleasant climate. The area forms the geographical centre of the country and its rich soil also makes it the centre of agriculture. Driving through the Cochabamba Valley we passed fields of wheat, grazing cows, fruit orchards and vast vegetable plots. We were there just long enough to remember what warmth felt like before we started climbing again, heading for La Paz, the Highest Capital in the World, which lies in a canyon below the freezing 3700m Altiplano. This barren and windswept plateau, formed by sediment washing off the eastern and western chains of the High Andes it lies between, is actually a basin. Infrequent rain never finds its way to the sea and collects in shallow lakes, many of which evaporate into saltpans like the huge Salar de Uyuni we had crossed. Aymara Indians still scratch a living up on the Altiplano, mainly herding llamas and alpacas, but also succeeding against the odds to grow a little grain.

We hit roadworks. South American roadworks are in a different league from their European counterparts. They often mean a total rebuild. The road, they told us, would be shut until 6pm, by which time we would have had to camp anyway. Driving back down to the Cochabamba Valley, I found a grassy meadow by a cool shallow river. *Perfect. One more warm night.*

While some swam and others started an early dinner, I joined Barbara on one of our photography expeditions. I had long struck up a good translingual banter with Barbara, particular concerning her penchant for photographing the minutiae of South American life – I had never once seen her snap a person or the land-scape. On this occasion a butterfly, a cactus, a wild red flower and some llama shit were all captured for posterity.

Hearing familiar voices in the tall grass by the river, we crept up on David and Helga, giggling with our intention to spy on them. David was talking: "Blah blah… and the Potosi mines were like a daytrip through a sewer with shit for lunch... blah blah blah ... the truck's still all broken up, and Tim nearly drove us off a cliff …blah… I say we leave in La Paz, get our money back and do it on our own – don't worry, I can sue 'em." My giggling stopped.

"We were nowhere *near* the cliff," I hissed. Barbara clapped a hand over my mouth.

"OK, but let's just try it from La Paz to Cuzco first," I heard Helga say. "If we don't like it we can meet them there."

"Sure, but I'm faxing my complaint from La Paz so we're covered."

Sue us?… Slimeball fuckin' lawyers.

186

Forewarned is forearmed. Back at the truck, I wrote out an Incident Report, a normally rather neglected part of our paperwork kit.

Back up on the Altiplano next day, we had to stop when we got a puncture. While the two of us struggled with breaking the wheelnuts at altitude, the group watched a game of football. On a desolate village pitch with llamas wandering around as commonly as sheep in Wales, the locals sprinted to and fro with no apparent difficulty. They're a hardy bunch up there. By the time we'd finished it was too late to get to La Paz, but the closer we got to the capital the more populated the Altiplano became. We ended up camping by a village, something it was usually prudent to avoid.

This was a red village – others had been either red or blue. With some sort of election going on, two parties appeared to have split the vote on a village-by-village basis across the whole district, support indicated by party colours. It's quite a normal electioneering method, even in the UK, but here absolutely everything was spray-painted in one colour or the other. Red llamas nibbled at the grass by our tents; a pack of friendly red dogs came for a nose about; the town secretary came out of his red house in a red costume to ask for money for our stay. Unlike the dogs, he was remarkably unfriendly.

"He wants a hundred bollies a head," I called across to Al, who was still sitting in the cab.

"I know, I heard – that's too much. It's only a patch of red grass covered in red llama shit."

"I'll give you fifty," I said to the secretary. He nodded.

"Give him the worn notes," Al advised. Worn, torn or holed notes had proved impossible to shift – it would be a good opportunity to get rid of them. The secretary refused. He disappeared and then came back with a small army of angry-looking farmers holding rakes and hoes like bayonets.

"Fuck me. Watt Tyler's back with the boys!" Al exclaimed, having seen them first.

"They look a bit annoyed," I observed.

"You're right, hombre. You were doing so well – you talk to them." He wound up the cab window, then pressed a fleshy nose and wet lips against the glass.

I argued for a short time, but it quickly escalated to the incomprehensible. Shouting above the clamour, by now willing to pay up with good notes as gardening equipment was being waved around dangerously, I tried to restart negotiations from scratch.

"Listen, sorry. I don't know what your problem is, but let's work something out," I pleaded. Suddenly it went quiet, and I was just congratulating myself on my evident gravitas, even in Spanish, when I noticed the entire crowd looking past me as if I no longer existed. Following their eyes with my own, I saw they were looking at Al. The cab window was down again now. Just a little though. In fact, just enough to be filled with Al's head. Sideways on, he was grimacing in pain as he slowly crushed his face in the narrowing gap.

"Que es el problema?" I repeated. It took a moment or two to get their attention, but the atmosphere felt significantly less confrontational when the secretary eventually spoke again..

"Problema? Problema aqui!" He was pointing at the truck. Sky blue and still shiny following a good hosedown at the Sucre workshop, I realised it clashed rather violently with the surrounding buildings, animals and clothing.

"No. No." I wagged my finger. "Somos touristas." I ran to fetch a brochure. As I showed the secretary photographs of other bright blue trucks and their happy inmates traversing his wonderful continent, he slowly got the message and began laughing. Al then appeared with two bottles. The men accepted our liberal offerings of pisco and, when they finally left many party political toasts later, the dirty notes.

If I had thought Potosi a city steeped in steep streets, then La Paz made it look like a Fenland town. Attempting to park outside the Hotel Continental on a narrow street that resembled a cobbled cliff, my customary method of remaining stationery without a functioning handbrake failed. Even with the front wheels at 45° to the high kerb we rolled up it when I let the footbrake off, straight into the hotel's low surrounding wall. Four breezeblocks, lifted from the damage, secured us long enough to hustle the group inside.

As we'd been warned in our notes, the traffic police were on our backs in seconds – reasonably so, as we had blocked a whole street of this incredibly busy city, so that the resulting cacophony of klaxons sounded like it was under imminent attack from cruise missiles. Having fought my way back through the traffic, I drove back up the long hill – the single route into town to and from the Altiplano – the road running parallel to the railway track. Up there, a full hour away, I reached the nearest truckpark.

From the lip of the Altiplano I could see why parking a truck was impossible and driving one so difficult. La Paz sits in a deep bowl, the bottom of which is entirely full of city. Builders had erected dwellings as far up the sides as possible, but at some point had inevitably reached vertical where gravity put the mockers on further development. By any estimate La Paz was already at capacity but poor campesinos still kept arriving, rattling down into the bowl by the bus and train-load. Due to the near impossible farming conditions on the Altiplano, many have had to leave their traditional homes for the big city.

Every one of them was friendly. Not normally tempted into souvenirs, that night I found myself with Matthew and Phil buying llama-wool jumpers, colourful waistcoats and stupid hats from the campesinos-turned-craft-sellers who manned stalls parked on every inch of pavement. With the legs of their stalls crafted to the exact height required for keeping their particular textile display horizontal – two short, two long – the availability of the same pitch the following morning was guaranteed. The ruddy-cheeked women laughed and joked while they held up mirrors, and didn't mind at all if we walked away without buying anything.

Al and I were in the queue for the Post Office first thing in the morning. Finally getting inside, I had faxed London with the parts request and Incident Form, writing on the cover sheet that we would telex live in fifteen minutes. Al, meanwhile, had queued for the Post Restante. There was nothing for either of us.

"Right. That's fucking it. Me and Barbara. In my bed. Tonight," Al announced, hands on hips when he joined me in the telex queue, my third excruciatingly lengthy line-up that morning.

"You might have to let Marco in there too."

"Good point. OK, Annie then. Maybe Lena as well."

"Why the sudden shift, Al? You've been as good as gold."

"Pauline said she'd write – nothing in Santiago, nothing here. She's obviously fucked off with some Aussie while I haven't even had so much as a wank."

"Maybe Cuzco?"

"The next Post Restante is Quito, and that's cocking yonks away."

"Well give it 'til then mate. Stick with your doggies – some of them are so pretty."

The telex operator opened a line. We declared our cash in hand, and the usual 'Group all AOK'. Dean started as always with a greeting, then went straight for our now customary bollocking.

The spares list is of concern. Not only late, but long. Can u cut back?

No, Al typed.

Understood. We'll look at it with Tony. He may come out to look at the truck. Costs are running high.

Itd be great to c him. Say cheers n beers

Next concern is Tim's incident. Any injuries?

None. All poles still long and straight.

Concernd Al you not taking seriously

Sorry. Group all AOK

Good. Tim to leave in Cuzco for Quito. Contact from there for instructions. Drive safe. TX b4 leave LaPaz to cnfrm spares list

OK bibi - love and cuddles

BIBI

So I had my leaving date, but no info' as yet. Would I be driving alone? Which way – round the top to Rio or back this way? And more to the point, would I finally get to finish a *whole* trip?

Before we left for a pizza dinner that night, David proudly announced his and Helga's decision. As I quickly furnished him with dates and addresses and said how I hoped he'd reconsider, he looked surprised at my apparent preparedness. He was very civil, however, professional almost.

"I'm not claiming compensation yet," he said steadily, "but I must tell you I've faxed your office to tell them the reasons."

"Which are?"

"The truck mainly, and your driving."

"Oh, too slow?"

"No, I mentioned the crash before Cochabamba."

"Oh yes, sorry about that, but no-one was hurt. London know the details already – we always send a report if we have any incidents."

David looked as if the wind had slipped a little from his sails, but said nothing more.

"The Post Office pisses me off too much," remarked Al at breakfast the next morning, "but check the Restante for me eh?"

Two queues and two hours later, I informed London that we were leaving the next morning minus David and Helga, but would meet them in Cuzco. I also asked if I could do the Inca Trail before leaving for Quito. Dean came on the line.

Rcved a fax from David citing incident as one of reasons for leaving trip - good you reported previously. All seems AOK. Just take all care driving. Tony has Ok'ed all spares, arriving in Quito with EMs.
Re: I Trail. Will decide by time you arr. Cuzco
BiBi

OK BIBI

I felt a little sneaky. Dean was right though. Safety first. It had been another timely lesson before starting a trip of my own again. I didn't want to end up dead at the bottom of a ravine – or, worse, responsible for a truckload of broken bones.

No letters from Aus.

We arrived at Tihuanaco ruins three hours after leaving La Paz. David, who was already up there with Helga, waved with a smug expression on his face, glanced at the nippy-looking Nissan that waited for them, then went back to his photography. Kevin went over to join him while Helga retreated back to our group.

Although there is little left of the ancient city that some two thousand years ago housed over 50,000 people, the history of the Tihuanaco civilisation is fascinating. A well-organised society, it spread its influence over an area comprising much of modern Bolivia and parts of Peru, Argentina and Chile. Their success is believed to have come about due to an enlightened, intensive agricultural system that produced a surplus – vital both to cover lean years and to free up labour for building projects. The reason for their sudden decline over a thousand years ago is yet another mystery, though most archaeologists blame climate change. The reason for the ruinous nature of the ruins is much clearer – when gold was discovered on the site, the Spanish authorities granted licences to tear it down.

Lake Titicaca, now some distance away, had once reached the original town and part of the ruins had at one time been a port on the lake. Looking across to the snow capped mountains beyond the site, I found that the most enjoyable sight there was simply in what nature had created long before any civilisation had ever existed. For me, those grand Andean scenes were most of what South America was all about, and in that regard, the continent trumped Africa at every turn.

With a slog we hoped to reach Puno the same day. The long drive on bad roads – which included a border crossing – was made bearable by the continued beautiful views east across the lake. At 4000m, the Highest Navigable Body of Water in the World mirrored the landscape behind it in its deep blue calm waters. The inverted picture postcard scene of hills, high mountains and blue sky was as clear as the original, and followed us as we skirted the lake.

As an introduction to Peru, Puno leaves a lot to be desired. Fortunately, we arrived at night, thus avoiding our first perusal of Peru's urban charms for an extra twelve hours. Our notes guided us to a large government run hotel a few kilometres north of town where we could camp.

Due to the long and bloody Sendero Luminoso insurgency and a reputation for pilfering, Peruvians have suffered bad press. Yet our hosts were charm itself and, in a surreal display of dedicated professionalism, the uniformed waiters brought drinks held aloft on silver trays out to our camp. Admittedly, we were the only customers that night. Surrounded by llamas and piled pellets of llama shit, we drank our beer and stared at the colourful flashing of the empty hotel disco. It was like watching a wide screen TV showing a documentary on the Northern Lights, especially with the waiters standing stationary around the dance floor like penguins.

First thing in the morning we drove through the dreary rundown town. We parked by the port and were immediately swamped by boat-trip touts. But we had a name – and that was good enough for them to cease the clamour. One signalled a three-wheeler bike, gabbled some instructions, and Al and I were peddled off back to town.

Down a dirt road, with kids playing in the huge puddles that swamped it, we stopped at a blue metal door. Andreas answered our knocking from a balcony above. From there, in a set of gold silk pyjamas, he conducted his side of the bargaining for an overnight trip to Amantani Island. Deal struck, he was down in a jiffy – jeans and jumper – and hitched a lift on the back of our three-wheeler.

Our boat chugged along with an enthusiasm reminiscent of our truck, but at a higher volume. Ingenious in its simplicity, a long propeller shaft was attached directly to an upturned diesel engine. It had no protective cover. Equally noticeable in its non-existence was any sign of the safety equipment normally associated with waterborne travel. Storms on the lake were known to be frequent, sudden and violent, and despite the current weather demanding sunblock, I kept a sharp eye on the whereabouts of buoyancy – the single wooden oar.

We stopped off first on the floating islands of the Uros people. These manmade islands are made of reeds, as is everything else, including the boats and houses. The Uros have lived by hunting and fishing for generations, but now appeared to be living from tourist donations for photographs. It was perhaps the most depressing example I had seen of the travellers' ability to destroy the very culture they had come to see.

With relief we thundered on, far into the lake. At Amantani Port the inhabitants gathered at the jetty to receive us. Like refugees we were split up amongst them by the assertive village secretary and led off to our respective hosts' homes across terraced potato fields. Only Al put up any protest. He didn't care which family he stayed with, he said, as long as he was alone. I was teamed up with Sam and Kevin – not the companions I would have chosen, but I was to gain a further understanding of the joy people find in overlanding, or, in David's case, the difficulty: by relinquishing control of their lives they allow wonderfully memorable occasions to enter into them.

The farmhouse was a rude stone dwelling with a thatched roof; the situation, idyllic. Offering a panoramic view of the lake, it was fronted by an attractive planted terrace from which the port and village could still be seen down to the right. Several generations of the extended family lived in various outhouses. They seemed unwilling to divulge much information, no doubt as we were just one of a constant stream of groups who arrived there; when the secretary decided their turn to host had come round they would house us and feed us, nothing more. But they did that well – if you like eggs and potatoes. The secretary had told us a recommended sum, and to pay the families direct. Impressive. Not many of the world's town leaders would adopt a system that spreads tourist income so evenly.

In our dark mud-floored room, Kevin took the opportunity to talk openly about himself. He had a lot to get off his chest. Sam twittered and interrupted but was silenced by a steady hand held up at intervals by Kevin. As we'd both been on the road for over a year, I found I could sympathise with many of his emotions and, once cleared out, Kevin cheered up immensely. He suggested a hike up one of the island's two peaks.

Though we were by now well acclimatised, it was still a difficult climb. Some islanders, toiling individually on separate terraces, stopped work and raised a welcoming hand. None spoke. At the top we met half of the group, who'd had the same idea. Looking around at the whole island, no other possibility for entertainment sprung to mind and I wondered what everyone else might be doing.

Kevin and I hiked to the island's second peak, it too topped by ruins. There we rested. I shut my eyes and listened to silence. Amantani is beautiful, but above all it is peaceful. The atmosphere calmed my truck-busy mind and I fell asleep, until Kevin woke me for sunset.

As we watched in companionable silence, my thoughts turned to Charlotte. She hadn't replied to my letters – but that wasn't surprising. Any hint of misery dispersed, however, when I thought about what Kevin might be recollecting in his own reverie not a metre away. He wasn't the most approachable of characters, but he'd had a lot to deal with. The truck, I thought, was possibly not the best place for doing it.

After an early supper of boiled potatoes and poached eggs – lunch had been mashed potatoes and boiled eggs – we took a candle each to our room and sat on our beds, not really knowing what to do with ourselves. Sam put on his Walkman and lay back. Grimacing, arching his back and thumping his bed, he injected his poor brain with devil-worshipping heavy metal, the metallic bit of which we could hear in tinny snippets. Kevin then decided to produce a further part of his life story. It didn't sound like one I wanted even a bit part in. Contrary to my opinion though, he told me that escape *had* been the right decision. Now he felt ready to go back and face life again. He hadn't solved anything, he said, but he had found the space to gather his reserves of strength. Many overlanders are running from something, and I had run too. But as Kevin said, the experience, the overall warmth of our travelling community and the way we lived – hand to mouth, rarely looking beyond the day – "it all must lead somewhere. The challenge," he added, " is to find out where."

Omelettes and potato cakes for breakfast, and a hasty ushering from our temporary abode once cash had changed hands. Our end of the goodbyes were said with some emotion – it had been a memorable stay, a welcome respite from the group, and I had learned a lot from Kevin. Back on the boat we found that the other half of the group, lodged nearer the village, had found a party where the locals had made them very welcome. It amazed me how quickly lives can diverge once a different path is first trod. It sounded an excellent occasion, but I wouldn't have swapped it for my own Amantani experience.

It was a marked contrast to the way we would feel over the next two days. We were about to enter a Sendero stronghold. The rise of the Sendero Luminoso, or Shining Path, seems an almost predestined reaction to Peru's political and social history: Having wrested power from the Incas in the 1500s, the Spanish continued their brutal reign until independence in 1824 when the Criollo (mixed race) elite simply took over where the Spanish left off. Only by rising against an invasion by Chile in 1881 did indigenous Indians gain any political influence, that date marking the start of a struggle that still continues today.

In 1919, a more sympathetic president took power. In trying to implement his policies, however, President Leguia ran up massive foreign debt and eventually abandoned social reform. He departed in 1930 and the country then alternated between military and civilian governments until 1980, each contributing some of the industrial development we see today, but also much of the continued dissatisfaction. For the last two decades civilian democracies have held power.

Against this backdrop of exploitation and poverty, the PCP – the Peruvian Communist Party – was formed in 1970. A related guerrilla movement, the Sendero Luminoso, began an armed revolution in 1980. Led by Guzman, a philosophy professor, millions of marginalized Peruvians were attracted to the cause. Guzman was a Maoist and imposed a tough moral code on his followers, instilling in them a belief in Mao's central premise: power must come through the barrel of a gun.

During the twelve-year Sendero insurgency, it is estimated that 30,000 people were killed: half by the guerrillas themselves, the other half by the military, the Sendero's violent tactics having invited repression in retaliation. In theory, Sendero killings were always targeted. By killing town mayors and civilian leaders, for example, they hoped to create a power vacuum to be filled with 'popular committees'. It worked – many more resigned than were killed. But many campesinos were caught in cross fire from the more indiscriminate military.

After a series of attacks on the capital Lima, the government, under a recently elected Fujimori, stepped up their campaign, resulting in the capture of Guzman in 1992. In 1994, he agreed a peace accord with Fujimori's government and Sendero militia activity immediately stopped. Guzman had been close to victory, but his mistake lay in his dogma. The very existence of the campesino demands his pragmatism. Dependant on weather and fate for their survival, they weren't interested in his philosophy. They simply wanted the promise of a better deal.

Fujimori might well have assumed that the years of disruption by revolutionary socialists were behind him. Now, however, rather than in the mountain peasants' areas, it is the jungle communities that have turned to violence. While the government grants prospecting rights to wood, gold mining and oil companies, they live in poverty and deprivation, the profits never seen by Peruvian Amazon peoples. Their reward is more direct: they are routinely driven off their land, their rivers and land are contaminated, and deforestation chases them further and further into the jungle. Future leaders of Peru may well pay a price for continuing to ignore the message of the past.

The story of Adam's night at the hands of the Sendero was, like the driver himself – ten years behind the wheel – overland legend. It was also well documented in our notes. Whether really Sendero or not – banditry always increases where insurgency prevails – the Central Highlands of Peru were a dangerous area. While camping in the area several years previously, Adam's group had suffered a long night of beatings. But they were lucky. In the end they were only robbed of every cent on the truck, and escaped without serious injury.

The advice in the notes applied specifically to the road that runs through a desolate mountainous area between the towns of Juliaca and Sicuani. As in Nigeria, bandits sometimes set up roadblocks to pick off their prey. Our notes indicated two choices to avoid Adam's fate:

Camp at the Sillustani ruins outside Puno, then leave very early to camp in safety near Cusco; or stay in Ayaviri town halfway along the road. Either way **– only drive in broad daylight.**

Al's demand for a lie-in had put paid to option one, so, arriving safely in Ayaviri the next evening, we asked around for somewhere to stay. People seemed very wary of talking to us and little help was forthcoming. One or two people, on looking at the truck, talked about a previous incident. We took this to be the enduring story of Adam and smiled as one silently drew a line across his throat with a finger. Eventually, aid arrived in the shape of a priest. He had a lockable church compound which we were welcome to use. The Lord had certainly provided. He opened up, we moved in, and we spent a quiet, alcohol-free night parked up in the graveyard.

Skipping breakfast, we continued on towards Cusco at first light. Nervous of every oncoming vehicle or the occasional group of men standing at the roadside, I decided that the roadblock method of highway robbery was unnecessary. As the appalling state of the road kept us at a constant 20kph, a single man stepping out with a gun would have been entirely sufficient to stop us. It was strange to be expectant yet completely impotent. Without stopping even for lunch, we eventually arrived at the villages lining the road into Cusco. Any danger was now passed.

Hungry and relieved, we stopped where we could see smoke coming from a spit-roast on the side of the road. To the delight of some and the disgust of others – namely Isabel – the food on offer turned out to be one of Peru's national delicacies: roast guinea pig (cuy). Lined up on a series of revolving metal bars with their little heads, arms and legs sticking out, they looked like a row of charred table-football players. I bought a whole team and shared them out. And guess what? They taste like chicken.

Cusco is the centre of tourism in the Andes and the ancient Inca capital is unparalleled in its diversity of fascinating offerings. Architecturally, the mix of Inca-built first-storeys topped by Spanish colonial buildings is intoxicatingly attractive, and the Inca ruins that surround the city – Sacsayhuaman, Pisac, Ollantaytambo and the favourite Machu Picchu amongst others – are so well preserved, so extensive and skillfully built that they cannot fail to impress. I was riveted by the history of the Incas and read about a family-based society of sun worshippers who were rigorously controlled by their monarch Pachacuti. Their civilisation displayed skills in building, metalwork and textiles to standards higher than the people who caused their ultimate ruin, the Spanish conquistadors. Had the Incas had the frame of mind to create what the Europeans managed with their inferior metalwork, things would have been quite different; indeed, to speculate on what might have become of this continent without the invention of the gun is to rethink the history of the world.

Our entrance to town included a stop at the Post Office and three circuits of the magnificent centre – the Plaza de Armas – as Al and I squabbled over which street to take to our hotel. As he was driving, Al finally decided. Annoyingly, he was right. At reception we found David and Helga waiting for us, all smiles and happy to see us. At their insistence I included them on our latest room request, which the group had spent most of the day sorting out.

"I didn't realise you got so much discount travelling as a group," David gushed. "The agents wanted twice what we pay through you for the Inca Trail. And you end up climbing with a great big group anyway." My turn for a smug expression, I'm ashamed to say. "And I gotta tell ya, we really missed those fires and rough camps."

Finding our room along the labyrinthine corridors of the Hotel Cahuide was even harder than finding the hotel in the first place. Outside the shuttered window the streets were already crammed with the evening food-stalls. The smell of cuy filled my nostrils.

"What do you fancy to eat? They've got the lot here."

"I don't care. I'm fucked, and I'm fucked off." Al leapt onto his bed and started thumping the pillow like a toddler in a tantrum.

"Aaaahhhh, Alboy, what's up? You won the bet on which street, so I owe you a dinner of your choice."

"There's" – bash – "no" – bash – "fucking" – bash – "letter."

"Letter? You said yourself you weren't expecting one till Quito."

"Yeah, but then I read the rules. This place is on the trip fact-sheet I sent her."

"Are you sure she got it?"

"She told me she did before I left."

"Well you're shafted then, aren't you? It's seven in the morning over there; she's probably having an early morning shag with that surfer as we speak. So let's celebrate freedom, eh? Que comemos?"

"Como nada amigo. I'm going on the Caipirinhas. I'm going to get lummoxed. I'm going to prove those Brazilians right tonight."

Given all the choice of atmospheric local bars, we went straight to the Cross Keys, an English pub on the Plaza. Crass, brash, full of gringos but great fun, they've got pool, darts and do a mean Sex Drink. Al was 6:3 up, on both pool and the lethal cocktail.

"It ain't right, Matthew, it just ain't right," Al slurred, sitting round a table with some of the group.

"What ain't right?" Matthew looked confused.

"That you've got a bird with the best T-shirt in the world, an' I ain't got nuffink." Al went cockney for no apparent reason.

"I think we'd better try and catch you up," Matthew said decisively, then downed his proper English pint. "Caipirinhas, anyone?"

He had a full round to buy, but still came back with far too many drinks. Standing over the table he counted them off a tray.

"Two for me, two for Annie, Isabel, Lena, Richard, and you, Tim. None for you Sam, you're too young. And none for you Al, you're too grumpy. Down in one, everyone."

He polished off both and shouted for Al, who was now at the bar, to get him another. I quickly filled everyone in about the lack of a letter. Al came back with the drinks. Matthew waited until he had sat down before saying, "Right, where were we? You wish to remove Isabel's clothes, is that right?"

"No, no, no. I'm not interested in her any more. Annie, how about a shag?"

"No, not tonight Al. You don't look up to it these days."

"Lena, you've been waving those firm breasts in my face for weeks now. You want some?"

She grabbed me. "Too late. Tim just popped the question."

"Hey, what's going on here? No-one wants me." His eyes rolled back, then focused again. "What have you been sayisng, Tim? I saw you whispering a minute ago."

"Nothing. Just that you refused a dinner. Bets don't carry overnight, so it's now or never."

"Never. I need another drink. If I can't get a shag here, there must be something at the bar. Anyway," he added, "I've got a dose of toilet love so I'm never eating again." Al downed his drink, stood and weaved his way back, shouting his next order from half way.

Sadly, the mood caught and everyone skipped dinner. A hideously raucous team of drunkards arrived arm in arm at a club, having sung our way through the empty square like football louts. We danced outrageously to a selection of music remarkably similar to our own. Staggering back to the hotel in the early hours, the last thing I remember was Al's voice piercing the silence of Cusco's ancient and beguiling streets.

"Wait for me you wankaaaaaaahs.... Lena? Annie? You don't know what you're miiiiiissiiiiiiing."

COLUMBIA

Rio Coca
Quito
Banos   Coca
ECUADOR
Cala   Alausi
   Cumanga
   Machala
Zarumilla   Huaquillas
               Iquitos

Rio Napo

Rio Amazonas

BRAZIL

   Huanchaco
Trujillo   Chan Chan

   Lima   PERU

      Puerto Inca   *Macchu Picca*
Islas   Paracas   Aguas Calientes
Ballestas   El Chaco   Cuzco
      Nazca   *Vn. El Misti*   Juliaca
         Colca Canyon   Puno   *Lake Titicaca*   BOLIVIA
            Arequipa   La Paz   Cochabamba

               Salar de Uyuni   Sucre
                     Potosi
   Buenaventura   Uyuni

         Calama
      San Pedro   PARAGUAY
            Salar de Atacama

CHILE   ARGENTINA

               URUGUAY

   Viña del Mar
      Santiago

The room was cold; the stone walls bare. Beyond the badly welded security grille I could see and hear little. As on the previous three nights, old town Quito had emptied promptly at 6pm. Walking the streets after that hour wasn't dangerous, but nothing was open. The centre, as impressive or more so than any other colonial-built Andean town, was depressing.

With my head crunching against stone, I was sitting on my bed reading letters, some for the fourth time. Beside me, on a concrete bedside cupboard, lay two unopened ones. They had Australian stamps and were addressed to Al Casey. With the news from London confirming that I was leading a southbound Andean Adventure in ten days' time, I judged it quicker to deliver them directly; Al and I would meet in Banos. I had no truck as yet, but it was due in at any moment from the north. Meanwhile, I was to wait. Waiting meant intensive Spanish lessons: one on one, three dollars an hour, five hours a day. Taught, as I was, by a talented and extraordinarily beautiful Ecuadorian university student, my days were brim full of distraction. It was these long evenings that were the killers.

With time to reflect, I put my letters down and thought back over the trip. I loved South America. The continent had so much variety: deserts, mountains and beaches; fine food, friendly people and fascinating cultures. And I hadn't even seen the jungle yet. But strangely, I missed the intense hassles of Africa. Which did I prefer? It was impossible to say, as you simply can't compare two such diverse continents, each with their own internal distinctions too: cultural, economic, historical and geographical. But I could sum up the difference in overlanding terms. South America was *softer*. Softer driving, softer sleeping, softer eating; softer animals, softer officials and softer weather. Even the group had been softer. Al and I had softened too, particularly around our beef and beer-filled bellies.

The Inca Trail, just outside Cusco, had been superb – and again, soft. Well organised and well lead by our guide Manolo, an embarrassing twenty-six porters had climbed with us – useful, as for half the group it had been struggle enough to haul their own arses up the mountains, let alone their kit. The porters had also brought us morning tea in bed. Nice. Although it had rained for most of the three-day hike, it was spectacular and beautiful throughout. Linked by the precipitous Inca pathway, in places still distinct with good paving and carved steps, we'd camped by a series of astonishing ruins. As back-marker, I'd stayed behind with the stragglers: Matthew, Annie, Lena and Sally. At Matthew's suggestion we had taken dolly steps up the passes, the highest a wet and cold 4200m, arriving at camp well behind the rest of the group. We were convinced we'd had the most fun though, as we'd reserved enough energy to chat and laugh our way up. An almost complete city, Machu Picchu was only uncovered from the jungle, which surrounds it still, in 1911. It occupies perhaps the finest site in the world. We had all got there in time for sunrise, but it was rained off. We had explored regardless, and in a satisfying mix of myth and speculation, excellent guides had explained the city's extraordinary history.

What a place to be.

Below Machu Picchu lies Aguas Calientes. This small, rickety-looking town on the river has a unique atmosphere, partly as the main street is a railway line. Shops, cafes and stalls line high pavements facing the rails, and without cars to disturb the quiet or pollute the rarefied air, I'd found Aguas a charming place. We had spent the evening in the hot springs on the edge of town, ideally positioned to relieve descending hikers' aching limbs. The waiters had served us Caipirinhas as we were slowly brought to a simmer in the pool.

The train journey back had been spectacular too, as was my departure, celebrated in a Cusco 'cevicheria'. It had taken a while, but we'd finally discovered the perfect food, in fact the commonest type of restaurant in Peru, particularly on the coast. 'Ceviche', and its mouth-watering cousin 'escabeche', is made of raw fish and seafood marinated in either lemon and chilli peppers or onion, peppers and olives. Served with corn on the cob or deep fried plantain, it is quite delicious – and a fine accompaniment to Pisco Sours in number. In a repeat of my Kano departure, I was helped into a pre-dawn taxi and waved off by a suitably inebriated group. This time Al there too, a boot waving in time with his hand.

Wrapping myself in an extra blanket, I began to wonder again about the overland groups I'd met. None could function perfectly of course, but on the whole it amazed me how well perfect strangers of different ages and nationalities got on. In normal life you can usually just walk away from social situations you don't want to be in, but overlanders have to deal with them. Also, it was clear that the more each group member was involved in the functioning of the trip, the more he or she got out of it. And I felt I could identify another basic rule – the groups roughly followed a normal distribution: two didn't really fit in, two got into everything, and the rest showed varying degrees of involvement in between. In terms of compatibility, a rough pecking order nearly always developed, based, much as it would be in an office, around humour and attractiveness but also ability and self-respect. Quiet had often proved to hide confidence. Furthermore, the relationship with the leaders was interesting. Some thrived on it and couldn't wait for their turn to come up to the cab, but most couldn't care less; they just enjoyed the group as a whole. One more thing, I felt, looked abundantly clear as well: an overlander's memories of the group they travelled with would be much more lasting than those of the route they travelled.

After two more lonely days, brightened only by over-the-desk conjugation and under-the-dress contemplation with my lovely Spanish teacher, reception gave me a message with a number: ***Call Craig.***

"Hey, mate, what are you doing there?" A cheerful Aussie drawl brought a smile to my face. On the blower was The Golden Boy himself.

"This is the Quito hotel."

"Not any more, we're in the new town."

"Who's 'we'?"

"Four of us. We've been here a week. I just heard you were in town too. London told me."

"They might have bloody well…" I stopped. Craig Hutchinson was the kind, I'd heard, that didn't even understand the concept of whinging. "Which hotel?"

"I'll show you. Meet us at Adam's Rib for dinner 8 o'clock. Mind the cat."

The cat in question was an ocelot – a beautiful jet-black creature the size of a cheetah. Tame but menacing, it glided silently around the restaurant while we ate. Craig did the introductions.

"Hugo, Colin, Rob. This is Tim. He opened the Mauritania route. Too late for me though, eh?" He was grinning and, true to his reputation of friendliness, had quickly found something flattering to say about me.

Rob was Craig's trainee. He had just got the sack. "Too much bad behaviour," he shrugged. "But I always went for the ugly ones. I thought I was doing them a favour." He seemed cheerful about his curtailed career on the road, but I suspected there was more to it than his remark revealed.

Colin had been in South America for two years. He and Craig had just travelled the northern route in tandem, meeting in various centres along the way. Tough looking and witty, he aimed his humour at the others, until Craig slid his chair nearer to mine, forcing Colin to include me in his field of communication.

Hugo was only 21, 'the youngest driver in the history of overlanding', as Craig introduced him. Quiet, but very entertaining when he spoke, he had an air of total coolness, as if nothing would fluster him. This was confirmed when he told a story that hadn't yet reached Al and me, and which revealed the reason for the recent truck-pointing from the locals in Ayaviri.

Hugo had spent several months running six-week trips along the Gringo Trail – La Paz to Quito. On a truck relocation between the two capitals a month previously, he had been in a hurry to get to La Paz in time to pick up a group. Risking the Sicuani-Juliaca road late in the day, he was held up at gunpoint, despite the hitchhiker he'd picked up for extra security being a policeman.

"We were both standing there with our hands on our heads when the cop took off. He just legged it into the grass, dodging and weaving like a full back going for a try. The boys were taking pot shots at him and he went down. I thought they'd killed the sod. They asked me for all my money, so I turned my pockets out. There was no bugger at all in there, and only $300 in the safe. But the boys didn't believe that was all I had. 'Take the keys', I was saying, 'take the truck, it's yours, a present, cadeau, the whole bloody thing. Strip it back at Terrorist HQ and find whatever you think's there.' They weren't interested. I don't blame them. It's another heap of shit like the rest – except yours of course, Colin."

"No one's touching that 'til I leave South America," Colin chipped in. He had the company dream machine, a Ford Cargo he had personally built at the Northampton workshop and later picked up at Rio Harbour. With its supposedly unbreakable ten-litre Cummins engine "she could drag Concorde up Everest," he boasted. The Dream Machine also featured a bed in the cab and best of all, no trailer. Colin looked after "the old girl" as his own and was very proud of it. He was shortly heading over to Africa, however, and in a rash decision by London, the Cargo was coming my way. Later in the evening, Colin let slip his knowledge of my reputation for having only a nodding acquaintance with spanners, a fact that no doubt accounted for his continued dismissal of both my presence and my contributions to the conversation.

Hugo continued. "They pushed me into the grass, put a foot on my back and my hands behind my neck. I was chewing dirt like Clint himself had caught me. Then one pointed a gun here" – he put two fingers to his left temple – "and fucking fired the bastard." While Hugo laughed uproariously at the memory, I searched for signs of holes or a recently exploded brain.

"'Bollocks, I'm dead'," Hugo continued. "'Fuck. *Fuck*. FUCK. They've fucking killed me!' I was saying to myself. Then I realised I *was* saying it to myself. The bastards were laughing while I felt the side of my head. It was burnt, so they must have used a blank. Anyway, then they buggered off, an' you know what? As soon as they did that lousy cop came back and picked me up off the road. I still gave the sod a lift to Juliaca."

He paused, then repeated, "'Bollocks, I'm dead ...' I was a right git, wasn't I?"

Hugo almost sounded ashamed by his reaction to reincarnation. I looked at his youthful face. He was blushing in self-admonishment but was otherwise totally composed, like he'd just been relating an embarrassing comment passed at the office photocopier.

Colin laughed at my suggestion that I might go back to Spanish school the following day. "I think you might find you've got a lot to learn before you can even drive the Cargo out of the truckpark." He was right of course, and I'd just confirmed his worst suspicions. I kicked myself for even thinking it.

There in the truckpark, I was in my worst element and he in his heaven. We didn't get on from the first passing of a screwdriver, and I found myself regressing to subservience. In fairness, Colin was thorough and patient in explaining the unfamiliar air system; the myriad valves controlling the brakes, suspension and the split-range gearbox. But for me, the modern technology involved made me feel like I was starting mechanics again from scratch. I just longed for the week to end.

On the afternoon before my pre-departure meeting, my opportunity arrived to fully understand Colin's comments about driving the Cargo. During a supervised test-drive, I found that the clutch was either non-existent or didn't work. In a demonstration, Colin had passed smoothly up through the first four gears, judging the pitch of the engine to engage each perfectly, and had then flicked a switch before going up through the next four. I, on the other hand, stamped uselessly on the clutch pedal whilst crunching and grinding my way from third to sixth, fifth to second and any other combination of eight in between. Once, after bullying the gearbox from seventh directly into first, I nearly sent Colin through the windscreen. His laughter didn't last long. By the time we got back to the truckpark he was furious, while I was sweating from the tension of being watched and judged. That was the last moment we spent in each other's company. He handed me the keys and walked off.

In an effort to avoid Colin, I had spent most of my evenings with the new group. They were another youngish bunch, and there were no couples. Joanne, an ever-smiling Tasmanian, had arrived first with her Canadian friend Jean. They were both very keen on outdoor activities and, by their positive attitude, showed quick promise of being excellent trip participants. Two more Australians had arrived together on the same flight, but were evidently not *together* together. Kylie was a social worker, Dylan a mineworker. She was calm and reserved; he, animated and gregarious.

With the arrival of four New Zealanders, the Antipodean contingent accounted for exactly half of my group, thus boding well for co-operative involvement. Maria, a loud woman, liked to be centre of attention, probably as she was used to it – she had all the outward appearance of a catwalk model. Julia, her travelling companion, was much funnier but her Irish descent had let her down in any competition for looks: she was ginger, freckled, pale and round. Eric, a tall, friendly teacher with a moustache and military air, quickly befriended Ed, a hefty-looking builder who, like a boxer keen on collecting teddy bears, waxed lyrical about his pet newts.

The Brits – Liz, Rod and Simon – seemed as laid back as the Antipodeans, Simon in particular because he was permanently drunk. Ruth, a very sweet Swiss girl, looked a little delicate, but had quickly volunteered for a vast pre-departure staples and wine shop. Carrying the huge boxes through the truckpark, she had suddenly looked rather more robust. Nancy, the New York dancer and actress who had helped her – sleeves rolled up and muscles bulging – obviously liked to think she was dangerous to know. Very fit, and very entertaining with her crafted Big Apple accent, she had the air of a spider waiting to trap whomever she chose in her web.

The end of March and there I was in front of them all at my pre-departure meeting. I was not happy. Well over a year and a half into my job and a simple ambition was proving elusive – I'd yet to complete a single trip. And my time in Quito had ground me down. I had lost confidence. Craig had bolstered me, saying he couldn't drive the Cargo either, but I somehow doubted that. As I spoke I was watching Geoff. He had spent some time picking his nose with a deep corkscrew action of his thumb. The generous extraction was currently hidden in a loose fist and I was wondering where it would end up. Geoff had arrived unexpectedly just before the meeting. Showing me his confirmation slip and a note from London, he'd asked, 'Does the bus go tomorrow?'.

I carried on reading from the headings I had prepared: warnings, the route – the half I knew of it – and finally jobs. One by one, hands volunteered their owners for them, but Geoff's stayed firmly put on the table warehousing his nasal effluent. After Joanne accepted the job of nurse – well, she was a physiotherapist – there was only one left: Rubbish Burier. No movement.

"Well, Geoff, you're the only one left. Looks like it's you and the shovel."

He looked alarmed, like he had just been handed sole responsibility for Ecuador's waste removal, but he nodded. We were still in eye contact as the thumb came to his lips. He pretended to be nibbling the nail and I watched, riveted. First the surreptitious transfer, then the chew, finally the swallow.

Only a quarter the size of Peru, Ecuador still features incredible diversity in its Amazon, Andean and Pacific Ocean zones. Even its main cities are poles apart in their differences. The political capital, Quito, lies 3000m up in the Andes, while the people of the economic centre, Guayaquil, sweat it out on the humid coastline. The rivalry between their inhabitants reflects not only their different way of life, diet and climate, but also their history of political struggle to dominate a divided nation. That struggle, however, pales when compared to the differences between the two sets of city-dwellers and the predictable story of an indigenous rural population in search of rights, respect and of course, land. It is their beautiful homelands that we would spend three weeks exploring as we headed first to the jungle, before climbing again into the Andes.

"He's a bit pretentious," I said.

"No he's not. He's the genuine article, mate." Joanne looked at me and laughed, which she did after most things she said. She and Jean were with me in the cab.

"Was it bad?" I asked.

"Bad enough. He'd been winding everyone up, complaining about someone taking his seat. Then that was too hard when he got it back."

Jean pitched in, "Yeah, and Nancy just told him to shut it. Then he just rips into her. Ed had to stop her from hitting him."

"Lucky. I think Nancy would've knocked him clean out," interrupted Joanne.

Geoff had been arguing with the rest of the group for the two days we had been on the road. Initially about having to be 'binman', but thereafter on most other topics too. He hadn't done it in front of me so I was trying to get some facts. We had been to Otovalo market, north of Quito, and had then driven east into the thick, hot jungle. Two rough camps – one freezing, one humid – had been fine, the group already nearly up to speed with the routine. That afternoon we expected to reach Coca from where we would go on a five-day jungle trip.

"Was he actually abusive?"

"Not really, just whining and annoying," continued Joanne. "He knew what to say to Nancy though. And it was smart in a way – he didn't swear at her at all."

For now there was nothing much I could do except ask him to be more co-operative, and maybe swap him out of his job. He wasn't helping my continued low mood. I was still crunching every gear, frequently stalling, and fielding comments like 'Have you ever driven a truck before?'

Adonis was far from looking like one. Fat and bearded, he was our jungle trip guide. He was very friendly, and ruthlessly efficient – all I had to do was hand over the cash. "Drivers", he had said, "usually have a holiday when they're with me. They're either at the end of a long trip or tired from their Quito turnaround. Just relax and I'll take care of everything." Comments in a book had verified his boast, so I was hoping that a rest, particularly from the truck, might make me feel better. And so far it had.

Stretched out in a long dugout, trailing my hand in the Rio Napo as we sped through the jungle, I watched birds fly overhead as Adonis identified them. Another boat drove just behind us. At the stern of each stood a 'boatboy'. José drove our boat, Eduardo the other. Their job demanded full concentration as we dodged sandbanks, half submerged logs and whole trees at high speed. Defying the law of randomness, the girls were all on Eduardo's boat, and unlike us they were all lying facing one direction. His. Brown, dark-haired, muscular and impossibly handsome, I imagined that in their eyes Eduardo was the *real* Adonis.

After five hours, having negotiated narrow tributaries and wide swamps, we arrived at a longhouse on stilts at the edge of a lagoon. Idyllic.

"Swim now if you like," offered Adonis. "There are piranha – they only nibble – but mind the Willyfish. They'll swim up your urine and set up camp inside you if you give them the chance. Same goes for you girls." Most of us dived straight off the boat. I kept a full bladder full.

Adonis was a superb guide. Armed with a spotlight, we took the boats out at dusk to scour the riverbank where we saw capybaras – giant guinea pigs over a metre long – sloths, and many of the five hundred species of bird Adonis assured us were there. During the day he took us on long treks in the jungle itself, explaining the tribal customs and hunting methods of the Indians, as well as the flora and animal life – in this instance, mainly mean insects.

He had his tricks. One was to stand in the path of some inch-long ants. He waited until they'd swarmed all over his legs, and then squashed one. On cue, all the others clamped onto his skin with large pincers. It looked excruciating. As he picked them off, some hung on so tightly that they lost their bodies. "Indian stitches," he grinned. Another trick I tried. Putting our hands in a swarm of 'lemon ants' until they were coated, I followed him in licking and sucking them into my mouth. They tasted exactly like their name, and would have gone well with a gin and tonic.

Moving on to our second stopover even deeper into the jungle the following day, we stopped our boats at a small village and bought a pig. Strung upside down from a pole, it was carried between the shoulders of two villagers and dumped unceremoniously near me in the back of the boat. Its intelligent eyes looked up sadly. It seemed to know its fate. At our second stopover, this time directly on the Napo riverside, Ed and Dylan lifted it onto the shore, struggling under its weight. Eduardo walked behind them holding a hefty looking axe. After the Dogon goat slaughter, I really didn't want to watch.

We had all bought hammocks at Otovalo market and most of us busied ourselves setting them up in the open sided longhouse. The squealing started, the pitch making me wince. I heard the thwack of the axe hitting the pig's head, but the squeals got louder. A second thwack cut them out of the air. Shortly after that I was puzzled to hear the sound of flames.

Dylan came over, satisfied with the outcome. Only he, Ed and Kylie had watched. "How do you make a pig go woof?"

"I dunno, how?"

"Cover it in diesel and put a match to it."

To the sound of a long groan, Dylan was pelted with various missiles emanating from hammocks. He shrieked with laughter, batting off pillows, tubes of toothpaste and a hairbrush. Anyway, it explained the sound I'd heard. That was the procedure Eduardo and Jose had used to get rid of the furry coat before roasting the pig on a spit. The boatboys did all the cooking too and, given our primeval surroundings, were very talented at it.

Despite a lack of concentration during my Quito lessons, my Spanish had improved enough for me to talk at length with Eduardo. At only nineteen he had been on the river five years already and wanted to become a guide. His home village was still deeper into the Ecuadorian jungle and if you came from there, he told me, education was poor, so you either worked in tourism or laboured for oil companies. He had chosen the lesser of two evils. Both, he said, were endanger-

207

ing the ecology of the area. Obviously highly intelligent, he explained how the whole of the Amazon area, including Indian territories and national parks, has been designated an oil extraction zone, and how the production process causes huge devastation. Due to the building of access roads and helipads, initial prospecting causes massive deforestation. And then the pumping begins. Crude oil and heavy metals despoil once pristine rivers, and pipelines leak due to lack of maintenance. When the indigenous population tried to sue Texaco in 1993 for 'negligent operations', the Ecuadorian government backed the US company. Eduardo explained that they feared losing foreign investment. Our tranquil paradise was untouched, but Eduardo said he could show me vast tracts of wasted land only a short distance away.

With the pig-roast came rum, and with the rum the beginnings of a party. At our end of the table, Adonis was pushing the subject of weird or amusing sexual encounters, to which most had already loudly contributed. At length, Nancy told a story we found it harder to laugh at.

There had been a violent prelude – including punching and belt lashing – to a tabletop experience, and with continued expressions of lust, it had broken beneath them. Her now dumped boyfriend had been knocked out and she had had to remove a long sliver of wood from the bottom of her back. The story was funny, but it was the way she'd delivered it that had caused the rather stifled reaction – with such evident relish of the pain and violence. Adonis moved the subject on after that; to the effects of the narcotic potions that could be procured from the jungle.

Later, Dylan organised a shoulder-fight. Geoff was beneath me and I was fending off blows from two other pairs of wrestlers. Geoff had caused absolutely no arguments in three days and I had begun to think his behaviour had been exaggerated. Suddenly he went down, and I landed on top of him with my leg in an awkward position. Dylan then landed on us, followed by Ed. With both impacts I felt a twist in my knee and heard a sickening crunching noise. Picking myself up after we'd unravelled our limbs, I found I couldn't put weight on my leg. With the anaesthetic effects of too much rum, I nonetheless joined in the subsequent dancing, gyrating on my single functioning pin. At the party's end I hopped to my hammock.

The first movement of the morning brought a searing pain. Looking down, I saw my knee bulging like a rugby ball. To get out of my hammock, I had use my hands to lift my leg over the side. As I dropped it down the bottom half hung loose, dangling almost independently of my body. Touching toe to ground brought another flash of pain.

The realisation of what I had done immediately flooded my mind, making me feel physically sick. I was responsible for a fifteen person trans-continental expedition, one that I was desperate to actually complete, and now I couldn't walk.

And it was totally my fault; the result of abject irresponsibility whilst pissed up at a jungle party.

Joanne, who had seen many such injuries, had diagnosed a snapped cruciate ligament. While Adonis took the group on various trips, I spent the final day on land. I then had to be carried to our boat for the journey home. During the three-day drive to Banos, I had to be lifted in and out of the cab. The lifting felt humiliating and I felt more ashamed of myself than I had ever felt in my life.

Three things had saved me from having to leave the trip. The first, by some improbable inversion of luck, was down to the Dream Machine's lack of a clutch – I only needed one leg to drive. Better still, the gearchange technique had finally clicked too. The second was Joanne's expertise as a physiotherapist. She had put me on a programme of exercises to build up my quads and I spent the day at the wheel with my left leg sticking out at right angles, my thigh quivering with the effort. She then coached and coaxed me for two hours each night. The third was the group's benevolent support. While I tortured myself over my stupidity, they appeared to have reserved judgement and had simply taken over every chore apart from driving. In a strange way, I had finally turned a trip into a genuinely team-lead expedition.

"Well who's a stupid wankaaaah then, eh?"

When I hopped into the Banos Hard Rock Café, Al took the decision to dispense with his normal mode of greeting. We were back up in the Andes, and Al and his group had just been on a horse riding trip in the beautiful hills around the hot spring town. I had found a note telling us of his whereabouts on his windscreen. Fluttering in the breeze below his pink swordfish-print shorts that he'd hung above the cab as a flag, he had written it along two metres of bog-roll.

"Tell me about it," I replied. "I've only just stopped kicking myself."

"That's pretty tough with only one leg." Al got up to do an impression of such, falling onto the table and spilling drinks. Sitting down again, he glanced at me over his beer. "That's my entertainment done for the night, mate."

"Why? I thought it was me who had the problems."

"One-legged driving is nothing, pal. That'll fix. But my truck's a lifelong disease. The bastard's stopping me having fun with the group – an' that's about the only thing I'm any good at."

"Well, I've got something that'll cheer you up."

I gave Al the letters. On seeing the stamps, his eyes bulged with delicious expectation and he ripped them open. While he read he chuckled occasionally and absent-mindedly rearranged his balls.

"You'd better read that one," he said when he had finished both, starting the first again. As we both read quietly, the two groups around us edged towards another party night.

I skimmed over much of it, noting that Pauline was more positive about their future than he had indicated. I soon came to the bit Al had referred me to:

I heard from Charlotte. She's back in Sydney and back with her old boyfriend as well. I'm going to their wedding next month! She mentioned that Tim had really crapped on her in London – something about that Kathy woman. I don't know if Tim told you about her, but he told us he'd met her on another trip. Anyway, she says she's glad it happened coz she's back with Sammy and very happy. I'll get the full story when I see her in Sydney and let you know. Tim's as bad as you are!

I swiftly ran the gauntlet of emotions. Further guilt, jealousy, a pique of defensiveness at the final comment, and finally relief. She was happy and it had turned out for the best. I then felt a sudden lifting of my spirits after a two-week gloom. Even though it hadn't been associated with Charlotte, the letter felt like a trigger for me to start enjoying myself again, leg or no leg. I felt exonerated, released without charge from my own lengthy personal trial.

While Al read on, I called my group to some sort of attention, explained the nature of Brazil's national drink – it appeared on the cocktail menu – and offered the first two rounds of Caipirinha "as a thankyou to you all for getting me this far!" Dylan did the honours with my money. I hadn't had a drink since the jungle party, but my resolve quickly wavered when the group encouraged me into a beer. Presently Al put the letters down.

"Good news?" I asked.

"Well, there's no mention of any muscle-bound Bruces, and it sounds like she's having a good time."

"Come on, the bit I read was better than that."

"You nosy git... I pointed out your bit!"

"So, I bet you feel terrible now after that threesome with Annie and Lena."

"In their dreams – I never touched a thing, your Honour." His hand was held up in oath. "But I'll wager you're about to have an affair with that one over there." The hand was now pointing at Nancy, who was arm-wrestling Rod.

"I don't think so, mate. She's a bit scary."

"Who cares? – as long as she doesn't use her teeth. Anyway, I'm off to check your lot out now." Al leapt up, then turned to me with a familiar smile. "Like the old days, eh?" He winked.

Al did a tour of my group, entertaining them with stories and, instead of handshakes, mooning each in turn as he left them. His renewed exuberance made me suspect that the other letter had been even more generous with compliments than the one I had part read. As for me, I had to sit where I was all night while people came up for a chat. Matthew and Isabel were happier than ever – they had got engaged in an Andean hot spring – and David, totally smitten with Helga, now proclaimed the trip "the best choice I've made in my life". It was great to catch up with the old group and presently, Al came over with his arm around Nancy.

"I'd like you to meet the world's toughest woman. She beat me in an arm wrestle. Then beat me up."

"That doesn't surprise me. She was about to kill Geoff over there the other day."

"What? The wind-up kid from Cambridge, England?" Nancy spoke with her Mafia accent. "He's a pushover. I ain't got the time to waste on him." They both sat down, Nancy on Al's knee. "Tell us a story, Big Al," she drawled.

As always, he had one at the ready. After I had left the trip they had gone back on the Sicuani-Juliaca road to go to Colca canyon to see the condors there. They got through safely again, but on the long descent down towards Arequipa, his brakes had failed. He was only in 2nd as usual, doing no more than 15kph, so he had time to think. And his solution was brilliant. He had driven head-on into a huge truck that was struggling up the hill towards him.

"Death, my friends. There it was in front of me. I only missed it by a fore-skin."

"I bet it hurt ya though," Nancy said, stroking his crew cut.

"Not me, not the group; not my truck or my cock. But it did hurt my pocket."

We drank more Caipirinha, as did everyone in the bar. People were dancing and there was some evidence of the drink's alleged effects taking place between the two groups. Al eventually lifted Nancy off his knee and placed her on my good leg, stretching his own out and sorting his balls with relief.

"Hey, that's where I've wanted to be for two weeks now." I was shocked at Nancy's forthright comment, and then remembered it was well within her nature.

"Well as long as you stay on that one, it's fine," I said.

"Why? Don't you like pain?"

As the night went on Nancy stayed with me, no longer on my knee. We talked and laughed with everyone, celebrating the great news from our happy couple, but she kept one hand firmly under the table. It travelled around my lower body, eliciting pain and pleasure in equal measure as she pinched, stroked, squeezed and tickled. I hadn't expected it, but I wasn't about to stop it.

Even Al had gone home by the time Nancy and I ended up in one of the ground floor rooms of the next-door hotel. The night was more than I'd bargained for as I succumbed to some of her peculiar habits. Short of her usual props, she was quite inventive, and at one point I found myself at the mercy of a coathanger. Whenever I twisted my knee Nancy matched my pain with little cries of pleasure. I couldn't bring myself to return her favours but she seemed to enjoy the dominant role. We left the hotel at dawn and Nancy half-carried me to the campsite.

We cooked our group some breakfast and slowly everyone surfaced. Al got his group moving quickly and I went over just before he left.

"See you in Rio then, Hopalong... I told you you'd end up with her. That was all set up, by the way. She asked me to bring her over. She's great, isn't she? A bit wild."

"I thought you two were getting on pretty well actually."

"Well we would have, mate, of course, but I told her the new union rules: closed shop. Pissing only."

"Well, stick to that. Just keep it focused on Australia."

"No worries, mate, that's the plan," he said in an Aussie accent. "But we might have to see what happens with my next group, eh?"

As he drove away, Al's improvised flag flapped in the breeze, visible against the backdrop of the lush hillside for miles.

After our own horse riding trip, which I spent doing leg exercises in the hot springs, we left Banos and continued down the Andean spine of central Ecuador. It was cold and we could see huge volcanoes, but I knew if I took any road east and drove for a day, we would arrive in hot, steamy jungle. Melted snows from those very volcanoes form the rivers that carve up the vast forests, which eventually come out at the mouth of the Amazon 5000km away with such power that they push fresh water over 100km into the Atlantic.

At Alausi the group boarded the roof of a train and travelled down the Andean foothills on the Pacific side. I drove back to Cala and picked them up again in Cumanga, then we headed towards the Pacific coast. Near Machala we visited a shrimp farm where my notes told us we could camp. The owner, Rudolf, was harvesting that night and we watched under huge spotlights as he pumped his produce out of two of his ten huge, shallow pools. He encouraged us to swim and laughed as we got used to the feeling of being nibbled by thousands of little fishy lips. This seemed to set Nancy's mind thinking and I later found myself back in the pond for yet another bout of abandonment to her bizarre instincts.

The Huaquillas-Zarumilla border with Peru had a bad reputation for obstructive officialdom, but I wasn't braced for the peasants' revolt that I inadvertently drove into. Hundreds of striking farm labourers had barricaded the border and were stopping trucks in the main street. They had punctured the tyres of several and stripped them of their cargo. Part of the 'levantamiento indigena', the Ecuadorian Indian uprising, they were protesting against the government on several issues: land rights, the oil industry, public spending cutbacks and the rising prices of basic goods. Under International Monetary Fund conditions attached to massive debt rescheduling – ironically incurred by successive governments' borrowing against future oil revenue – a reduction in health and education spending had been forced, and subsidies on fuel and food banned. Typically, the governments' policies were totally opposed to the needs of indigenous people and one of their most effective tactics in protest was to block main highways, and therefore the delivery of supplies to the big cities.

At first the protesters ignored us, and the officials – who were avidly ignoring them – went slowly through their stamping motions, shaking me down for a few pesos. I wasn't about to argue over cash. It was an ugly scene outside and the group looked somewhat vulnerable perched above the rake-wielding crowd who had begun to mill around our truck. My leg had improved to the extent that I could get in and out of the truck unaided, but I still found movement quicker on one foot. The protesters made way for me as I hopped through them.

When I made to drive off, however, an angry man, who I took to be the leader, stepped out. He came to the window and shouted that no trucks were to go through to the border. I tried explaining that we were tourists and nothing to do with their protests. He carried on shouting, attracting a large mob that started banging on my door and the sides of the truck. A policeman looked on with his hands in his pockets, a smile on his face. I couldn't think what else to do except try and drive to safety, very slowly so as not to make the men even angrier.

As I edged forward I could see in my wing mirror a crowd gathering around the back wheel. They were dangerously close to getting injured, so I stopped again. Unfortunately this gave them the opportunity to do what they'd been trying to do. The hammer lifted and the long spike went through my tyre, followed by a cheer. I gunned it – the Dream Machine had double wheels at the back.

The border itself was out of town. Before it, more strikers manned a further barricade; a set of spikes filling the gap between two huge heaps of earth. There was no making a run for it. Pesos in hand, I hopped over to them, smiling, "Pasemos por favor, somos touristas." Cash and some leg sympathy did the trick. The spikes were removed and we flew through the gap. In the mirror I could see the mob from town reaching their now slightly richer comrades, but by then, all bar the stamping, we were in Peru. Our very own break-for-the-border.

If Chile is remarkable for having the whole world of landscapes in its huge length, Peru is comparable, plus it has an incredible wealth of history. In terms of variety it must surely be the single most interesting country on the planet – and excellent for overlanding. I had already seen the lake, the mountains and some Inca ruins on the way up with Al. Now we were in the desert that occupies a thin strip between the Andes and the Pacific in the far north of the country – any right turn would take me to a Pacific beach and a beautiful deserted rough camp. Although some water runs down from the mountains to create oases in the desert, most of the rain falls on the Andes' eastern slopes and the jungle that makes up half of Peru's territory.

The long coastal drive south was punctuated by fabulous roadside cevicherias and the odd swim. At Huanchaco, near Trujillo, we stayed at a hotel opposite an excellent surfbeach. Local fishermen rented their little pointed reed boats for the group to ride the waves; their wives sold their morning catch for our poolside barbecues, or supplied delicious ceviche from little beachside stalls.

More culturally, the ruined pre-Incan city of the Chimu was just up the road. Its Chan Chan ruins are in a bad state of repair, but excellent guides bring the history of the twenty-eight square kilometre site to life. Preceded by the Moche people who built the neighbouring Sun and Moon pyramids in the same area, the Chimu constructed these huge royal compounds between 900 and 1400 AD. An artistic people, they have left many ceramics and wall carvings, from which archaeologists try to decipher more about their mysterious rise and fall. Between surfing and barbecuing, we spent three fascinating days there, me being wheeled around on a bicycle.

Lima was next. It was decidedly dodgy but nonetheless worth the visit. The centre has endless interesting historic buildings and the nightlife reflects the frenzy and heat of the city. Not far south of the capital lies the beautiful bay and beaches of Puerto Inca. Inca fishermen who docked there would have seen their fish heading off in the direction of Cusco – the city leaders were said to have organised a relay of runners to get it to their mountaintop tables in twenty-four hours. Camped on the beach, the group walked part of that very path, or explored nearby rocks upon which seals splashed and played.

Still further south is the Paracas marine reserve. Leaving at speed from El Chaco jetty, we found ourselves on a high-powered boat racing out to sea towards the Ballestas Islands. Even without wildlife the islands would be spectacular, but the eroded rocks – carved into pinnacles, enormous arches and caves – are home to thousands of seals, sea lions, pelicans, penguins and numerous other sea birds. Dolphins joined the happy party, swimming playfully around our boat. If you can stand the cacophony of shrieks, snorts and screams, you can get as close as you wish to the animals, as they show no fear – a significantly cheaper version of the Galapagos island trip from Ecuador.

Finally we reached the lovely desert town of Nazca, a place I had wanted to see since watching a documentary on the Nazca Lines as a child.
Nancy and I weren't the only ones who'd been caught out by the Caipirinhas in Banos. Booking into our little chalets in Nazca, I counted five couples. The chalets circled a sandy courtyard in which we could cook at the truck as usual.

Sitting under the shade of a palm reading my trip notes, I looked at the group as they set up our equipment. They were superb. They got on excellently, were fully involved in the expedition and really looked after one another – and me. All except Geoff. Ever since we had left the jungle I had heard constant reports of his arguing, but had still not witnessed it. I had spoken to him several times but nothing had changed. He was now isolated and excluded.

The target for the majority of his antagonism was still Nancy, probably as she rose to it quicker than anyone else. Joanne filled me in on each near-fight in the back of the truck, describing how Geoff always started it. Now that I was with Nancy, however, I was in an awkward position. Geoff claimed that she was the antagonist and accused me of bias. I had spoken to Nancy too. She was adamant that she had done nothing wrong but agreed to try and control her reactions.

Nancy was a troubled woman. But the more I got to know her, the more her complex personality fascinated me. Her desire to feel pain stemmed from places deep within her that we were slowly trying to reach. It was traumatic for her and difficult for me, especially when I found her on one of her purges – when she would scream self-abuse, and kick and punch the air with trained movements until she fell, exhausted. We communicated a lot in letters, which seems strange when we could talk all day and night if we wished, but in her written ramblings – enormous missives in beautiful handwriting – she was finding a more direct route to the source of her pain.

She was by no means always woeful. Much of the time she was at the centre of the group, entertaining us with funny stories in her great accent. Having witnessed her strength and temper, some of the group were wary of her, but most enjoyed her company enormously. As a couple we had quickly come to depend on one another. Where I was in some ways her counsellor, in the absence of Al, she was my co-driver – I needed her to talk through problems, ideas and decisions. I would think about her a lot while driving and would sometimes have little brainwaves about her problems. But they rarely made it as far as her – it's hard to reconstruct insights. In our bed, which on that stretch had frequently been a real one, I continued my embargo on violence, endeavouring to heal her with tenderness. It wasn't always successful and I had a few choice bruises to show for it.

On that first evening in Nazca, we were all relatively quiet. After dinner we sat around the courtyard watching one of the many extraordinary sights that seemed commonplace on an overland trip. As he lay across three stools with his head hanging off the end over a bucket, Joanne massaged Eric's back. It was no lover's touch. He had contracted pleurisy and, as I understood from Joanne's apparent vast medical knowledge, his lungs were full of mucus. No longer. With every other push he coughed up sheets of fluorescent snot into the bucket. Riveting stuff.

The Lines were extraordinary. On a walking tour the next morning we saw how they had been scraped into the flat, stony surface of the desert pampas. Later, from a tower, we could see some of the enormous pictures that had been drawn in the same way: a lizard, a tree and a pair of hands. The full extent of these ancient works of art, however, was only really clear from the air.

At first we flew over the Lines – arrow straight for kilometres, even as they climbed up and down hills. Then we headed back to the pictures. Up to a 100m across, we could now also spot representations of a condor, a huge monkey and a dog. The pilot gave us a completely different theory on their origins from that of the guide on the ground, and their dates ranged from 1000BC to 600AD. Clearly, as with Machu Picchu, no one actually has any idea. In a world where science has an answer for everything, the enduring mysteries of South America are very appealing'.

At the meeting that night I offered the group an extra day, just to relax, and they voted for it. This obviously created the right atmosphere for a party. Liz and Maria made a huge bucket – not Eric's – of punch out of masses of pulverised fruit. It was delicious and as the evening wore on, more and more rum was added. It was all down to the Dream Machine that I could do such things – I could catch up the equivalent of the day in just a few hours.

Getting up late the next morning, I felt very content and relaxed. The shoppers wanted to go into town, so I asked if anyone else wanted to come. I got about eight takers. After shopping, Simon surprised me with a special request. He had already surprised me simply by being there; on a free day, particularly after a party, he never usually woke up until after lunch. Today, however, he wanted to look at the Inca-built irrigation system that still keeps the desert arable.

It was a superb idea. We walked along the line of the aqueduct for some time, peering down the funnel-shaped brick wells that somehow aid the flow of water under flat land. Nancy was the first to climb about six metres down one. She shouted up that the air was clear and the water sweet, and then disappeared. About five minutes later she popped up about a hundred metres away, having climbed up the next well. We all then had a go, even me, my leg now all but healed, wading waist deep through the expertly built metre-high tunnels in total darkness. I would never have done it had Nancy not shown it was possible. We stayed for a while, just messing about, before heading back to the chalets in the early afternoon.

' For more information, check out this link: http://www.incalink.com/nazcalines/ NAZCALINES4.htm More recent archaeological digs have uncovered textiles created by the Nazca that are lighter and of a closer weave even than present day parachute material. This backs up one of the theories that the Nazca had constructed hot air balloons with which to construct and view the Lines. From a sculpture point of view Richard Long has created visually similar pieces, based on walking in landscapes: see http://www.richardlong.org/sculptures/sculptures.html

It started as a grumble. Those that had missed the aqueducts were annoyed, especially as those that had gone were so eloquent in their description of the fun we had had in their absence. I explained that it had been unplanned but still got the wrong end of a few sharp words. I was annoyed now too.

Geoff started arguing in my presence for the first time. I knew, because it was aimed at me. It quickly became obvious how expert he was at winding people up, but given the atmosphere, I chose to ignore his comments about taking my favourites for extra fun. I went for a walk, hoping to have a proper meeting when everyone, including me, had cooled down.

When I got back the atmosphere was as though someone had died. No one was talking and only Joanne would look me in the eye.

"You'd better go to Geoff's room. He's a bit hurt. He and Nancy have had a fight. I think she's gone off for one of her sessions." 'Sessions' was her word for Nancy's purges, which she too had seen.

Geoff had a black eye and showed me bruised ribs. He had obviously been crying. I found it hard to feel sorry for him though, and was short and to the point.

"Do you need any medical attention?"

"Nothing's broken," he replied.

"Who started it?"

"Nancy just hit me. I wasn't saying a thing." Somehow I doubted that.

"I've spoken to you about your arguing, Geoff. It's a real problem. And above all it stops you enjoying the trip. This is the best country I've ever been to and all you do is complain. What's wrong?"

"I hate it." He started to sob a little.

"Why?"

"Because I want to be at home, that's why." He was openly crying now. "But if I go back my father will be furious."

I can't deal with this! Driver, mechanic, doctor, and now family counsellor. It was one job too many. I made to leave.

"What are you going to do about Nancy?" he asked, drying his eyes with his fists.

"If she did hit you first, she'll get a written warning. It's company rules."

She had. They had been arguing for over five minutes, publicly and loudly, about my supposed favouritism. Nancy had decked him with one punch and then got his ribs when he stood back up to fight. *That's my girl*, I thought.

The group were firmly on her side, but I had to write out a warning and fax an Incident Report to London. We talked and talked that night. It seemed to have opened some doors in her troubled mind. When she had finished, she sobbed while I held her, matching my strokes of her head with a tenderness I hadn't felt before.

I got lost again in Cusco, ending up at a dead end at the top of a snaking hill that was just the width of the truck. It was dark and it took half an hour to reverse back down. When I finally found the Cahuide it was past eight o'clock and I was exhausted. Pointing the group in the direction of the Cross Keys and the cevicheria – they were all firm fish fans by now – I chewed on a guinea pig from the stalls outside the hotel and went early to bed.

Next morning I parked the truck at the workshop on the edge of town. I was completely mobile now, and had a lot of work to catch up on. Nancy came down and helped for two days. While I was underneath, she worked with the man who was going to respray the truck while we did the Inca Trail, pulling out the windows and masking everything up with tape.

I didn't finish my work in time, so the group set off to the Trail without me. Finishing late, I got a taxi, but night had already fallen when I got to the trailhead. It was clear and cold, and there was a bright half moon lighting the path. I found that I could run.

Running alone at night in the mountains felt fantastic – I had a sense of total freedom. After a couple of hours I arrived at a small stone house that I remembered sold sodas. I knocked on the door. A woman, showing absolutely no surprise at my late sweaty arrival, invited me in. Sitting at her wooden table with a Coke, I looked around at her sparse candlelit dwelling. All she owned were a few pots, a pile of clothes, a cot and a mattress. The cot was empty. Underneath it, scampering about on the dried mud floor, were guinea pigs.

She offered me food.

"What have you got?" I asked.

"Cuy."

Cornering one with a broom, she picked it up and smashed its head against the table. In the back of the room she expertly bled and skinned it, then started roasting it over the fire. Half an hour later I was eating a cousin of the furry animals that played at my feet.

Well after midnight I found the group's campsite. Nancy was waiting up for me and even though I had loved being on my own, it was nice to snuggle up with her in the cold mountain air, the door of the tent open to the stars and moon. Sometimes she could be as soft as a puppy.

For reasons unknown, the next day she took off to one side of the trail and violently conducted one of her purges. I hung back, not watching, but listening to her cries of abuse. Presently she rejoined me.

"Why are you waiting for me?" she hissed. "I want to be alone."

"I'm supposed to be the back marker."

"We did all right without you yesterday."

Suddenly she was like a different person, and it hurt. But I knew it was best just to leave her be for a while. I went ahead and caught up with the back of the group.

With no repeats over the next two days, Nancy stayed back with me, Liz and Maria, chatting and dolly-stepping our way up the passes. Arriving at camp late in the afternoon, we would spend the evenings talking with Manolo. I had talked a lot with him on the last trip and found he had a particular charisma. Very quiet and thoughtful, he spoke gently about the mountains and what they could teach us. Nancy and he quickly formed a bond; it was as if he had some sort of healing power over her. Often I would leave them while they talked, but while I was around he never talked specifically about her, just about the wisdom, peace and happiness to be found in respecting and understanding nature.

I had already started warning the group about how cold it would get on the Altiplano, but I was to be in for a shock myself too. We were in the dry season, which meant clear blue skies and very cold nights. Sunrise over the ruins of Machu Picchu was magnificent, the mountains in the background covered in snow.

Down in Aguas Calientes we had the traditional post-hike laze in the hot springs, then wandered around town or slept. I went to my favourite little table outside a café on the train-line main street and wrote back to Nancy's most recent letter. In it, I said I hoped she had found peace under Manolo's tutelage. In the pizzeria that night, we toasted his expert leadership and presented him with a tip that we hoped would be large enough for him to buy the new boots that our cook had told me he was saving for.

Back in Cusco, another day's work with Nancy and the painters finished off the truck – it looked fantastic. As thanks, I took her to a churrasceria for dinner. It was on the second floor of a building overlooking the square. There, she presented me with an envelope. In it was a polaroid photo of Manolo squatting, chin in hand, deep in thought, the image perfectly framed by the Andes behind him. In her neat handwriting she had written below the photo: 'This man knows'.

We talked a little about what she had been thinking, but she seemed so full of happiness that I changed the subject. On hearing us talking about South American music, a distinguished looking gentleman dining alone on the next table asked if he could join us. He turned out to be the proprietor and we spent a fascinating night being educated by his encyclopaedic knowledge of music. He had a waiter change tapes and explained all about the singer and the style of each. His favourites were a Chilean – Lucho Gatico – and a mournful Mexican – Javier Solis. Finally the musical gaps had been filled in for me. The next day I bought two copies of each – one set for me and the others I posted to Al.

The Inca Trail marked the start of a prolonged spell of stability for Nancy. Geoff was apparently still sniping but she was in a considerably better frame of mind to deal with it, which in turn curtailed him. We travelled south as a harmonious group.

Safely clearing the Juliaca road, we dropped down to the relative warmth of Arequipa. Situated in a valley below El Misti, a 6000m snow-capped volcano flanked by two smaller mountains propping it up, Arequipa is another wonderful old colonial town. As usual I got lost on the way in, this time having asked Jean to guide me.

"But how can I? I've never been here before."

"Well, isn't that what the map is for?"

In truth it wasn't her fault. The centre of Arequipa is a grid of almost identical narrow streets dividing up terraces of little white houses. And there's a vicious one-way system. After driving the wrong way down a street, then through a market where everyone had to move their displays for us, we eventually arrived at our hostel. An old Spanish building with a lovely lawn and mature garden, it was close to Arequipa's highlight, the remarkable and peaceful Santa Catalina convent. A miniature walled town within the city, the convent has flowered cloisters, beautiful houses, fine paintings and interesting photos – all in the most serene of atmospheres.

Nature can always go one better though. After a night camping at a hot spring we found on the steep road back up to 3000m, we arrived at Colca Canyon. Twice as deep as the Grand Canyon, its dramatic views are embellished by smoke signals puffing up from a live volcano beyond it. Terraces tumble into deep valleys surrounding the nearby villages, and to complete the idyllic mountain scene, enormous condors float up from the canyon on thermals each morning and evening.

We spent the afternoon hiking around the villages, then got back to our camp right on the lip of the canyon to wait for the big birds. They were truly enormous and much more impressive in flight than standing on a wall in a town. As they swooped around the truck I could hear a buzz as their great wings cut through the air. In the morning perhaps thirty circled the truck, satisfying their own curiosity while we watched and listened in rapture.

By the time we had been through La Paz, it had been well over a month since I'd had any major disasters. The group were enjoying themselves – even Geoff – and Nancy was on a near permanent high; and the new paintjob had proved to be the ideal choice of maintenance for the truck – it gave me no trouble at all. I had briefly courted trouble by putting the truck on a small flat-bottomed boat to cross Lake Titicaca – it was only so I could play 'you can't catch a boat to Bolivia', a ditty by the Martin Stephenson And The Daintees, while doing just that. In the middle of the lake, waves had whipped up and we rocked violently, water coming dangerously close to the lip. A big one and we'd have flipped.

Everything's running smoothly, I made the mistake of thinking, as, now in the section I had covered before with Al, the trip was about to collapse like a house of cards.

Outside Cochabamba we got stuck at the same roadworks, this time on the high side. The road would be open for an hour between six and seven in the morning, I was told. It had been getting colder and colder at night and when I woke at 4am and tried to start the truck, I found that the diesel had frozen. I had in fact anticipated this, and had elicited a list of five solutions from Colin in the early days when we were still talking. Out it came. Unfortunately, I got a little mixed up with the different methods.

I tried pouring boiling water over the block, but to no avail. While the group sat in sleeping bags on the truck, I worked on, frozen, in the dark. Next up was the tin-of-sand-soaked-in-diesel trick. I think it should have gone under the sump, but I put it under the fuel tank.

Deciding to have a cup of tea while the fire warmed the claggy fuel, I used up the remaining boiling water, my fingers grateful for the warmth. Suddenly I heard a whoosh; the sound the pig had made. I turned to see flames licking up the side of the truck. The group were already on their way out, sprinting for their lives. Eric was a bit more on the ball. Last out, he had grabbed the fire extinguisher. He played it over the fire and put it out. A post-mortem revealed that the diesel tank's wooden support was soaked in years of spilt diesel. Naked flame in its vicinity hadn't been a good idea.

The coast clear, the group filed back into the truck. *Next, next, next – ah!* – diesel-soaked-rags-burnt-around-the-injector-pipes. It might have worked, certainly there were eight cute little fires dotted about my engine, but a sudden 'pssssh', again reminiscent of something, but this time of the CAR cab-fire, revealed my mistake. In the darkness I hadn't noticed the proximity of the black plastic airlines. The brakes of course clamped tight. *Hmmmm – was Colin winding me up?*

The next attempt was my own concoction, an amalgam of several others, and it worked remarkably well. I took off the diesel filter and, eschewing flame for a while, popped it in a bowl of boiling water. The diesel warmed to a nice temperature, the metal filter-casing holding the heat as I replaced it. Once that warmed diesel had reached the injectors, we were in business. Apart from the brakes.

Group out again while I rummaged for spares, they enjoyed a nice sunrise. Ironically, had I waited that long the first few rays might well have warmed the engine sufficiently anyway. We had half an hour before the road shut. With numb fingers and an extra twenty from the helpful but too numerous hands of Dylan and Ed, I fumbled with the fiddly connectors. Five to seven – all done – but we were totally empty of air. It took ten minutes for the compressor to build up enough to release the brakes. With a choice of waiting till lunchtime or a hefty bribe, I chose the latter. We got through, dodging JCBs and trucks, which had started work on the dot of seven.

The receptionist's scalp problem hadn't subsided, but otherwise Sucre was as fun as on the previous occasion. After long lazy breakfasts at the market, Nancy and I spent two days working at the truck park. The taxi system to get the group out of town when we were leaving was a bit of a pfaff, so I decided to risk driving the truck into the centre. I was caught only yards past the notice clearly banning trucks, the police motorcyclist exceptionally pleased with his work.

"You will follow me. I will take you to the police station."

"Which way?"

"This way." He pointed into town.

"But that's what you just arrested me for."

"It's too far around the ring road. Come."

The group would be milling in reception, cluttering the place up. I was in a hurry and impatient.

"Haven't Bolivian policeman got anything better to do? Rounding up drug dealers or terrorists or something?"

"You are a very rude Englishman. Come with me. Now."

We sped through the beautiful streets of central Sucre, scattering pedestrians, carts and taxis, the only vehicles allowed on the cobbled roads. It was great fun actually. I felt like an ambulance driver must.

At the station my truck was impounded, no one would let me phone the group and I was flung into a cell. Two hours later, the same policeman came to fetch me.

"You will see the commissioner now." He escorted me into a plush office in which sat a stern looking man in a crisp white uniform.

"Sit." I sat. "You have something to say about my police force?"

"Only that they are very efficient with enforcing the road-use laws."

"And you think there is something wrong with that?"

"No."

"Then why?" – he stood and slapped his desk with a deafening crack – "do you insult us!?"

Time for conciliatory tones.

"I'm sorry. I have a group of tourists. They are keen to see more of your beautiful country. I was in a hurry and I was rude. Please accept my apologies." He stayed standing.

"Stand up!" I stood. "Look at your clothes. You are disgusting. How can you call yourself an Englishman?"

I looked down. My cut-off shorts were covered in oil, my Chan-Chan ruins T-shirt ripped and equally dirty. The commissioner was right again.

"I'm sorry for that too. I'm a mechanic" – my biggest lie of the conversation so far – "and I had problems."

"Sit!" I sat.

"What would your English policemen do if I, a Bolivian, broke one of your road laws?"

"Well, Sir, if you were on holiday there, they would understand that their laws were different from yours. They are kind, friendly and very understanding – particularly with foreigners." Beats the mechanic lie hands down. "They would explain your mistake and wish you well on your journey."

"Is that so?" He was musing now. "And would I like a holiday in England?"

"Very much, but it is not as beautiful as your country."

The conversation changed tack. In a long drawn-out comparison of the two lands, we almost became friends. Certainly I offered him a bed at my parents' house should he ever find himself in Lincolnshire. It was pleasant but I was now four hours late for the group.

"May I use your telephone?" I asked at length.

"Please. Go ahead, my friend."

I called the hotel and asked for Joanne. She laughed when I told her I was just trying to extricate myself from jail. I told her to sort taxis for everyone and go out on the Potosi road until she found a suitably obvious roadside café and there to have lunch. When I was freed I would find them.

"Thank you, may I go now?" I asked now the flow of conversation had been broken.

"But you haven't been punished."

"I know, but I don't think you want to punish me any more."

"You are right, but you will apologise to my officer, and I will watch to make certain it is sincere."

He was right to watch as I found it very difficult. The officious man had only been doing his job, but he had a huge smirk across his face. I would rather have tried to wipe that off than grovellingly wipe the slate clean.

"I accept your apology," he said, "now I will escort you to the hotel."

"What, through town again?"

"If you are with me, it is OK."

"Thank you both, but my group are waiting on the Potosi road."

"Then I shall escort you there."

Once again we sped along in convoy; this time the motorcycle policeman had his siren on and blue light flashing. Now I felt like royalty must. Cars and trucks scattered as we belted down the centre of the busy highway out of town. The group had made themselves obvious by piling their rucksacks on the side of the road – besides, they saw us coming from miles off and were waving and laughing as I skidded to a halt on the gravel forecourt of the café.

"Many thanks," I bubbled, shaking the policeman's hand. Another friend now too.

"Please come back to Sucre. But look out for the signs." Bolivians are so charming.

"That's a deal." I grinned and waved as he roared off back to town.

"Was he the one who arrested you?" Joanne asked, having watched the happy scene.

"Yep. And his boss is coming to visit me at my folks' house next year."

After the table-football, chicken-and-chips and mines of Potosi, we had to cross the Salar de Uyuni. Now the dry season, we could go straight across the huge salt lake. Hitting 90kph on the smooth, shimmering surface, it was an exceptionally good fun drive, almost like ice-skating. I saw an island in the distance and aimed for that. We hiked around it, wondering at the giant cacti, and then took photos of us and the truck on the salt, everyone wearing sunglasses as the glare was more blinding even than from snow.

Continuing on from the island we reached the mud flats and stopped on the edge for lunch. I switched on the pump to transfer fuel from the reserve tank into the main tank, but heard a strangely high-pitched hum. When I hit the reserve tank with my dipping-stick, it rang out with an empty echo. *Strange – have I already transferred it?* I dipped the main tank – about an inch of fuel, maybe forty kilometres' worth at best.

Oh God! What have I done now?

Knowing there was no fuel available until Calama, I had been to the diesel pump in Uyuni that morning. Fuel had almost immediately spurted out of the reserve tank, so I had assumed it was full – it usually was. I had tapped the main tank – about half full, plenty. Busy anyway – I had to stock up on Golpes and Dinovos – I had left, just handing over a handful of Bollies in change. It must have been an airlock. I hadn't thought to check.

So, I had plenty of bubblegum but no fuel. Too far across the salar back to Uyuni, I had no choice but to go on. Trying to make it sound funny I admitted my mistake to the group after they had packed up lunch. No one fell about laughing. My fault too – I had drummed into them how cold and uncomfortable crossing the salt-flats would be and how we might get stuck, possibly for days. Now I was presenting them with a near fait accompli, but not as a result of the forces of nature.

Selecting fifth as the most efficient gear, I kept the truck on constant low revs. I might have been improving petrol consumption, but it was hurting both the truck and group as we banged down into mud-holes and bounced over the rough tracks. I found a village, possibly San Juan, but there were no signs. No diesel, they said, try Uyuni. A few minutes later, feeling sickened by the damage I was doing, I saw a truck in the distance and headed in his direction.

I flagged him down and explained the problem. For a hefty sum, he siphoned out enough diesel to fill a twenty-litre container. I funnelled that into my tank and carried on. I tried again with a pickup I saw but he had nothing to spare. He did, however, know a man who did.

"See that mountain?" I looked where he pointed – it was at least 30km away. "Go round the back of that, turn left at a graveyard and there's a village. Ask for the secretary."

The directions sounded as sketchy as our trip notes, and it was in the wrong direction, but I knew there was nothing on my route bar the army base, and that was too far away. Apologising to the group, most of whom had taken to standing and holding the overhead bars in the back of the truck, I set off towards the mountain. *Bang, Crunch. Smash.*

It was just as he'd said. A road did indeed go round the back of the mountain; I found a graveyard and about ten kilometres later, a village. As it was nearly dark by now and bitterly cold, I asked the first person I saw if there was anywhere to stay. We were guided to a village hall. It had a fireplace, which we filled, and we brought in all our cooking equipment. I manoeuvred the truck next to the window and fed our lights through. Cosy and comfy, we were faring better than we normally would have. According to my watch, the cab in which I slept to guard the truck reached minus 15°C. In the morning the village secretary came and introduced himself. I explained our problem; if he had no diesel we were to become permanent residents of his little village.

"No problema. Venga." Only twenty metres from the hall, he climbed over a stone wall – no gate as the llamas might escape he explained – and opened his barn. Stacked up in front of me, in my eyes like a cornucopia of gold and jewels, were dozens of drums of diesel. After negotiating a price about three times its normal cost, I siphoned a two hundred-litre drum into my thirsty truck.

It may have been the intensely cold nights or the long bumpy days, but since Potosi Nancy had begun her purges again. I had been enjoying implement-free nights since the Inca Trail and cold had put paid to any activities post-Potosi anyway. It was herself she was beating up again, not me. The letters started up and made frequent reference to 'the man who knows'. Whatever Manolo had said had clearly made a deep impression, but the magic was fading. I did my best to listen, talk and write back. Her mood would lift, but then descend quite rap-idly, leaving me feeling inadequate. We had been together nearly two months and were very much a good team, a proper trip couple; but there didn't seem to be any way in which I could help.

The night after we solved the fuel crisis, we had a party. I knew it would be cold, and I knew the Chilean salt flat that Al had found on the way up from Calama was beautifully white – almost like snow. Back in Sucre I had asked Joanne and Jean to buy the entire wherewithal for a Christmas party, my theme. It was May.

Arriving in plenty of time, we set everything up. Lights, tinsel, loads of candles and a tree made out of a railway sleeper with bits of branch and tufts of tough grass nailed into it. We had tinned chicken and plenty of vegetables which I'd gone to great lengths to sneak across the border; customs had only impounded a few carrots left as a decoy. We had good contraband Gato Negro from Uyuni, and Liz and Maria baked a superb pineapple upside-down cake. With the wine mulled and a big fire blazing – I had bought some telegraph poles from the old man at the mine – we could just about stand staying outside. Dancing helped us warm up.

Our early Christmas was just becoming suitably festive when I heard shouting over near the cab. Looking over, I saw Nancy and Geoff arguing. Then I saw the punch – he went down impressively quickly. I felt a tear in my heart and groaned audibly; a second violent incident demanded that she leave the trip. Nancy would have to be dropped off at the next major centre.

This time he didn't get up for a belt in the ribs, and by the time I got there Nancy had already run off into the darkness. I picked Geoff up and asked him what had happened.

"I don't know," he spluttered, "she's a nutter, your girlfriend. If she doesn't leave I will, and I'll bloody sue you and your company for the money."

I barely listened to the suing part. I felt deeply stung by his description of her. She had problems, but she was trying to deal with them, and there was no way she'd have hit him unless he had provoked her deliberately. He had made his own life a misery and then tried to drag everyone else down with him.

But he was within his rights.

"Don't worry," I said. "Nancy will be leaving from Santiago."

Five days away.

She came to the cab about an hour later, her whole body shaking with cold. I had searched for a while, but with the darkness total and scrub or salt in every direction, I knew she wouldn't have been found until she chose to be. The party had stopped in an instant, Joanne killing the music as soon as I had finished speaking with Geoff. The group had all gone to their tents.

Lucho Gatico was playing when she climbed in. Despite both being on one small seat, we found a way to hug until she stopped shivering. We said nothing – Lucho was saying everything we both felt in his poetic Spanish. When Nancy finally spoke it was in a whisper.

"I know I have to go. I know you've got to make me. I'm sorry."

"Will we see each other in Rio?" I asked.

"I don't know what I'm going to do."

"We've got five days until Santiago. Please let's try and enjoy them. We'll work something out."

"We will," she whispered, giving an answer, I thought, to both my comments.

"She's gone," Joanne announced as I pulled up to the campsite gates in a taxi.

It was the second morning since the fight and we were back down in Calama. I knew exactly what she meant but still said the words, seeking, I suppose, an extra moment of denial.

"Who's gone where?"

"Nancy. She didn't say where but she took a taxi to the bus station. I tried to stop her but she wouldn't let me. She wouldn't even let me go with her."

"How long ago?"

"About an hour."

As I got back into the taxi Joanne climbed in with me. The bus station was crawling with people; dozens of buses revved, sounded their horns and left. We searched amongst all the activity. Fruitlessly.

"I'm sorry, Tim. I tried to stop her."

"Thanks, Joanne. Don't apologise – there was nothing you could do."

We drove back in silence, my mind trying to digest the facts. Nancy had disappeared and could have gone anywhere. I didn't even have a home address – we hadn't got round to that. At the campsite, the atmosphere was gloomy. Nancy had been a key part of the group. She was already missed.

In my cab I saw an envelope on the driver's seat. I opened it. Inside was a polaroid of Nancy and me in front of Machu Picchu. Arm in arm, we were smiling at the camera. On the back was her familiar handwriting;

I've gone to find the man who knows.
I'll write when I have something to write.
All my love, Nancy.

Well, at least I know where she's going.

Three long days drive brought us to our rough camp in forest not far from Viña del Mar. I had been working on some sort of autopilot, but in my head the same things kept going round and around. How could I have helped avoid the situation? Where might she be now? On the trail? With Manolo's family waiting for him to come back from a trip? Would she be welcomed or sent packing, to feel even worse? When would she write? While I ruminated, the group had picked back up. The gap Nancy had left had already been filled; the group had closed in, each taking on a tiny part of the role she had played.

In the morning, with an easy run to Santiago ahead of me, I went to find a Fallen Branch. They didn't come in ones and twos this time – I was suddenly enveloped in a cloud of bees. I didn't even wipe, but pulled up my trousers taking just enough care not to trap any bees inside. Then ran.

The memory of the attack in Africa made me panic. A frenzied cloud was trailing me, front-runners diving at my head. It must have looked like a comedy sketch as I sprinted past the truck slapping my head to kill those that landed. I was being stung on the scalp and could feel the bees buzzing in their own panic, stuck in my dirty hair. Then they suddenly disappeared. Stopping, gasping for breath from my still rising panic, I thumped the last few struggling bees with over-zealous punches.

After waiting a while to compose myself, I went back to the camp. Joanne was waiting with Piriton. She picked little furry bodies out of my hair and I shuddered as I saw each one on the end of her tweezers. Suddenly, another came. I saw it. It went past Joanne and straight at my eye. I batted it off once, getting my hand in front of my eye just in time, but it swung back round and stung me on the other one. I shouted that we were going – the group had packed up while I was off running in the forest – and drove off as soon as they were all aboard. Joanne was in the cab with me.

"You'd better stop and let me look at that eye."

"Not yet." I wanted to get clear of any trees. To look at them reminded me of CAR.

"Then take some more Piriton."

"It'll make me sleepy. It's only two hours to Santiago. I'll have some more there."

We got there without stopping. Incredibly, I got us straight to the Hotel Maury without getting lost, and then parked the truck up. I was supposed to telex and go to the bank, and I also wanted to check the Post Restante in case any letters had made it from Cusco in three days. Instead I went straight to bed.

I was woken by knocking at my door. The feeling was familiar. My head pounded and my hands, arms and face were painfully swollen. Where I had stings on my wrists, red welts were running up the veins of my forearms.

"Piriton time, every four hours." Joanne was jolly as usual.

"Oh my God," she said as she saw my arms. "That looks bad. How do you feel?"

"Bloody awful, but I've been here before. It'll go by tomorrow."

"Did you have those marks last time?"

"Yes, but not as bad. These are much darker."

"Take these antihistamine and drink lots of water. And whatever you do, try and relax." She left.

I woke up in hospital on a drip, Joanne and Jean by the bed. I asked what had happened.

"I called a doctor and you wouldn't wake up," Joanne began. "He took your pulse and it was very fast. He thought at first you had asthma but I explained."

"So I called an ambulance," Jean added. They always shared stories. It made me smile.

"How long have I been here?"

"Ten hours," said Joanne

"What's happening? Why am I on a drip?"

"You've got low blood pressure," said Joanne.

"Your body's fighting the poison from the stings. It overcompensates and makes it worse, apparently. You can die of anaphylactic shock." Jean liked a drama – and new vocab.

"Your body's been sensitised to bee stings by the previous attack," continued Joanne. "That's what the marks are" – I looked at my arms; they were red up past the elbows – "something to do with mast cells in your blood."

Too much detail. I must have fallen back to sleep. When I next looked around I was bathed in sunlight. No one was there. Presently a nurse came into my cubicle. She told me it was eleven in the morning, more than twenty-four hours since the attack. I felt worse than ever. A few hours later, Joanne and Jean arrived.

"I called your office last night," said Joanne guiltily. "I'm sorry, but I had to look in your diary. There was a number saying 'Hotline'."

"Yeah, she spoke to someone called Graham," Jean added.

"I told him what the doctor said. You'll be here for a week at least." Joanne said them, the words I didn't want to hear.

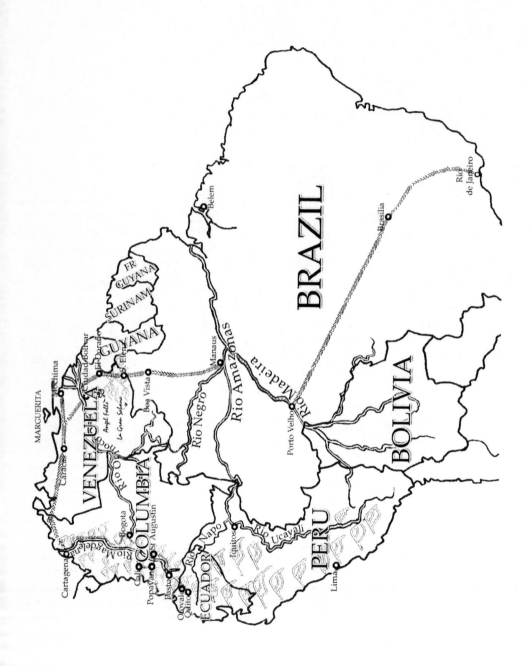

It was Hugo who took over. I didn't meet him, but Graham told me when I called London the day after he'd left with my group. The group had spent only one unscheduled day in Santiago. Once again Graham had proved himself a maestro at minimising mayhem.

I was five days in Santiago Hospital. Discharged, I flew to Rio – the Marajo seemed a more familiar place to hole up in; at least there I had a chance of seeing people I knew. Hugo wasn't due in for two more weeks, but I expected Al before then. Then again, with his truck, going across the Amazon, anything could have happened. London had told me that two trainees were on their way out, and Craig would no doubt show up at some point.

My only company therefore – apart from Maudlin Michel, who helped me out whenever I needed anything and constantly asked when Al would arrive – was an enormous turkey that lived on the balcony of the fifth floor flat opposite my room window. In old-town Rio the tenements are packed so close together that I could almost touch my fowl friend. I remembered Judge, Robert's Zairian chicken, whose head I could now picture dangling at right angles after being stretched past snapping point for the benefit of our tastebuds. With grisly images of stripped goats and flaming pigs also populating my internal TV, I sometimes seriously considered vegetarianism.

Due to his imposing stature in comparison to Judge, I named my new poultry pal Chief Justice, quickly shortened to Justice, then Justy, Just and finally J. The reason for J's roller coaster ride through nomenclature was our communication problem. While he happily gave good gobble at dawn, the minute the sun was up he would zip up, and then stand to attention like a soldier, staring through my window or through me if I went for a chat. But I loved the sound he made so I would continuously call his various names in a bid to elicit a friendly squawk in return.

My own gobbling – I had been woefully short of practice in my life – was more of a gargle, and J didn't even bother to feign indifference. He was blatantly and brazenly unimpressed. Of course it became a challenge, and it was when I moved on to other animal noises that I saw the first signs of a breakthrough. A moo, if I did it with my mouth closed, got a shake of J's obscenely ugly labial growth. A hippo grunt made him stand on one leg. But it was my best duck that got the gobble going. By the third morning, J would even look at me.

The extensively extended Brazilian family who peopled his apartment apparently found nothing untoward in our morning and evening conversations. On the balcony themselves in the evenings, they would raise Antarctica beers and smile, gobble and laugh with us. Still having no Portuguese to speak of, the father of the family and I also communicated in quacks.

When I wasn't talking turkey, I was wandering the streets and sights of Rio. The advice is wrong. It shouldn't be 'don't walk in Rio' but 'don't carry anything in Rio'. I kept my shorts' pockets turned out like little dog-ears and the street kids loved it; they were really friendly and funny. I got addicted to fruit drinks, fresh 'vitaminos' from beautifully presented juice stalls. Stacks of fruit and vegetables are fronted by a couple of sharp-looking guys doing the cocktail shaker thing but with blenders. You can order anything, with or without milk. After endless experimentation, I finally came up with my perfect combo: three parts maracuja, one part cerise, and a smattering of natural yoghurt. In Rio you really could easily go veggie, if they only would close those churrascerias.

I wandered the Copacabana, Flamenco and Ipanema beaches. I climbed the Sugar Loaf and Hunchback mountains. I thought about hang-gliding, which was on offer, but decided to wait to do it with someone else. Apart from that, I thought about thinking about Nancy as little as possible.

She won't even know where I am now either, I didn't think.

Eventually London gave me my orders. Al and I would be doing a double-depart – two trucks in tandem. I would have my third crack at finishing the Rio-Quito southern route, the Andean Adventure. Better still, my trip was a full South American Circle, nearly six months Rio to Rio – a *real* overland trip. With continuing bad news from Al in the Amazon, however, departure dates had been put back six weeks. Meanwhile, Craig was indeed coming – to supervise a major rebuild of Al's truck. I was also to pick up Matt from the airport that day – he was the trainee who would be going with Al. With just over seven weeks to live and work in Rio, therefore, I could imagine no more enjoyable future life event than announcing at a dinner party: 'Rio, ah yes, I once lived there for two months. Lovely spot.'

Al was delayed still further, so both he and Hugo actually arrived on the same day. The booths in the large Marajo reception area were suddenly full to the brim with overlanders swapping stories of the different north and south Quito-Rio routes. South generally got the larger thumbs-up. My group had really enjoyed the rest of their trip, and Hugo had done an excellent job with them.

Over the next few days the groups slowly dissipated and Craig organised us into a team to sort Al's truck out. Unfortunately, the one thing we lacked was an engine rebuild kit. Currently unavailable, London said.

The routine was excellent. A cab ride with Paulo to the bus depot, a morning's work, lunch at the Office 2, knock-off at five, a beer at the Office 1, a few more with the irreverent regulars at the Marajo bar, then off to one of Al's chosen restaurants. We tried everything but punctuated adventurous eating with liberal visits to the churrasceria and a great cevicheria Al came across. Weekends were spent on the beach; the evenings in the samba clubs where teams practice for the carnival. Twice we hired a minibus and drove up into the mountains behind Rio to go camping. It was great to get out of the city and breathe cool air, but it was always good to get back.

One weekend we tried to arrange a barbecue at Ronnie Biggs' place. Al had heard he entertained for a fee, but we didn't know how to contact him. Michel came to the rescue with an enlightened idea. Lifting a hefty Rio and Environs directory onto his marble desk he ran a finger down – "B, B, B, B, Biggs, R." He was there, one of the world's most wanted men, in the phonebook. We got shy all of a sudden. 'You call' – 'No, you call' – 'You sound more like a criminal'. Eventually Al, bored with the quibbling, stepped forward. We crowded around Michel's red receiver. "Shhhhhh, it's ringing."

"'Ello?"

"Ah, could I speak to Mr. Biggs please?"

"Speaking."

We all descended into fits of nervous giggles. Only Al kept some demeanour and had to relate the conversation after it had finished.

"Ah. Hello … erm, Ronnie. May I call you Ronnie?"

"Whaddya want?"

"Err… we were wondering if we might come for dinner. You know, a barbecue one night. There's a lot of us. Erm ... we'll pay."

"Not this mumf, mate. Me memwah's comin' ahht. I got The Sun 'ere naaah an' the rest of the press lay'tron. Give us anuvver ring Septembah, an I'll sor' chaahht."

The accent was Al's.

"Oh, OK. Thanks a lot, erm … Ronnie. Err, bye. Oh … and good luck with the memoirs!"

Arriving at the depot at dawn one Monday morning, we each stepped over a man's body lying in the gateway. It was trussed and badly beaten up. The guards told us it had been dumped there, probably after a fight in the favela nearby. They were leaving it for the police to pick up. I couldn't believe how nonchalant I had become. Only Matt had said anything. He saw it first. "Hop boys, there's a dead 'un." Ex-French Foreign Legion, he was the last to be ruffled by such things.

Matt was tattooed, crew cut, bearded and tough. He was fine, quite sweet actually, until he got too drunk. We'd had to pull him out of a few fights. He was very guarded about his Foreign Legion days, only saying that he had been part of a team evacuating VIPs from Kisangani, Zaire, in the battles that had left it how Al and I had seen it. In fact, his history as we knew it was quickly summed up by Al: "He had a happy marriage apparently, then one day he put his away kit on and shacked up with another bird. That titsed up, so he joined the Legion. Now he's here. He's a bit scary, eh? Especially after a Caipirinha … and he's one for the ladies, I think."

"One for the ladies, eh? That's rich coming from you," I countered.

"Not no more, mate. Still fully zipped up. I get a letter a week now, and they've spiced up a bit since you read one."

"They keeping you going, are they?"

"Yeah. But I told London that's it after this one. Unless they give me some non-truck trips for a while." The company also ran long-haul jungle trips using local boats to cross the Amazon from Peru to Brazil, or across the Darien Gap from Columbia to Panama. "It's the only way I could get back into enjoying the groups."

Broken for two blissful months in Rio, my own string of problems was already laid out ahead of me, stretched taut across South America. I set off on a coast-to-coast deluge of disaster.

After an overnight trip to one of the islands off Parati – we could charter a whole boat with two groups – and an excellent party, Al and I split up. More accurately, I left him behind. The attentions of six mechanics for six weeks had done little to improve his truck's performance and we certainly hadn't uncovered the hill-detector. An overtake on the first rise out of Parati, a smile, a wave, a dot in my wing mirror, and that would be it until Chile.

At Foz campsite someone cracked their head open on the slippery poolside and had to be flown home; in Ascunsion there was a general strike and I couldn't get my funding; and just outside Residencia in Argentina I was nicked for speeding – a horrendous $2000 fine, out of my own pocket. I was on my way to Salta at the time, on a ridiculously long detour north. I had felt I could afford to try and liven Argentina up a bit using the speed of the Dream Machine. After the fine we got bogged for a day in the Chaco and were chewed on by a crack cohort of carnivorous bugs while we dug. In Salta itself, which boasted the Largest Outdoor Swimming Pool in the World, we were rewarded with the dismal view of a vast empty concrete pond populated by skateboarders.

Going over the Andes, I got talked into taking off the snow-chains I had spent three cold hours putting on. Busy, I had fallen for the old man-in-a-uniform trick at the giant, indoor, centrally heated border post. It was dark by the time I began to descend the torturous pass into Chile, and there was no place safe to stop and put them back on. In crawler gear it took the whole night to get down, the terrified group freezing in the back of the sliding truck.

We spent two days in Santiago, during which time I picked up double-money from the bank and a month-old letter from Nancy at the Post Restante. The envelope was post-marked New Jersey and pre-printed with the name of a theatre production company. In it was a long letter but no address. She sounded happy, and had written about our time together and how she missed it. She had done the Inca Trail again, in fact a longer version, but not with Manolo. There, she said, she had found the space to realise that what she wanted was at home. She had flown back to New York from Lima and said she might have a surprise ... *'I don't know which way you're going, but I'll write to Quito and Manaus – it's odd that I don't know which one you'll get to first.'*

Give me a bloody address and I'll tell you!

During the long drive up through Chile I began to wonder again what people got out of doing overland trips. There was the adventure, of course, and the experience of other cultures, albeit peripheral, that would surely affect their lives in the future. More and more, though, it looked like many people were looking for a change in their lives, or at least a break; a blank page to give them time for reflection. It certainly gave them that, and new friendships that would last a lifetime.

Fate was about to trivialise such musing. The dust plume behind the Dream Machine, pelting across the flat sands towards San Pedro de Atacama, was so good that the group wanted photographs. I dropped them off and took a good run up. I wanted them to get the truck and its sandy appendage against a background of the purple Domeyko Mountains. To complete my enjoyment I was smoking a Marlboro, vaguely hoping that a good lens might pick it up as it hung from my mouth with a nonchalance matched by my elbow hanging out of the window. I finished it, I flicked it, and I heard a tremendous 'whoosh'. That barking pig again.

Oh No! Not again!

Don't get it? Let's run through it again, frame by frame. You've got the camera:

Dust plume behind the truck, mountains in background, zoom in. Fag in driver's mouth, elbow out of the window. Last deep inhalation. Cool glance out of the window at group of admirers previously shown. Cut to close up of cab-top air intake positioned above and behind the window. Zoom in on very small holes in the mesh. Cut back to face profile. Catch driver's eyes slightly squinting in the sun. Hand goes to mouth, pulls out fag. Follow hand out of the window. Hold as it flicks the butt. Double slow-mo now as the butt spins upwards and backwards. Keep running as it shoots with the accuracy of a sniper's bullet through one of the holes in the air intake mesh. Cut to whole cab shot. Flash of flame in the air filter cylinder below and behind the door. Zoom out. Brakes go on. Plume drops. Zoom in on face. Cool expression now turns to one of puzzlement. Driver jumps out.

'Yeah, so what?'

As soon as I saw the melted blue paint on the outside of the cylinder – it's big on a Cargo, about two feet long – I knew what had happened. With the hot desert air flowing at speed into the intake, the paper filter had instantly combusted on being touched by the cigarette end. I traced the route in my mind. The filter efficiently prevents even the tiniest dust particle from going into the engine, the clean air ending up helping diesel combust against the pistons. My filter had just turned into the equivalent of a whole bag of soot. Millions of abrasive carbon particles had suddenly shot into the engine.

I came out in one of my cold sweats. The implications for running the South American Circle were too many, so I concentrated on the immediate problem – getting a new filter, as I didn't have a spare. In San Pedro they laughed. In Calama they offered me an astonishing assortment of shapes and sizes. In fairness, all they had to go on was two different-sized, blackened rings I held up hopefully – the top and bottom of the filter, the only surviving remnants. No luck, try Antofogasta. It was too late to get there that day.

"Waaankaaaaaahh." A familiar call rang out across the quiet campsite as a truck drove into Calama campsite; a booted foot waved at me out of the window. Al hopped out – *purple tartan? Where the hell...?* – his troupe scurrying to erect their camp where he had stopped. Matt waved and climbed under the truck. Well trained.

"Heard you had trubs, hombre."

"How did you know?"

"The whole of sodding San Pedro told me you'd been looking for a filter. Even the condor had a word. What happened?"

I told him.

"Well, Captain Fagend, I'll still swap trucks if you like. This thing's got me fucked. I faxed London and told them – if you don't sort me out I'm quitting right now. I've not spoken a word to the group since Parati, and you know that's not like me." He had a major oil-leak and the Bedford could hardly get up the hills. Emergency pistons and rings had been couriered to La Paz, but before he could get there, he and Matt would have to work on the truck in Calama before heading up into the high Andes.

"How's Matt doing?"

"He's turned out a blinder. He's cool with the truck, and cool with the troops, thank fuck. I've had to grab the bottle from him once or twice, mind."

Matt came over to help, but as always I found true experts irritating – "Too long ... you'll have to go back and get another one made."

The filter I'd had made during my lonesome two days in Antofogasta at – of all things – an air-filter factory I had found, stood proud of the cylinder by an inch or more. It was no good if I couldn't seal it against the lid.

Matt stayed with me, tutting at my efforts to fill the gap: tape, a T-shirt, even bandages. They failed the seal test one after the other. *Time to get serious – I'm not going back again.*

236

The truck seats were made of very dense foam. I measured up and sliced a long strip to match. I cut it, and then glued the ends. Putting my makeshift rubber ring in place, I pressed the cover on and flicked the clamps down. It looked snug. My test was to hold a Rizla paper against the seal; if it stuck, air was being sucked in – a failure. I got Matt to fire the engine. The Rizla fluttered in the breeze, then dropped from my fingers. That would do. Whatever damage the soot had done would now at least not be made worse by incoming dust.

Al wouldn't let me stay to help him. It was only a gesture anyway and we both knew it. Besides, he had Matt. It took a while to stock up with fresh food at the supermercado and even longer to hide it all from the keen Chilean border guards. We set off late, leaving Al and Matt knee-deep in oil and surrounded by unidentified metal objects.

I had forgotten the lonely Chilean checkpoint until I saw the two mean dogs Al had tried to befriend barking in the road. Staying in the truck I waited until the policemen came to the cab. They were different but just as friendly, so I asked if we could stay – it was late, 3200m, and only up from there on in, as the memory function of my alti-watch showed me in a graph. They happily agreed and moved their two Landcruisers out of a shed. That memorable evening – apart from the problems inherent in tipping a bag of soot into an engine, namely vastly increased oil usage – was to herald a respite from trouble.

He was as good as Lucho Gatico. In the tin shed, shut tight from the cold, a fire in the centre, a portly moustachioed policeman strummed and sang. I understood most of the words, but he filled his temporary auditorium with such emotion that even the most monolingual in the audience shed a thimbleful of tears. Lachrymose himself, he stopped between each song to wipe himself down and explain the meaning of the next one. He had some time back introduced his wife in both words and song; now, many years, two children, three distant postings and a long Toyota-drive home later, they were about to get divorced. My hand was covering my eyes like a visor. Each time I looked up I stretched my arms, mimicking a deep, tear-inducing yawn. When I rubbed my eyes it was through tiredness alone. And I think I speak for all our group's boys in all of that.

Crowds of Quitenos lined the streets, cheering and throwing garlands under the wheels of the truck. Ticker tape fluttered like flying ants from colonial windows. *What a feeling!*

I had made it, all but two of my group crossing the finishing line with me. The second missing party was Anne-Marie, a Dutch woman who had expressed an interest in Latino men way back in Parati. "I know just the man if you can wait

237

that long," I had said. After our jungle trip Anne-Marie had gone off with Eduardo – the Real Adonis – to his home village. Things were serious. He wanted her to meet his mother.

The only real problems, apart from oil usage steadily increasing to five litres a day, were a bogging on the salt flats and further jungle disaster. On the Salar de Uyuni, in a freezing wind, we were four days stuck in mud, the truck buried up to its windows until its monumental last effort after many previous disappointing attempts at extrication. Under the truck with a bottle jack for much of that time, I had sobbed for the second time in my overlanding career. It was truly horrible to be working in a mixture of glue and cold porridge for such a duration.

And as much as I love it, the jungle is my nemesis. This time, avoiding the knee-snapping effects of rum, I tried the hideous white sap that Adonis assured us took the Indians to nirvana of a night. Personally I just went floating off down river, having assumed that my new-found superhuman strength could drag a drifting dugout upstream against the vicious current of the Napo. Eleanor – the doctor of the trip – and myself had been skinny-dipping, she too loosened up by the 'tree-blood'. Eduardo's boat had worked loose with our playful splashing and off it went, me in hot pursuit.

A fact that should be made known to any potential experimenter of natural narcotics is that the effects wear off with fear. Pretty sharpish, in fact. Naked, cold and clinging to a fast-moving tree trunk carrying me ever further towards Brazil, I felt as sober as I felt stupid. Luckily, Eleanor had clocked my unexpect-edly swift departure and had raised the alarm. Eduardo was peeled off Anne-Marie by Adonis, bollocked for his clearly insufficient knotting abilities and sent off after me in Jose's boat. I got back for breakfast. Warned by Eleanor, Eduardo had brought me a towel.

Of course I hadn't 'made it' at all. I had completed a section, and was well over two years doing that. In reality I was only half way around my South American Circle. Meanwhile I had a week in Quito.

Sid was to be my trainee, so he announced when I sat next to a shortish gringo at the bar of our hotel in new-town Quito. London hadn't mentioned it. Sid told me he was an aircraft mechanic; perhaps London thought he would be helpful in keeping the high-tech Cargo in pole position. Unfortunately, powerful though it was, the Dream Machine didn't have a jet engine and Sid had little more of a clue than I did. There was certainly nothing we could do about the oil usage without a full engine rebuild, and that would have to wait until Rio. Jets don't run every-thing with air-valves either. On the Dream Machine they controlled absolutely everything – brakes, suspension, gear change, probably even the indicators; and contaminated airlines were clogging the whole system up. It was the Christmas-tree lights theory of breakdown – if one went they all went, and the source was unfathomable. It took us the whole turnaround week just to map the forty-three valves, then dismantle and clean them.

Al and Matt had arrived five days after me. Their truck finally fully fixed up in La Paz, the trip had improved enormously. Al had been granted his wish and told me how he was getting himself prepared for his trans-continental non-truck jungle trips.

"I'll have to be fit as fuck, hombre – half the way we're sodding walking. So if you need me, I'll be in bed … I've got a week to get some kip."

Matt was to set off back the way he had come as a trainee again with a new leader who was coming out from Africa. This was a typically nifty solution by London – an experienced leader from Africa could use the geographical expertise of a trainee who had just done the route. Both would benefit, and the group would get an excellent combination. We had yet to hear who the driver was.

Nancy had written. An old letter dated only a week after the one I had got in Santiago. Still no address other than the theatre company, which I had tried without success. The surprise, she said, would have to wait. I allowed myself a happy thought – would the surprise be her?

London was in contact too. A bollocking for going over budget in Argentina – expected; another for not keeping in enough contact – expected; and a birthday greeting – not expected. They even said they had sent me a present with the driver who was coming out.

Later that week, I had another surprise. Amongst the arrivals for Matt's southbound Andean Adventure were a couple celebrating their engagement. I had detected the facts of their status before even being told. In the hotel bar one evening, hands had covered my eyes, a woman's voice saying, "Guess who?" The accent and the feel of warm bands of metal on my cheeks was enough for me to know. As Katrina moved her hands away from my face, I saw the Djenne ring – gold amongst all her home-crafted silver ones – on her engagement finger. Struck dumb, I turned and looked at her. Her eyes laughing, her smile wide; both displayed the joy and artistry I suddenly remembered her exuding.

"Congratulations," I said to Charlie, having used the time it took to hug them both to pull myself together.

"It sure is a shame we ain't got you to drive us," Charlie drawled.

No, Charlie. It isn't.

With the promise of an ocelot for entertainment, I took them to Adam's Rib. We had a great night catching up. The rest of their Africa trip had been superb. Much to Charlie's delight, they had got a good bogging in Zaire, and had avoided malaria – during and immediately after the rains is definitely the time to avoid. More news: Adrian, my replacement driver, had indeed got together with Clubfoot Heidi and they were going to have a go at living together in Norway. Charlie and

Katrina had both recently been working in London and had gone to their leaving party in Leeds.

The unidentified leader of Matt's trip turned up on the day before his departure – he'd had trouble getting flights out of Dar-Es-Salaam in Tanzania. Collier looked five years older than when I'd last seen him briefly in Niamey. Two years Africa driving had taken its toll.

"Hey, you ponce, you look five years older than you used to. What the hell happened to that little lad with the shits in Niger?"

God – me too? I had never stopped to think about it. Mirrors weren't a common feature of overlanding life.

"You can bloody talk. You better start planning your fortieth by the looks."

"Cheeky sod. What's it like out here?"

"Superb in most ways, mate, but you'll miss Africa."

"I can't believe that for a minute. I've had enough over there." Obviously it happened to everybody.

"What's this?" I said in one-hundred percent enquiry as he handed me an old army helmet along with my spares and funding he had brought out. It had squiggles of black marker pen all over it and looked like the sort of thing you would get in Camden market for a fiver.

"Your birthday present. A 'mechanic's hat' mate, signed by everyone in London. What the hell do you think it is?!"

When we left Quito, the group was made up of seven from the first half who'd stayed on and four new arrivals. Erika, a very tall Swede, was permanently flushed. Whenever I saw her she was pounding the pavements with furrowed brow, looking remarkably busy. Freda, an equally tall but much rounder German lady, did the opposite – whenever I saw her she was sitting with either a beer or a book. Melita, a very talented Swiss photographer, was there to research some locations for a book she was planning. And Jonathan, a teenaged Brit, reminded me a bit too much of Geoff with his early remarks about the 'bus'. Overland drivers don't hold out for high world ranking in the professional stakes, but they do tend to insist on their one tool of the trade being called a *truck*. Eleanor the Doc then booked on at the last minute. An excellent addition, she made it a nice round dozen.

I hadn't summoned the energy to get to know the old group that well and knew I wouldn't try hard with the new ones either. A lot of people had flowed through my life in the previous two years and in many ways it was the hardest bit of leading trips. The early getting-to-know-you conversations were draining. The more tired a driver became, the harder it was to start up real friendships, particularly in the knowledge that they would be unnaturally terminated after three months. Drivers would do their jobs, but only rookies and real naturals like Craig could keep up the entertainment. I had even watched Al's enthusiasm wither. Withdrawal, particularly if the truck needed constant attention, was natural and was perhaps why drivers, from whatever company, were always so pleased to see each other. We had a natural bond, our own understanding of the highs and lows of the job. Overland groups had their bond too, their own sub-culture, and even years in the future – like mountain-climbers meeting in the Alps or surfers on a Cornwall beach – they would always be able to relate when they met one another.

We weren't long in Ecuador. We crossed the Equator, went to Otovalo market, and then crossed the border into Columbia. Columbia is famous for three things: coffee, cocaine and civil war. As far as I knew, drug barons controlled Cali, Medellin and much of the surrounding area, their gun-toting gangsters killing anyone who so much as looked at them in the wrong way. Terrorists, be they FARC or any other group, were either with them or against them, depending on what I wasn't sure. They controlled the rest of the south and most of Columbia's vast portion of the Amazon. More guns, more swaggering bullies; hardened criminals who had known nothing but decades of violence. To me, it didn't sound like the best place for a dozen camera-toting tourists.

But my sketchy media-based understanding just was not true. Outside of Bogota I never met anyone without a smiling face, a welcoming handshake and a ready joke. If Columbia rivals Peru for bad press about its dangers, it rivals Brazil for the friendliness and fun of its folk. And their country is consummately beautiful. The mountainous drive to the attractive mainly Indian town of Pasto, then through the coffee plantations around Popayan, was sublime. It stayed that way for the drive through the Purace National Park to San Augustin, although our armed police escort through the purportedly terrorist infested park distracted me from the scenery a touch. Even they were friendly, and had a penchant for tea and biscuits. We had to stop and brew up four times that day, providing a nice stationary target.

In a beautiful, green, mountainous landscape, perfect for hiking, lies another of South America's unsolvable mysteries. Dotted around the Valley of the Statues below San Augustin are hundreds of large – well, statues – hewn from rock by an unknown culture over five thousand years ago. Oddly enough, they too disappeared with the arrival of the Spanish, only this time totally, with no information documented.

We decided to visit the statues on horses. I find horses have strong minds of their own, and if they sense a hesitant rider, generally display that strength in a contrary fashion. We were descending a narrow track cut into a steep hillside. I was lagging behind and wanted to catch up, but I couldn't get my mount to do any more than sway a fat arse in a saunter. I gave it a good double back-heel in the ribs. The horse instantly speeded to a trot and veered dangerously close to the edge of the track. Once there it wouldn't move away or slow down, however hard I tugged; in fact the tugs just triggered further rapid acceleration.

"Ooh look, you're cantering!" enthused Eleanor as I bounced on and off the horse's back going past her. I was getting a headache.

"How do I stop it?"

"Just pull."

"I tried that, it doesn't work." She was gone, further advice carried off on the breeze.

I reached our front-runner, Jonathan, and overtook him too. By now I was thinking of jumping off, but we were going downhill too fast for my liking. A bridge formed a corner before an uphill stretch ahead and to my mind we were approaching too fast to take it safely. *He won't skid though; he must know what he's doing.*

Wrong. The horse's legs went from underneath him and I was thrown into the stream. The horse picked himself up and galloped off up the hill, not evening looking back to see if I was OK – the selfish beast.

Drying out and tending my grazes over lunch by the stream, the guide turned up with my horse. Jonathan said he wanted to swap, as he wanted a big one. Despite his being (A) a good rider and (B) much taller than me, I had been given the biggest – I was the 'esteemed leader'. I gladly accepted and after a good picnic, cocked my leg and settled into the saddle to enjoy a docile amble in the Andes on my dog-sized pony.

On the way back to camp in the late afternoon, we were passing a campesino leading a cow. Suddenly surrounded by horses in number, the heifer panicked, pulled its rope from the man's hands and ran for it, udders swaying painfully wide. Jonathan's big horse decided to follow suit. It reared, whinnied, and then disappeared in a cloud of dust as if being chased by a posse of Crow Indians.

Normally I would expect to get involved in such situations. I was, however, severely handicapped, by both a lack of equestrian expertise and a diminutive steed. Clippety-clopping up last to the scene of Jonathan's crash – also on a corner, I noted with a nanosecond of satisfaction – I found him lying flat on the ground being tended by Eleanor. No doubt slightly reluctantly, as she had made it clear she considered herself on holiday, but she was under the oath.

"He's hurt his back."

"Can he ride?"

"I wouldn't think so."

"Is he OK otherwise?"

"I don't know, but he didn't hit his head, which was lucky."

"I'm OK," groaned Jonathan, "I just have to stay horizontal. It's happened before."

The solution was a bit messy, but the best I could do. Eleanor stayed with Jonathan; I got on the back of the guide's horse and shut my eyes as we flew back down to town. Melita volunteered to lead the group back at normal speed, taking the extra horse. Personally I thought it should have been put down on the spot. That's what happens to dodgy dogs.

I found the town taxi driver, who made me pay double for driving along the rough track, and soon Jonathan was stretched out in the back. With Eleanor sitting in the front I wobbled dangerously on the boot, hanging onto a tiny roof sill with sore fingers. Back at the campsite we lifted him onto a camp bed and into the truck. I took him to hospital.

We had two more days exploring the valley and its statues – all on foot – and a spit-pig party one evening. This time, the pig, having been dropped in headfirst, was boiled in an old oildrum to remove the offending fluff. On both evenings, Eleanor and I visited Jonathan.

"It's worse than before." He still couldn't get up and sounded surprised. "It's usually fine after a day in bed."

"What did your parents say?" On my insistence, Jonathan had called them that morning.

"That if it was no better by tomorrow, they would pay to get me home and deal with the insurance later." His eyes were downcast, but he knew more about his injury than any of us, and knew we couldn't help.

It wasn't any better, so I prepared Sid for dealing with the evacuation of an immobile patient, after only his first week on the road. It involved private hire of an ambulance, phone calls to a bank in Cali to arrange the Colombian end of a money transfer, flights for both of them from Cali to Bogota with extra seats for a horizontal passenger and another for Jonathan to the UK.

What a drag, I was thinking.

"I hate to say it, but I'm enjoying this," said Sid guiltily as he set off.

One down.

Just past San Augustin, at Altavisva, the Andes split into the Central and Oriental Cordilleras. We would follow the Rio Magdalena Valley between them all the way to the Caribbean, the third South American coastline I would visit. I was tempted to pop east over the mountains into the jungle, but word had it that the FARC and ELN, Columbia's two major armed revolutionary movements, wouldn't take too kindly to my curiosity. There, they control much of the territory – and the people. Some of Columbia's small population of indigenous Indians live there along with a huge influx of dislocated 'mestizos' – those of mixed race who make up the majority of Columbia's total population. Both groups struggle to establish themselves and their crops in this forested wetland frontier, and the politics of the area are unfathomable. While the guerrillas encourage local people to take care of their environment and build schools for their children, they fight armed right-wing paramilitary groups; meanwhile, the US sends personnel and arms to the Colombian government to fight 'the War on Drugs', wilting the evil weed with poisonous sprays and at the same time destroying the settlers' crops.

But is there a wider agenda? The guerrilla groups are communist, the wealthy landowners of the north who make up the government, emphatically not so. Didn't we see similar in El Salvador? Guatemala? Where the military – backed by the US – brought untold terror to the 'communists' eking out a living in the Central American mountains. Where exactly the truth lies it is difficult to say, especially as the oppressed retaliate with inhuman atrocities of their own. But there is a pattern. In many South and Central American countries, land distribution is appallingly inequitable, prospects for the poor dire. These real grievances need addressing, but whenever a progressive society is set up it is quashed in the name of 'freedom'. I'm no expert, but as our richer countries continually consume, hidden, hideous things go on across the world to keep 'them' in order and 'us' supplied with our primary products and cheap goods. CIA subversion or invasions of so-called rogue states haven't stemmed the desire for environmental common sense and a more equitable distribution of wealth. Perhaps nothing short of a radical rethink of the way the world is run will do, one that benefits the majority rather than the few.

We overlanders had all come to these countries for a 'life-changing experience'. And we all got one. If one thing becomes clear to anyone driving across a continent in a truck, it has to be that the people we encountered – be they croppers making the most of the Amazon, campesinos struggling to live in a communal society, or hawkers swamping a bus in Africa – all work twice as hard as we ever have. And get very little in return.

We crossed the Magdalene and climbed onto the plateau on which Bogota is built. Another frenzied capital, its beautiful but tumbledown colonial buildings stand side by side with towering, modern office blocks. While the group dodged muggers to visit attractions like the Gold Museum, I found Sid. Then we both found one of the few Cummins workshops in South America.

The diagnosis was grim and the engine actually a deleted design. We had problems all right, but they couldn't be fixed. And while we were at it – 'Where on earth did you get that air system?' We faxed my spares list for Rio: the whole rebuild kit for our design of engine, a turbo, mugs, bedlegs and mosquito nets. In reply, London told me that I was to pick up an extra person who was flying into Caracas, Venezuela.

Cartagena for Christmas. It had been my aim and extended driving days had got us there on the eve itself. But trying to balance progress with engine health had left me tired and fractious. By now we were using ten litres of oil a day – half the engine's capacity – and I had to top up every few hours. In an effort to cure the stress, I paid extra to camp in the garden of a hotel right on the beach.

It worked, but in different ways. I looked on in wonder at Sid as he led the group in joining the festive fun Colombians excel at. He organised their parties and extravagant meals; he spent hours talking with them, swimming with them and cooking with them, and he still found time to help me when I needed him. He was a whirlwind of positive energy. In contrast, I spent my time taking refuge under the truck, tinkering away, discovering new tricks and quick fixes. I couldn't face all the group activity and besides, mechanicing seemed to assuage the worry about the impossible real issue – the badly broken engine I still had to coax across the top of South America, and then right down through Brazil to Rio before I could fix it properly.

Too much partying can be a bad thing. Freda fell down the stairs of the fire escape she was dancing on – it overlooked the garden where Sid had installed a Colombian DJ for the night. Her left leg was broken. In the back of an ambulance, I reflected that at least there were good hospitals and an excellent infrastructure in South America. If either of our two accidents had happened in Africa, we would have been in real trouble. Freda was put in plaster that night and flown out the next evening.

Another one gone.

To pick up our new expedition member we were aiming at getting to Caracas, Venezuela's capital, for New Year's Eve. I was looking forward to meeting her; God knows, we needed a sub on the pitch. With two days to spare before that deadline, we reached the Tayrona National Park. There, we hiked in the beautiful coastal forest all day, swam on deserted Caribbean beaches each evening and drank fresh coconut rum punch at night. The group bonding process, begun in Cartagena, was now complete; the old and new members of the group now welded together, drawn as much by the loss of two of their number as by the fabulous environment.

We picked Gladys up on time. It's never easy to enter an existing group, particularly on your own, but with the group as relaxed as they were, it might have gone well. However, we had, to say the very least, just taken delivery of one very odd fish; indeed, Gladys' arrival was about to up my stress levels to unexplored heights and mark the descent of my spirit to a whole new low. Although she had nothing to do with my first worrying reaction to incident, the man in question certainly rivalled her for lunacy.

The streets of Caracas were empty. Completely so. Families were holed up in their apartments for close-knit New Year celebrations and all work had stopped. Sid had driven us from the airport to the centre in a post-apocalyptic silence where only traffic lights carried on their repetitive chore, holding us up to let light breezes pass safely before allowing us through.

The hotel was empty too. Up a steep alleyway with rough ground for a view, it was a dark and exceedingly ugly building. Inside, red mock-velvet wallpaper lined the tunnel-like entrance to reception. Maybe it is the long hours sitting on their own; or maybe it is down to never getting deeper than passing the time of day with the passing guests of the day; possibly it is the stale air and a lack of exercise, but South American hotel receptionists suffer skin problems – and social awareness problems to boot.

While the group unloaded their luggage from the truck and the receptionist dealt with our room requirements, Sid and I watched in horror as he pushed his cheek out with his tongue whenever he wasn't talking to us – *to help him think*, I thought. But that wasn't the case. In fact, the man was skilfully targeting the rear of mountainous zits, then creating sufficient pressure with his taster to induce them to pop. When communication required the renewed assistance of his mouth muscle, he would stem the yellowy seepage with the hairy back of his hand. I was waiting for him to lick it, thus to complete an unsavoury circle, but his blotchy trousers bore the brunt instead.

Leaving Sid to complete the transaction, I wandered back up the corridor in distaste. Outside I could hear screaming, so finished my exit at a sprint. The group were scattering, running away from an armed man chasing them. In his right hand was his weapon – a string, on the end of which he swung a bottle; a modern day mace. He stopped moving and started shouting instead, still swinging the makeshift mace above his head. The group started to drift back, curious as to his next move.

At first, I tried the palms-up, soft-talking approach. He lunged, scattering the group and me once more, so I decided the time for weaponry of my own was at hand. Taking a long detour around him I retrieved my machete from the cab, not really having a clue what to do with it. In such situations the moment makes the move, however, and mine must have been ridiculous to watch.

"Aaaaaaaaaaaaaagh…!" After a gladiatorial wiggle of the blade in his general direction, I charged at him. "I'll bite your bloody nose off!" I screamed. Out of nowhere, a phrase I was once told could scare anyone in any language, leapt into my mind.

I lunged and he swung. I parried and danced around him, crying, "Fuck off, fuck the hell off!" Lunge, parry, lunge, like my fencing teacher had taught me when I was ten. He ran at the group.

"Aaaaaaaaghhh!" I shrieked, louder this time, running at him and swinging my machete, aiming to slice the string. Miles off, the bottle shattered instead.

The atmosphere switched instantly to sad. Like a wilting erection, the string fell to the ground. The man dropped it, then dropped his head and shuffled away. Looking at myself, I saw only how stupid I looked – I had totally overreacted. We could have simply filed in to the hotel and shut the door behind us. The man was just ill. He would soon have gone on his way.

What's happening to me? – *'Bite your bloody nose off'* – *where the hell did that come from?* I couldn't think what else to do, so I ran after him and thrust money in his face. With cloudy eyes he looked at me and took it. "Gracias senor... Feliz Nuevo Ano," he muttered before wandering aimlessly away; the lone pedestrian on Caracas' supposedly festive streets.

The group agreed that we should get out of Caracas and spend the three days scheduled for it on the beach instead. Only Erika objected – she wanted to wait two more days for the Poste Restante to open – but was overruled. Later that day, in an argument with a tanker driver after he joined the coast road without looking, just missing my truck, I spat in his face – a massive insult in South America.

Tim, what's the hell's going on?

We found a beach to camp near. I just wanted to walk, to swim. Instead Sid and I worked on the truck while the team cooked. The brakes were getting unreliable, so we cleared the airlines and valves of the oil that was somehow finding its way into the system, and of course topped up with oil.

Dinner had finished, and we were all sitting around the fire when Gladys pissed right there next to it. She had squatted, giggled, and then lifted her skirt. I had noticed that she hadn't eaten, instead polishing off most of a bottle of gin. After her unsavoury performance, I lead her away to talk to her, but heard only gibberish interspersed with laughter. I tried to put her to bed but she ran off to the beach. Later on I found her sprawled there, the bottom of her body naked. A wig had fallen off her head.

We reached Mochima the next morning. There we hired boats and loaded them with equipment, food and hammocks. Three days away from the truck, on a deserted Caribbean island in a coastal National Park, near Margarita, with Trinidad just around the corner. That would surely do the trick – I could sleep, get into the group.

Well, not quite an island. The boatmen had tried to trick me, but I saw on the map that we were in truth crossing to a peninsular. I decided to keep up the deception as it sounded better their way. Gladys was lucid once more but couldn't remember a thing from the previous night, even though sandfly bites covering her legs and disappearing up past the hem of her dress provided ample evidence. I asked her to cut down on her drinking, just to keep herself safe at least.

She was out cold again. This time legs akimbo, no knickers and in the blazing sun. Her wig was still in place but she had an empty gin bottle by her side. Eleanor had alerted me, concerned about Gladys burning herself – surrounding her most delicate flesh, her skin was red raw – but she wouldn't wake up, so we made her a shade out of hammocks. Eleanor tried to make her a little more decent in her slumber, but her legs kept springing back apart. At my suggestion from the other side of the hammocks she tied a towel around Gladys' knees.

Unlike that sight, Mochima was beautiful; the white beach pristine, with shady trees dotted along it. I hiked up the surrounding hills, the earth scorched white and sparsely covered by thorny bush. From the top I could see the village and the boats that had brought us but I had yet to be rumbled – it amazed me how little notice people took of their whereabouts when they had a leader doing it for them.

"Listen, Sid, I'm sorry I'm so grumpy all the time." We were in a bar back in the village, not twenty minutes walk from the hilltop. I had asked him to come for a chat and a beer.

"It's OK. I hadn't noticed."

"Thanks, mate, but you don't need to be polite."

"It's OK, Tim. Really. You just do what you have to do. If you need any help, with anything, just ask. I'm having a great time – and so are the group. To be honest I really don't understand why you're not."

I felt a sudden rush of anger. I wanted to shake Sid into reality; to drum the enthusiasm out of him. But I couldn't understand my reaction, so I said nothing. I leant back, looked at the Caribbean and sipped my beer. Something was stopping me, but what? Dimly, I began to recognise in him the constant energy I'd had when I started the job. And Sid was just the same: he was extraordinarily helpful, did his fair share of work on the truck and had all but taken over as communicator with the group. Not for the first time, I looked at myself through the eyes of the group, and didn't like what I saw. I was concentrating purely on getting the truck, and everyone on it, safe and sound to Rio; I was getting ever more withdrawn; I was lost in a spiral of worry and weariness that I knew I wore on my face in deepening creases. *Shit! Like Pete!*

It suddenly dawned on me.

Gladys jumped up, threw her wig in the air, lifted her skirt and started dancing. It was our second night on the 'island'. Finishing her bottle, she disappeared into the bush again. We found her, half naked like on the previous occasion, some distance from camp. Earlier, Eleanor had told me she thought Gladys might be schizophrenic – certainly she believed she was on some strong medication that didn't mix well with alcohol.

The next morning I spoke to Gladys again, describing her behaviour. She refused to believe me and then refused to speak. As we finished our meeting, I noticed Erika hovering agitatedly by my side. She had on her backpack, a short orange skirt and a pair of white wellington boots.

"Going somewhere?"

"Yes. Back to Caracas to get my post. Then I'm going to travel alone." I had no energy to argue and correctly assumed that Sid would already have tried. If she didn't like doing what the group voted for, then as far as I was concerned she could go.

"Fine, but you'll have to wait until the boat gets here tomorrow morning."

"I'm not stupid. I know the village is just behind the hill there."

Rumbled.

I watched in fascination as she strode off, her powerful legs carrying her wellies swiftly up the hill Sid and I had climbed to get to the village. *Well at least she'll be safe – no one's going to tackle her,* I thought. Then, suddenly, I panicked… what if they did? Scrabbling around in the cab, I found our Voluntary Leaving Form and ran off up the hill after her.

"Erica, wait, Erica …"

She stopped and turned. I did the last few metres with my hands on my thighs.

"Are you going to take me to Caracas?" She looked even more flushed than usual.

"No. I just need you to sign this form please."

Three down.

Angel Falls were spectacular and, flying ten feet above a river in a DC1O even more so. The tepuis, the flat-topped mountains the area is famed for, looked exquisite out of the window, but I suspected the pilot himself couldn't see them. He was so small his eyes were level with his instruments. To take off, and later skillfully buzz the river as we landed, he had half-stood, his behind hovering above his seat like a boy at his dad's car wheel. The flight over, we made our way out to camp in the idyllic grasslands surrounding the mountainous area we'd flown over. It reminded me of the African savannah. Indeed, without the sight of Gladys' sun-baked genitalia once again, we might well have found the world's most perfect rough camp.

The situation was ruining the trip for everyone now. The remainder of the group were as worried as I was that she might fall into the fire, get lost, badly injured or attacked at night. Or just plain slash her wrists. While the nights revolved around her performance or listening to tearful stories from her bizarre life, the group took care of her all day, getting her off the truck at stops so she wouldn't wet herself. South America – the beauty of the Gran Sabana itself – was passing us all by, even Sid. No one had actually seen her take pills, but her stupors were so deep, her behaviour so bizarre, that we all suspected drugs of some sort. Eleanor and I had even looked through her handbag, but had found nothing untoward.

In a café in the original El Dorado, while the group went panning for gold, I could only draw monosyllables from Gladys. I was trying to find out what I could about her problems or any medication she was on, but was getting no-where. The interview over, I decided she had to go. I had the plan ready by the time the group got back – none the richer. Handing the reins – and oil jug – to Sid, I told him to drive slowly; to explore whatever the group wanted to see of the Gran Sabana. I would take Gladys back to Cuidad Bolivar and evacuate her on a plane. I would meet them at the Brazilian border as soon as I could.

We bussed to Bolivar and I booked a ticket out of Caracas. I called London so that they could notify the family to meet her at Heathrow. It was a delicate situation as she could be altogether lucid, so I faxed a report detailing each incident. The next afternoon I flew with her to Caracas, as she wouldn't get on the plane without me. There I saw her on to the plane home. She was crying when I did so, and suddenly talkative, saying that she didn't understand why I was making her leave. I felt terrible, but was sure of myself. Injuries were one thing, people not enjoying the trip another, but I was adamant: Gladys was a danger to herself and was going home while she still could. The next morning I got a plane back to Bolivar, then another down to Santa Elena just before the Brazilian border.

In an uncanny echo of Pete's Saharan Journey, the oil kept pouring, the group kept leaving and Sid started to avoid me, sensibly spending his time with the group. We weren't far into Brazil when I lost my fifth group member. With a wide, red gravel strip cutting almost dead straight through the tall green jungle, we drove, we stopped, I topped up with oil, and we drove some more. The Trans-Amazon highway proving too repetitive for the artist in her soul, Melita left us in Boa Vista. It had been a hard decision. While filling in her Leaving Form, Melita told me, "You know? I've lived with my family for twenty-three years, but I feel like I know this group better." But she was there for a specific purpose, and had decided to fly to the coastal town of Belem. There, the inhabitants are renowned for being raucous, vibrant and fun. They were probably a lot more photogenic, too, than our nightly centrefold had been.

Despite the lack of variety on our four-day drive to Manaus, Sid and the remainder of the group had an excellent time. But the endless distances were taking a further toll on the truck. Oil requirements had risen to the point where I needed to top up every half an hour if I was to avoid the 'bang' I spent my days dreading.

250

Perhaps that would be better though – get it over with. No. I had to nurse it to Rio. What had Pete said in Niamey? – 'Being in a hurry never pays'. Resigning myself to living with the anticipation, I recalled the trick with the old man's walking stick – shave off a tiny piece every day for a year and by the end he'll be bent double, unable to walk.

The day before reaching Manaus, at one of my oil-stops I saw a truck coming from the direction I had come. Bar logging trucks, traffic is thin on the Trans-Amazon, so I was curious. It slowed – and I saw the writing on the front. It was another overland truck.

"Waaaaaankaaaaaahhhhhh!" It was Mick. Baseball cap covering his bald head, he was yelling out of the window. The truck stopped.

"Hey, Mick – when did you get out of Africa?"

"Last week, believe it or not. I flew into Caracas. This is Johnno." He leant back and the driver's hand came out of the window. I shook it, but couldn't see the face for Poncherelli sunglasses. "He's the boss. I'm on my L plates out here."

"You got here quick."

"No hanging about on this trip is there – and bloody good roads. So what's with the truck?"

"Don't ask. Leave us some space and we'll camp with you later. If you're lucky I'll bore you then."

I did too. But Mick didn't seem to mind. Cracking jokes at every one of my whinges, he helped me sort through the junk that swirled around my mind. We were nearing the end of my stock of problems, three hours in and twice as many beers.

"At the risk of siding with an opposition driver, I think you did the right thing with that mad bint. I should stop worrying about it now."

"You're right. And thanks ... hey, it's Manaus tomorrow – it's supposed to be an excellent city."

"According to Al, Manaus is a vagina ranch, my friend. I heard from him, you know. He goes through there on his jungle trips – he's loving it. You reckon he's strayed again, eh?"

"As far as I know, mate, he's stayed focused since the day you told him to."

The streets of downtown Manaus are the sleaziest I have ever seen. Hookers hang out of mouldy-walled bars, music blaring behind them. The hot, dirty streets genuinely steam after every one of the frequent showers of rain. Totally isolated, the Capital of the Amazon is 1600km from the Atlantic and a little further the other way from the borders of Peru and Columbia. Until the highway was built recently, the only way you could get there was by riverboat. They still ply the Amazon, the Negro and the Madeira, and those three great rivers that drain most of the Amazon basin meet near Manaus. We would be leaving on one soon.

The city has never recovered since the rubber boom ended at the turn of the century, and the lost wealth is evident everywhere. One of the many extravagances of that time is the wonderfully ornate opera house. The whole square on which it stands was once coated with rubber at the whim of a baron – horses' hooves on the cobbles had disturbed his listening pleasure. Another is the customs building, built with stone imported from Scotland; perhaps by the same man who used to send his laundry back to England by steamer. He thought they did a better job there – even if it took six months for him to get his shirts back.

I loved Manaus. With a complement of three other drivers to explore with, I found I could relax a little – even after I picked up a letter from Nancy. It was a long one, and I read it over a lunchtime beer as sheets of rain barred exit from the open door of a particularly filthy downtown bar. It wasn't until the end that she revealed her surprise. She was getting married, she wrote, to the man she'd shared the table adventures with.

It was perhaps the perfect place to hear the news. Manaus – five days' drive to get there, another five on the river to get out. From there, Nancy's life seemed such a long way from my reality, where my major thought was the relief of covering the next swathe of the massive country by ferry rather than road. The letter tumbled out of sight on the overflowing waters of a gutter outside the ferry office. Leaping the rushing stream, I entered and booked our passage down to Porto Vehlo. I would go on the vehicle barge with Mick, taking the two trucks. Sid would go with Johnno and the two groups on the passenger ferry. He was more than delighted to be honoured with another week's practice at solo group leadership. And he'd certainly earned it.

I waved the group off. With its several decks painted white, and the ornate railings light blue, the whole ferry looked like a wedding cake with a giant spinning hamster wheel stuck on the back. In comparison, Mick and I had to laugh when our own river transport arrived. The barge was just a huge flat metal tray pushed by a tiny tug. We had to wait for some time for the dozen or so enormous Brazilian trucks ahead of us to manoeuvre into position; the little boat patiently puffing away like an excited, panting Terrier. Nearby, on the steep grassy riverbank, I caught sight of a team of some twenty men trying to move an enormous metal cylinder the size of my truck. Why and where, it would be hard to say, but in both South America and Africa, such inexplicable activities were not infrequent.

"Watch this, Mick, it'll be disaster in a minute." Mick turned to where I was pointing. The cylinder was bolt upright. Balanced on some sort of pipe on one end, it was wobbling dangerously.

"Oh Christ," Mick sighed. "Trev's out in force. Crash helmets on everybody!" He had obviously witnessed such things previously too, and I wondered why. At home, we wouldn't even need to try; there would either be a health and safety directive against it, or a machine to do it for us. But there, it was always the same process – and always the same result.

It fell and the men shouted at one another. It was raised another way, some ropes were pulled in one direction, some another; down it went again. A massive argument ensued – almost fisticuffs – then a new plan; roll it and chock it. Off it went down the hill, straight into the river, two men falling off the top as it accelarated. The team looked at the now impossible task, and then sauntered off in different directions. Did I imagine it? Or was each man whistling, like he had never seen a cylinder in his life – of any size or description.

Maybe it was the contrast to the state I had got myself into. Or maybe it was because, for the first time since I had been overlanding, it was impossible to actually *do* anything. There was no group, no cooking, no room to work on the truck, nowhere to explore – and no need even to talk if I didn't feel like it. Whatever it was, those five days floating through the Amazon on the wide waters of the Rio Madeira were the most sublime of my life.

The tug, slogging away day and night at its unfair task, was run by a husband and wife team. Ricardo drove and navigated, seemingly without rest, while Wanda cooked eggs for breakfast and trucker-sized portions of beans, beef and rice for lunch and dinner. She would even do a spot of clothes washing for a fee, hanging it over the hot engine to dry with impressive speed. The Brazilian truck drivers were great too. They spent happy hours at our communal mealtimes taking the piss out of our 'tiny' trucks and pointing out that Englishmen must be similarly poorly endowed. Their trucks were enormous semis. Between two of them Mick and I had pitched camp; a table, a cooker, a kettle and our hammocks slung under a shoulder-high chassis.

Even nothingness needs a routine: breakfast, banter, music, tea break. Short read, coffee, chat, long read, Wanda's lunch. Coffee, snooze, read, conversation, afternoon bug-swat, beer, snooze or banter. Climb on top of Mick's truck, rum, watch the sun go down and pink dolphins pop up. Wanda's dinner, rum, beer and more banter. Back on top of the truck, two sides of Mick's four-tape set of the BBC's Hobbit – the highlight of the day and rationed like Zairie chocolate – rum, rum, banter and rum. Sleep, complaints of lack thereof, mossie-swat, more rum, deep slumber. Awake to the view, the permanent backdrop to everything; the jungle, slipping endlessly by, broken from time to time by the odd village, the odd villager joyously waving, marooned as far from civilisation as it was possible to be.

What I read were my journals: memories of two-and-a-half-years spent in two continents. And as I read all that had happened, I forgave myself my mood and let my worries slip away. This was just typical overlanding. The truck would make it to Rio in one piece – 'pas de probleme' – and there we would rebuild the engine. I would finally complete a whole trip, and Sid would graduate to leader. With a rookie's energy for groups and hunger for action, he would keep overlanding what it should be: the ultimate road trip, with all the fun, adventure and disaster that such a description suggests.

Potatoes, I thought.

Eh? – Potatoes? … What the hell do you mean 'potatoes'?

Ah yeah – Amantani Island. Yes Kevin, you're right – it all must lead somewhere. And for me it's here. It simply can't get better than this.

"Mick," I said, rum in hand, as we sat watching the sun go down over a magnificent sweeping bend in the river, "I'm going to resign."

"It's your time eh? I'll be with you pretty soon."

Michel had it all planned out 'for my best friend', and Mick and I were ready. He was about to leave Rio on his company's version of the South American Circle, and Sarah was with him as unofficial co-driver again. Six months together to see the whole continent, then he was going to quit. They had lots to prepare, but neither of them was going to miss this.

We had just seen the taxi pull up outside the huge Marajo window. Mick and Sarah had gone to a booth in the semi-darkness of the back of reception; I stood in place behind the counter wearing Michel's jacket and bow-tie. Al paid the driver and lifted his backpack easily onto his shoulder. As he swung the door open I noticed that the jungle had obviously been good to him – he looked nigh on slim. He gave a quick double take when he realised who it was he had just asked for a 'special'.

"Christ, hey… get out here and welcome me properly, you wankah." He raised his arms.

"Hold on a minute," I said," there's someone over there with an important message for you." A look of concern crossed Al's face. He dropped his pack and strode over to the booth I had pointed to.

"Mick! What the hell are you doing here?" They stood and grasped each other round the throat, screaming their vulgar greeting through the throttling. Out of breath, they slumped down opposite one another, grinning.

"You remember Sarah, from Bangui?" asked Mick.

"Of bloody course – I wouldn't forget someone as gorgeous as you." Al reached across the table and pinched her cheeks. "Can I have a go when you've finished with this bald bastard?"

"Oi, you can get your hands off 'er for starters – you said in your letters you never touched a thing any more. Not so much as a shuffle, you said!"

Clearly puzzled by the voice, Al turned. A woman had just slipped out from behind the marble desk I was manning, and Al found himself looking at Pauline.

"What the ... for fuck's sake ... who? ... You're all bastards." He stood and hugged her across the back of the booth.

"What *are* you doing here?" Al asked at length.

"London told me which trip you were doing next, and that you'd told them it was your last one, so I booked on. As you said, we should see what's what, eh?"

Al was up on my desk in seconds, swinging his expertly removed fluorescent yellow shorts around his head in accompaniment to his own manic cheering. Opposite him, the doors of the bar suddenly burst open. Lead by Michel, the Marajo and the Office regulars flooded through carrying crates of beer. Michel held out his hand to shake his friend's. Al leant down and pulled him up on to the desk with him.

Wearing his new suit, and the biggest smile a kind face could produce, Michel made his announcement from aloft, the shorts wafting the last few hairs on his head with each gaudy revolution: "Today, we will party on *my* side of the Marajo."

Waving at the back end of a truck for the last time, I watched them turn the corner outside the Office at the end of Calle Amor. Al had been given a brand new Mercedes. London had decided it was time to update the South American fleet and all the old Bedfords were being retired – as well as their trailers. The Merc' truly was an impressive beast. Built in the workshop from the chassis up, it had taken a year to complete. After thorough testing, it had been shipped out to Rio. Al was entrusted with the job of reporting back any on-the-road improvements he could offer – they would be incorporated into the plans for the company's new generation of overland trucks. Sid drove the Dream Machine, which we had reconditioned during the Rio turnaround.

Suddenly alone, I turned my attention to my future. I had a free hand. London would provide me with a one-way ticket to anywhere as soon as I couriered them my accounts. They would hold my year's wages until I went to the Victoria office.

First stop was the Vitamino bar where they whizzed me up my usual maracuja and cerise. The second, the Post Office. Picking up a handful of letters, I headed back to the Marajo. Sitting in a booth nursing a coffee brought by the only other person there, Michel, I took my time examining each one, preparing to savour the contents. One was from Chile, which was unusual, so I opened it first.

After describing her trip down from Quito, the letter ended with news I hadn't expected:

I've left the trip. Charlie started drinking heavily again and finished up doing what he did in Bamako. I guess none of us ever change, do we? I'm travelling to Rio on my own. I'd understand if you don't want to, Tim, but if you're around still, I'd love to see you.

Are you kidding, Katrina?

"Michel," I said, "have you got any of those beers left? We've got something else to celebrate."